SPINNING AND PLUG FISHING:

An Illustrated Textbook

SPINNING AND PLUG FISHING:

AN ILLUSTRATED TEXTBOOK

Barrie Rickards and Ken Whitehead

THE BOYDELL PRESS

© Barrie Rickards and Ken Whitehead 1987

First published 1987 by The Boydell Press
an imprint of Boydell & Brewer Ltd
PO Box 9, Woodbridge, Suffolk IP12 3DF

ISBN 0 85115 462 X

British Library Cataloguing in Publication Data

Rickards, Barrie
  Spinning and plug fishing:
  an illustrated textbook
  1. Spin-fishing
  I. Title   II. Whitehead, Ken
  799.1'2   SH456.5
  ISBN 0–85115–462–X

Printed and bound in Great Britain by
The Camelot Press Ltd., Southampton

CONTENTS

PART FOUR

Introduction

Between the pair of us we have spent almost three-quarters of a century spinning for predatory fish, so we do overlap with tackle and tactics which, before the Second World War, went back a couple of hundred years or so. Such expertise was very gradually replaced in the 1950s and 1960s and today's lure enthusiast is not easily identified by his garb and equipment with those depicted in old Hardy catalogues. Whereas in ancient times most anglers did a bit of spinning, every now and again, (so that most corner tackle shops sold a few Colorados), today we have in addition successive waves of fanaticism, happily fuelled by a press on the look out for innovators. Thus in the 1960s we had the Wagstaffe-Reynolds era, although they no longer pursue the passion that once consumed them. Other names followed and *their* protagonists have left us also. Meanwhile we spin on; not on an 'every now and again' basis but regularly, with enjoyment, with enthusiasm, and with success. New lures come and go, new equipment, occasional improvements, very occasionally a seemingly sound philosophical standpoint. We examine them all with, it always seems to us, an odd mixture of cynicism and boyish enthusism: *one day* will come the lure to replace all others! Meanwhile our repertoire of lures and techniques grows, and we hope in this volume not only to bring the world of spinning up to date but to prepare the ground well for you, at least until well into the 1990s.

We do not intend to dwell to much on historical matters in this book, except where of strict practical relevance, so perhaps the introduction is where we should set an historical framework, beginning with tackle itself.

The history of spinning tackle is almost completely tied to the development of the reel. We fish today and never think of yesterday, and the tremendous problems of getting a bait out from the bank. In the early days it was very much a case of Hobson's choice, and there was nothing unusual in watching an angler strip yards of line off his reel to hang in coils at his feet. The coils were then reversed – and the line (in theory) flew sweetly through the rings as the cast was made.

In practice, every bit of gunge and grot on the bank got caught in the coils, or the line caught round the angler's clothing and after travelling about fifteen feet the whole thing came to a sudden stop, leaving the angler with a Natural Disaster Area on his hands. Of course, there were the clever people who could cast directly from the Nottingham reel; an art of flipping the reel just before the cast was made, supposedly giving the reel initial movement to cure possible overruns. But the 'reel' problem lay in stopping the line gently at the end of the cast.

The progression from this was the Silex reel that had a few knobs and dials which applied both drag and brake. Actually, many anglers still found this difficult to master, and there are Silex models in existence that have the outer edge of the back plate cut away so that thumb pressure could be applied to the rim of the drum as a brake.

It was the 1930 era that produced the cream of centre-pin reels. Allcocks's magnificent Ariel reel could, and did, cast well straight from the drum, and they are in demand as working items and collector's models today. In fact many anglers swear that nothing has ever been made to surpass it. Of course, the Malloch reel was also in vogue, but it took a chap by the name of Illingworth to come up with the answer to long-distance casting. The mass production of fixed spool reels has advanced to this day, latterly with aesthetically appealing models made of carbon. Whilst the fixed spool reel revolutionised casting for most anglers, the multiplier (originating in 19th century game fishing circles) continued with gradual modifications: Hardy's Elarex was a field leader for years. Today's multipliers are again of carbon. Ryobi do several left hand wind models which are sheer delight to use, and a good number of right hand wind models exist.

At an early stage of tackle development rods became polarised into long, double handed jobs and short singlehanded ones with cranked (or stepped) handles. They were often of cane or greenheart, later of split cane, and Ken has a magnificent six foot steel-centred Hardy Victor spinning rod dating from around 1910. Metal rods appeared after the war, such as Phluger's six foot caster, or several produced by Accles and Pollock in the late 1940s. Then came glass fibre, varying from abyssmal to beautiful; and last of all carbon which is with us today. Whilst anglers will search for old cane rods today or, indeed, make them, we doubt if anyone would search for glass in preference to carbon.

The lures used by spinning men encompass and hide an historical 'anomaly': it is certain that spinners in the form of something shiny revolving on a bar axis, go back thousands of years, but plugs, that other favourite type, has its origins shrouded in mystery. Just how the plug as we know it originated is really anyone's guess. Like Topsy, we consider that 'it grew', and was a growth between the natural fish and the spinner. When we look through some of our old angling books time and time again we notice the 'wobbled deadbait' mentioned. At its simplest – and easiest – this was a fresh-killed bleak or roach, with one treble mounted on a wire trace that was threaded with the help of a baiting needle, from vent and via the centre of the body through to the mouth.

Cast and left to sink, a slow retrieve produced the deadly wobble of a sick fish, or if a little lead was introduced into the mouth, a sink-and-draw action that was fatal. Now all that description was to make the point that the wobble was caused by the fish sliding down to the treble as the water pressure mounted during the retrieve. The bigger the curve in the body, the greater the wobble.

Let's leave those thoughts on the natural, and look now at progress on the artificial scene. There is no doubt that man has spun – cast and retrieved a spinning object – for centuries. But, with experience, it was gradually realised that an action other than the perfectly straight spin could also be deadly. Perhaps a good example of this is the Jim Vincent pike spoon. He used a spoon reported to have been made from a wooden original used by the American Indians. It was heavy, long and with a distinct curve at either end that produced a peculiar wobble singularly appreciated by pike. For several years it was produced commercially – and although not made now,

An in-between plug/spinner: the Cahokie spoon.

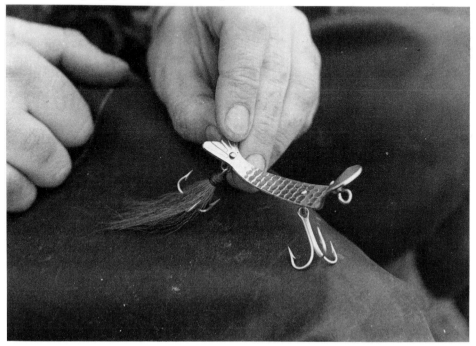

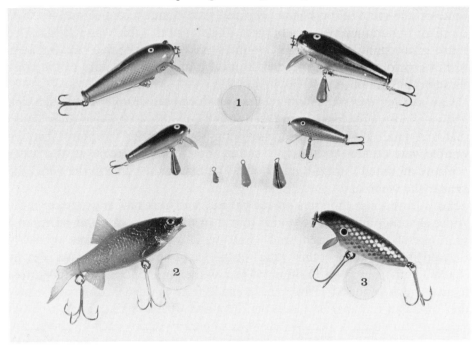

PLUGS FROM HISTORY.   *1. The Jock Scott, with weight attachments.   2. One of the first plastic plugs, rather tattered, but still usable.   3. Wooden plug from the 1940s.*

the Creek Chub Cahokie minus all trebles other than at the tail, looks remarkably like it, but has a different action.

Now, somewhere and somehow, someone got fed up with not catching live-baits, or carrying deadbaits that stunk to high heaven. At the same time either that same person – or his friend – got fed up with losing heavy metal wobblers on the river. So the wooden imitation fish that wobbled when it was pulled through the water and didn't get snagged quite so often was born. Or was it? Well, that's our guess, and anyone else's for that matter. The Ancient Egyptians used flies and it is not inconceivable that plugs developed at a very early stage simply by making bigger bodies for flies.

Early plugs to prove the point? The River Runt and some other American plugs have been going for some time, all originally made from wood, but generally it is considered that the Jock Scott plug is the 'Daddy' of the English models. And odd though it be, it still takes some beating. Made from wood, with the trace attached to the lower lip of the diving vane, it is a natural shallow diver. With the trace clipped to the upper part of the lip, and the addition of leads of various sizes it becomes a deep diver that can cope with a variety of waters. But its best asset is that the trace runs from head to tail fitting on to the outside of the body, and is secured to the tail by a turn or two of fine wire. When a big fish takes the thin wire parts, the plug immediately stands completely free and in this position it is impossible for a fish of any sort to lever itself free.

Naturally this innovation was copied, and 'improved' on by many people. One photograph shows a 1940s wooden plug with fixed diving vane and straight screw eyes into the body. In the same photo is shown an original 'plastic' type plug that Barrie found in the collection of Don Carter of Cambridge.

Compare these old-timers with today's products, and one can appreciate just how far we have come; and, indeed, we can see from what we have penned in this introduction, that spinning has not only a long history but a pedigree of innovative thought. That innovation is the hallmark of the successful spinning enthusiast will become clear from the following pages, that and the fact that there is so much still to understand. There is more than ample room for *you* to make your mark in a long history of sporting fishing. And we shall be more than pleased if we cause you to both think and act.

References

Bates, L. V., 1962, *Sporting Tactics for Coarse Fish*. Herbert Jenkins.

Bickerdyke, J., *Angling for Pike*, ch. 4. Thorson Publishers.

Buller, F., 1971, *Pike*, pt 3, §§ 6–14. Macdonald.

Falkus, H. & Buller, F., 1975, *Freshwater Fishing*, ch. 41 & 42. Macdonald.

Gammon, C., 1959, *Hook, Line and Spinner*. Heinemann.

Gay, M., 1975, *Beginner's Guide to Pike Fishing*, ch. 9. Pelham Books.

Gibbinson, J., 1974, *Pike*. Osprey Publishing Ltd.

Hampton, J. F., 1947, *Hampton on Pike Fishing*, ch. 3. Chambers.

Jardine, A., 1896, *Pike and perch*, ch. 4. Routledge.

Keal, W., 1972, *Bill Keal's Book of Fishing*. Clipper Press.

Lonsdale Library, 1930, *Fine Angling for Coarse Fish*, ch. 18. Seeley Service.

Marshall-Hardy, E., 1973 (10th edn), *Angling Ways*, ch. 30–3. Barrie & Jenkins.

Martin, J. W., 1907, *Pike and perch fishing*. Brendon & Son.

Maunsell, G. W., 1933, *Fisherman's Vade Mecum*. A & C Black.

Rickards, R. B., 1974, *Catch More Perch*, ch. 5. Wolfe Publishing Co.

Rickards, R. B., 1976, *Pike Fishing Step by Step*. Cassell.

Rickards, R. B., 1986, *Angling : fundamental principles*. Boydell & Brewer.

Rickards, R. B., 1986, *Big Pike*. A & C Black.

Rickards, R. B. & Whitehead, K., 1976, *Plugs and plug fishing*. A & C Black.

Spencer, S., 1936, *Pike on the Plug*. H. F. & G. Witherby.

Stoker, H., 1977, *Sea Angling with the Specimen Hunters*. Ernest Benn Ltd.

Venables, B., 1967, *Freshwater Fishing*, Barrie & Jenkins.

Wanless, A., 1930, *The Science of Spinning for salmon and trout*. Herbert Jenkins.

Wanless, A., 1933, *Thread-line Questions Answered*. Herbert Jenkins.

Webb, R. & Rickards, R. B., 1976 (2nd edn), *Fishing for Big Pike*, ch. 6. A & C Black.

PART ONE

CHAPTER ONE

Introducing Plugs

A plug is an artificial lure, usually made of wood or plastic, and most often designed to look something like a fish. We say 'something like' rather than resembling' because many plugs resemble almost nothing on earth – except in action in the water, where they may take on a vitality very attractive to the angler's prey. It should not be supposed that plugs are totally distinct from other artificial lures such as spinners and flies. They are not. In fact the three types are connected by a range of intermediates. Some 'spinners' have a fixed head, often made of rubber, situated just before a revolving blade. To British anglers the Voblex will be the most familiar in this category, but there are many others. Abu, for example, make the Morrum-spinner in weights up to ⅝ oz, whilst Bomber Baits of Gainesville, Texas, make a huge range of Gimmick 'spinner flies' which have variously-coloured heads including bulbous eyes, rotating blade, and feathered hooks. Again, many jigs are little more than simplified plugs with or without the addition of feathers: Bomber Baits make the Gumpy Jig for example.

At one time definition of a plug was fairly easy if all that was required was distinction from spinners: if it had a revolving blade it was a spinner. Nowadays, however, nobody in his right mind would term Shakespeare's Slim Jim a spinner since it is patently a plug, but with tiny propeller-like blades at the head and tail. Probably it is best to call an artificial bait a fly (using the word in a broad sense to include the modern reservoir anglers' 'lures') if it contains a preponderance of feather over hard body; and an artificial bait a spinner if it is built with more obvious blades than hard body!

Having said all that it remains to mention, of all things, a creature called the Spoon-plug. This is made entirely of metal, but on retrieve behaves like a plug, with a very powerful and vibrant wobble and a tendency to dive very deeply. Indeed, the diving ability is so great that casting and retrieving from the bank is next to impossible, and the lure is best fished from a boat. It is extremely good for trolling and has accounted for some big lake trout. Although it is not readily available in this country, it should not be beyond the skill of many anglers to make their own, experimenting with different thicknesses of metal and different sizes of Spoon-plug.

It will be clear from the above that the great variation possible in basic design will lend itself to inventiveness on the part of the angler – one of the great joys of plug fishing – and this we hope to explain more fully in the chapter on home-made plugs. Later we shall also give a fuller account of the manner in which plugs work in the water.

AMERICAN IMPORTS

Many years ago when wielding a battered and scratched wooden plug at Eastrington in East Yorkshire, Barrie came across a group of rather well-to-do gentlemen who had, in addition to deer-stalkers, a few dozen glossy, posh, colourful (colorful) American plugs. Since they didn't do as well as Barrie that day he dismissed their plugs as useless and gaudy to boot. This attitude stayed with British anglers for many years, with a few stalwarts such as Bernard Venables insisting that American plugs could be good, but resistance was eventually broken down by a handful of enthusiasts who proved beyond doubt that plugs from over the Atlantic were first class. We are thinking, of course, of anglers like Ernest Merritt, Fred J. Taylor, Fred Wagstaffe, Mike Muse, and Bob Reynolds. Some British tackle shops, Ken Latham's of Potter Heigham and latterly Ryobi Masterline for example, realised the value of these plugs and made a great effort to supply British anglers. Thanks to these anglers a variety of plugs is available in most medium to large towns in the country. Did we say 'a variety'? What we mean is terrific variety, with plugs to do things that grandfather would have thought impossible. But if you take into consideration the plugs available in all the catalogues, Heddon, Shakespeare, Abu, Bomber etc. the variety is quite overwhelming. Or is it?

THE GREAT VARIETY OF PLUGS

In the next chapter we attempt, perhaps unwisely, to give a basic classification of plugs in relation to other lures. But what we want to talk about here is the variety even within that basic scheme. Lay out twenty catalogues on the

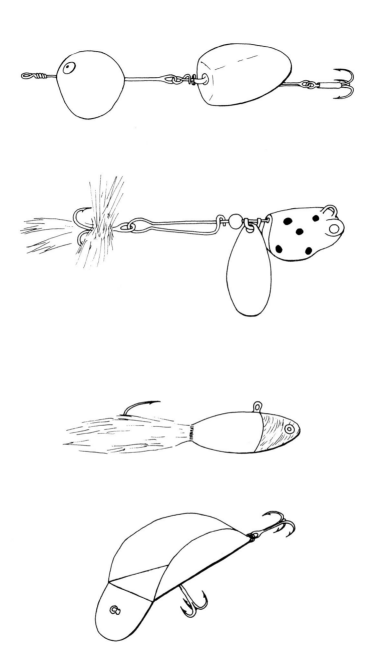

floor and prepare to gasp! The colour, shape and size variation is staggering. But wait, things are not quite what they seem: most of the plugs *do* fall into our classification, but furthermore it soon becomes apparent that very, very similar plugs are made by different manufacturers.

Thus Bill Norman's Shiner-minnows are very similar to Normark Vibro's famous Rapalas, and both provide us with moderate divers with slim, elongate, scaly bodies. Abu and Whopper Stopper make similar plugs although these tend to work at slightly different depths for a similar retrieve. Amongst the deep divers Bomber's Waterdog is not unlike Whopper Stopper's Hellbender. Both are available in a range of colours which are not, in fact, as similar as the bodies with their trailing tail-spoons. The Lazy Ike series of banana-shaped or 'flatfish' plugs have been made in very similar fashion by other firms.

And so it goes on: on the home front, Woolworth's did sell plugs which were at least comparable to the more expensive foreign designs. In other words, although things are at first sight bewildering to the beginner, all that the duplication from firm to firm achieves is to give the angler a wider choice of *colours* for his favourite design.

CHAPTER TWO

Classification of Plugs

We have already given some hint of the difficulties here in the section defining what we mean by a plug. But the flow diagram is a valiant attempt (we think) to draw up a basic classification of plugs, with examples, and at the same time show their relationships to other kinds of lures: spoons, spinners, flies and so on. No classification can be perfect, and an obvious drawback to ours is that the words FLIES, SPINNERS and SPOONS on the right of the diagram could be interchanged, since each can be used at any depth. On the other hand we prefer to retain the depth parameter for the rest of the diagram where it is readily applicable.

Let's have a look at the way plugs merge into spinners, spoons and flies: we'll begin at the surface and work down towards the depths. Some of the surface poppers such as Norman's Chuggerflash are surface plugs in the strictest sense, but others like small feathered poppers are little more than flies and are probably fished better *as* flies on fly rods and lines. In passing, we should mention that flies also merge into spinners as the blades get smaller and the amount of feather greater: the Abu-fly is a good example although there are several others.

Bomber's Gimmick and Bushwacker range have a small plug-like head, particularly the former, but otherwise are more nearly like fly-spoons, that is, with a considerable amount of feather and attendant spoons as well! Such lures almost defy classification, but you can see that on our flow diagram they are situated at the SPINNER end of the BORDERLINE group of plugs. They are really plug-like spinners with fly affinities, hence we have drawn arrows indicating their connections.

The same principle has been used with the placing of other lures of doubtful affinity. Thus Heddon's Spinfin has an almost plug-like body and associated spoon and hair: it is basically a deeper-fished spoon bait with plug affinities and we have it in the BORDERLINE group with arrows showing its relationships.

Going deeper than the Heddon's Spinfin we have Bomber's Waterdog, and Whopper Stopper's Hellbender. Both are plugs almost in the strict sense, with nearly horizontal diving vanes which take them on very deep dives, but they have small spoons appended at the tail end of the plug. Thus we place them, in our classification, deep in the water and with connections with both plugs and spoons.

A couple of lures which hold a similar position in terms of depth to the Waterdog and Hellbender are the Plug-spoon and Creek Chub Cahokie. These are all-metal and more spoon-like than plug-like and hence are at the spoon end of the BORDERLINE group. They work extremely deep and, unlike most plugs, are fast sinkers. Quite a few other lures are made which fall into the BORDERLINE group between plugs on the one hand and flies, spinners and spoons on the other, but it is not our intention to discuss them or their placings in detail. Indeed, it is useful for the user of our chart to try to place his own lures, look for exceptions, and then try to build up a better, perhaps three-dimensional classification.

There are two other relatively simple borderline types to consider in our groupings. Perks are *almost* spoons, *almost* spinners, and *almost* flies, depending on the type in use. They can be used at all depths, but particularly are deep-water lures. Jigs can be *almost* plugs in that they have a plug-like body even though they are often heavily adorned with feathers; they also merge into perks and flies! Jigs are operated at any depth, usually deep, and some, such as Rapala jigs, can be imparted with a very fish-like action by jerking them up and down with the rod end.

A few other borderline types are shown on the left of our diagram, and we hope their positions are more or less self-explanatory: they have a claim to represent 'natural' baits. The excellent Abu shrimps could be considered either as jigs or perks, whilst the bottom-crawlers like Heddon's Craw-spin and Lazy Ike's Craw-fish are probably closer to jigs than to anything else.

Returning now to the centre of our diagram, the 'plugs proper', we have tried to classify them in terms of the depths at which they work. Thus we have crawlers, plunkers and poppers at the surface; then floating shallow divers, followed by floating moderate divers coupled with slow sinkers; then floating deep divers and, finally, fast sinkers. Several things are apparent, such as the fact that the Abu Hi-Lo range and Creek Chub Dingbat transgress this classification because they have adjustable diving vanes and come into each of our depth categories.

Many other plugs *are* restricted, however, and one very obvious point is that whilst floating and shallow divers are made in abundance by many firms, fast sinkers, and even really deep divers, are far less common. Amongst the fast sinkers the Lazy Ike Sail Shark, with its 'sonic vibration' is outstanding, whilst Whopper Stopper's Bayou Boogie can be sunk to any

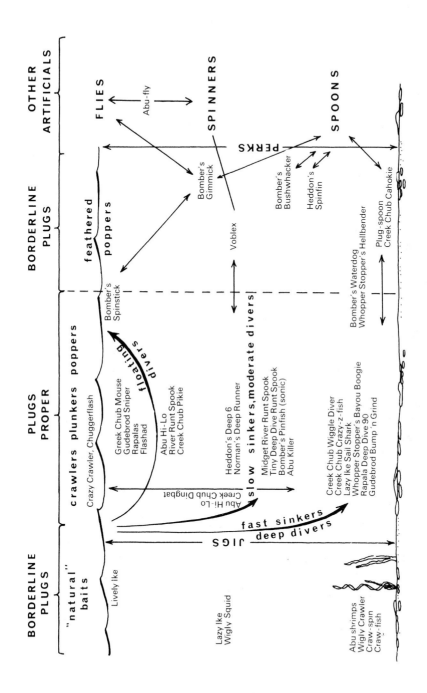

depth *and worked at that depth.* Creek Chub's Cray-z-fish and Wiggle Diver can be got down deeply and quickly, but having said that we have almost exhausted the readily available fast sinkers.

There are, of course, some good deep divers: Rapala Deep Dive 90; Gudebrod Bump 'n Grind. If these are used with the 'bordeline' Waterdogs and Hellbenders the angler has a useful coverage with deep divers, although nothing like that which he has with floating shallow and moderate divers. We have heard many anglers say that in British waters they cannot catch much on the Gudebrod Bump 'n Grind: contrast that with the reputation of the Gudebrod Sniper, and it is certainly no accident that most of the famous plugs are essentially shallow or top-water types.

We cannot emphasise too strongly that our naming of the above plugs and lures is merely for the purpose of explaining our classification, although we have tended to use the plugs we have found successful. We do not intend to imply that many other plugs are not just as good, and we invite the reader to attempt to classify his own favourites on our scheme.

LURE ACTION: PLUGS

So far we have talked about floating, diving, deep diving actions etc. The time now has come to sort out these in more detail to avoid confusion later on. When the manufacturer produces a plug he designs the model to work at, or rather between, certain sections of the water. His idea in this is to imitate a particular fish, or fish action, and the mechanics of the plug will give the best results when they are used within the tolerance he describes.

This does not mean that the plug *cannot* be made to work in a different section of the water, but if it is used in any other way than that for which it was designed, the action will probably be impaired.

As an instance of this, think about a surface lure. It is designed to work on the surface only. You can fix lead on the trace above the line and cause it to sink — but if you do, its action and attraction, i.e. sputtering around with bags of noise and fuss, will be lost. There are plugs on the market that can be adjusted to work at several depths by adjustment of the plug fittings, or where the use of lead is recommended, but they are few and far between.

SURFACE

These plugs always float on the surface, and are designed to remain there during the retrieve. They are made of wood, or plastic with in-built buoyancy. In shape they are usually pointed or with a 'pug' end sloping backwards, to give the plug lift as it is pulled through the water. Sometimes there are spinning blades at either end of the body, or metal vanes standing out from the head or body itself.

The idea with these is to cause water disturbance and strange though it may seem, this very noise (some of them kick up Hell's delight) is the very secret of their success.

They are designed to be retrieved slowly, or 'popped' back to the fisherman in small jerks that disturb the water – rather like an insect struggling on the surface. They fish best under trees, and around reed beds, fallen trees – places in fact where surface splashing creatures would be found.

SURFACE PLUGS. *1. Crazy Crawler 2. Sinner Spinner 3. Trouble Maker 4. Mr Thirteen*

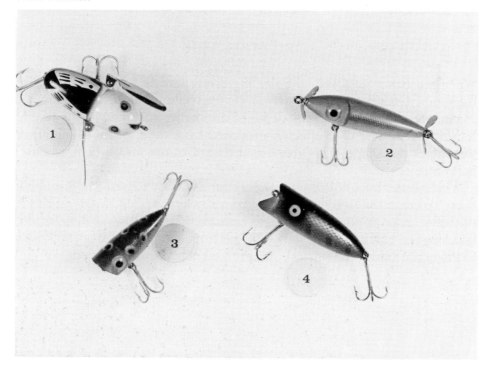

FLOATING DIVERS.   1. *Big 'S'*   2. *Flashad*   3. *Sniper*   4. *Meadow Mouse*
5. *Wood Basser*   6. *Tiger*   7. *Mr Thirteen*   8. *Tadpole*

FLOATING-DIVING ES

When not being retrieved, the floating-diving lure rests on the surface of
the water. Once a retrieve is started, or the rod top moved, then they will
commence a shallow dive, the depth of dive being governed by the rate of
retrieve itself. The dive effect is produced by a vane, or lip of metal, or
sometimes the shape of the nose at the head of the lure, which acts as a
paravane.

With a little thought this type of plug can be made to perform just about
every action in the fishing calendar, from a switchback up and down to the
sideways lunge produced with rapid retrieve. Sensible use of the rod top,
twitching and changing direction of the rod from one side of the angler's body
to the other during the retrieve, all promote a tremendous amount of life.

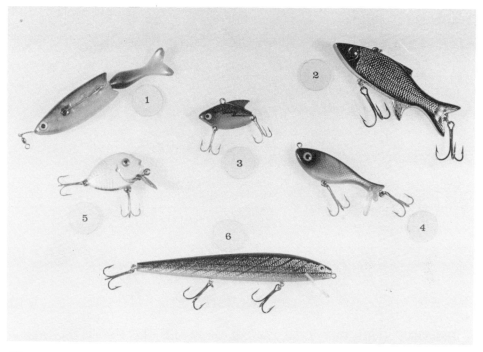

SINKING PLUGS. *1. Commando 2. Snoky 3. Sonic 4. Mr Murder 5. Punkin Seed 6. Killer*

SINKING

These are for deep water and holes where weight is needed to get the plug down into the fishing layer. After the lure has hit the surface, count the lure down, perhaps counting three – then start the retrieve. Next cast count four, and so on. Once the taking depth of fish is found, keep to that count-down, and you will be in their approximate feeding depth. Most of the plugs in this category really look like fish, although a few do have a vane or lip to help to keep them down. Often a fish will take on the drop. If the plug has an in-built vibrator – usually a metal ball inside a hollowed out section of the body – then the manufacturers advise a speed-up in the retrieve to make the maximum effect.

DEEP DIVING

These may have a floating or sinking body, but are recognised by the long, wide metal lip that planes them down quickly once the retrieve is started.

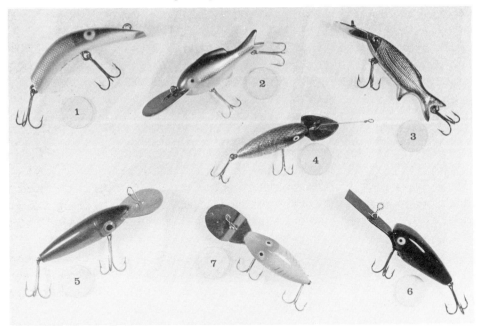

DEEP DIVING PLUGS. *1. Lazy Ike   2. Crackleback   3. Snoky   4. Cisco Kid 5. Bump 'n Grind   6. Deep 6   7. Deep Dive River Runt Spook*

The same lures – deep divers – seen in silhouette, as a fish sees them.

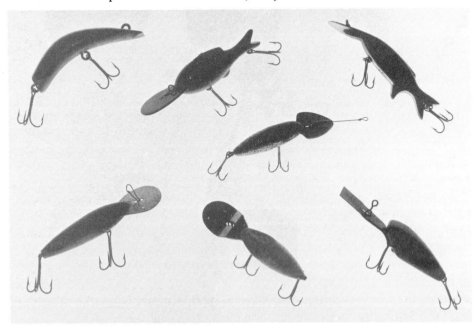

If you are using a sinker, then use the count-down method and start the action at varying depths until the fish are found.

Just how important *is* shine and colour, and where should it be? We carried out some brief experiments in flume tanks. The results were interesting and we give an account of them in the following paragraphs.

LURE ACTION: SPINNERS

The series of photographs accompanying this section show the light patterns made by spinners as they would probably appear to a fish. Lighting was set up over the tank to represent natural sunlight on a sunny day – lighting was not rigged to simulate winter conditions during any of the tests applied. To ensure that the camera recorded the pictures seen as a fish would see the lure, a neutral background was erected, which did not make the light patterns stand out in any way. In fact, the neutral colour as nearly represented a distant blank wall of water as was possible.

A current of approximately two knots was fed through the tank to represent a slow river or stream. The camera was set at right-angles to, and level with the lure, and a set of three photographs of each one was taken, the first two with an open shutter speed of one second, and the spinner moved across the plane of the lens during this time. The third was a one-second exposure with the lure held steady, only the current moving the spinner. The water in the tank was clear, eighteen inches deep, over a rippled clean sand bottom. Perhaps we should say a word or two about the tank itself. Thanks to the help of one of Barrie's colleagues, Peter Friend, we were able to use what is called a flume tank. In this case it was about ten yards long, a couple of feet deep, about eighteen inches wide, and the current controllable within wide limits. The flow is laminar, rather than turbulent, and is more akin to a long sweep of river or drain with a steady depth than, for example, the turbulence of a weir pool, or a series of pools on a small river.

What fish can see is, of course, open to some debate. Most zoologists, and beyond question most anglers, take the view that fish see colours quite well. Equally likely is that some fish, like pike, rely heavily on vibrations rather than sight, particularly in coloured water, whereas perch often give the impression to the spinning man of possessing really good eyesight. Be that as it may it is certainly possible, though perhaps unlikely, that each flick of a spoon or twirl of a spinner is seen clearly by the fish as a succession of sharp images. More likely, we feel, is that the hunting fish sees, and feels the vibrations of, an elongated disturbed area. What it sees is a series of flashes, and what it feels is a series of pulses on its lateral line sense organs. When we

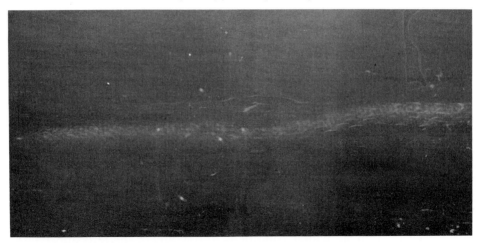

Patterns from the Mepps Rainbo.

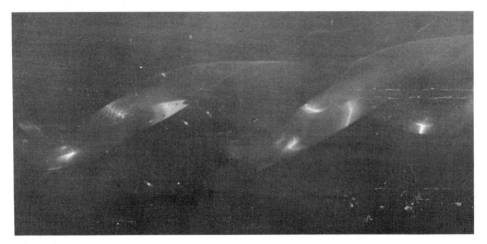

Abu Toby patterns.

viewed the spinner in action from the sides of our tank that is exactly what *we* saw, and the human eye is pretty good. So that most of our photographs, with an open shutter speed of one second, illustrate the light pattern characteristic of those spinners, and what we feel the fish actually sees in most circumstances.

Some interesting observations were made. Ondex bar-spoons for example, superb killers on Fenland drains and shallow lakes, actually have very little flash pattern and what did occur came from the 'upper' end of the revolving blade and would not readily be seen by fish on the bottom. This spinner, and some others such as Veltics, are very good vibrating lures, and it may well be that the fish home in on the vibrations, and then by sight on the red

Patterns from a Piker Spoon.

Light patterns from the Mepps Mino.

tag tail which most of them carry. Obviously then, you would use this type of spinner when you needed vibrations or a dull spinner.

The Mepps Rainbo, in contrast, sent out a constant light pattern of a tight circle from the multi-reflecting surface of the willow-leaf blade; the non-reflective underside breaking the pattern to give a light-and-dark effect that would be visible for some distance and over quite a wide arc of view.

Both Toby and Piker spoons, large lures in red and silver, show a striking figure-of-eight pattern that reflects light on the top edge (the shoulder of the bait). Only a few turns have been made in the same distance that the Mepps would make many, but the pattern is both clearly visible over a wide area and striking in nature. As already mentioned, the Toby actually spins

23

Piker Spoon patterns.

strongly in more powerful currents. Both show a typical tail-down position when retrieved slowly, but experience shows us that this is not unattractive to the hunting fish.

Colorado spinners showed the least light pattern of any we tried, and the red inside blocked what little light there was at every turn. Nor are vibrations very strong from this lure, yet we have caught hundreds of good perch on the smaller sizes, and good lough pike on the big sizes – which suggests that there could be other factors involved in its value as a spinner.

The Mepps Mino gave a small, tight light pattern though not so pronounced as with the Rainbo. Most of the light reflects off the *edges* of the revolving blade, and some off the plastic minnow which can be seen as a grey hue under the main light pattern of the spinner. This seemed the most effective of the gold coloured lures that we tried.

Our Russian weedless spoons, in effect two spoons mounted face to face gave light reflections from the shoulders of *each* blade, but produced a show visible only over a short distance. Vibrations nil: definitely a spoon for bright conditions if we are to accept the concept of bright lure for dull conditions and *vice versa*.

The general conclusion that we came to was that light patterns turn off the edge and shoulders of a lure as it revolves or wobbles. In terms of flash, the small leaf bar-spoons and Jim Vincent-type wobbling spoons are undoubtedly best. Round lures like the Colorado, and the large rounded blades as in the Ondex, do not show up well. Many of the red, gold and black blobs may count for nothing in the fishes' eyes once the lure is revolving. Coloured bars, on the other hand, *do* influence the light patterns strongly, the best being those that run obliquely or horizontally from nose to tail, breaking up the glint of the lure into quicker patterns. The 'stationary' photograph of the Piker spoon shows this quite clearly. Multi-reflecting surfaces on lures of any sort will obviously increase show. It seems a pity that none is yet on spoons in the really large sizes. Clearly, considerable thought is needed when painting your home-made spoons, the construction of which we have outlined elsewhere. The main problem concerns spots and blobs – are they really necessary?

CHAPTER THREE

SPINNERS: DEFINITIONS AND VARIETY

At a first consideration you might think a definition of spoon or spinner unnecessary, but anglers are notoriously casual people, we're happy to report, and use words and phrases which will give no clue to the beginner of their real intentions or activities. For example, we often say 'We're just going off to do a bit of spinning' when what we really mean is that we're going to hump a huge box of lures consisting of spinners, spoons, plugs (and a few others besides): we're not merely going to use spinners. Then there's that word 'lure'. Not so many years ago its usage was largely confined to plugs, spoons and spinners, the rest being baits and flies, but today it applies also to a special form of large fly (which some people would scathingly refer to as a spinner or plug!) used by reservoir trout anglers. So it is important, at least to us, to define what we mean by spinners, and spoons.

Almost certainly we cannot do this without upsetting somebody. When we wrote *Plugs and plug fishing* we included a definition of what we considered a plug to be. No less an authority than Brian Harris, the then editor of the monthly glossy magazine *Angling*, disagreed with our definition and defined a plug as 'a lure that attracts predatory fish at the surface and below it by wobbling or wriggling but not spinning'. In our opinion this definition of a plug also applies to big spoons that are bounced through big waves or across the choppy surfaces of lakes, techniques which, as we shall describe, have been shown in recent years to be highly successful fish-catching methods.

Our definition of a spinner would, therefore, be:
an artificial bait, usually made of metal (but also of plastic, wood, quill and rubber), *often in the shape of a blade* (but also as a tube) *rotating or spinning*

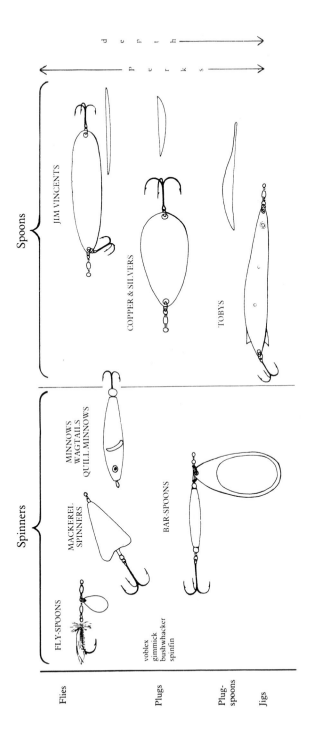

Spoons

Spinners

JIM VINCENTS

COPPER & SILVERS

TOBYS

MINNOWS
WAGTAILS
QUILL MINNOWS

MACKEREL
SPINNERS

BAR-SPOONS

FLY-SPOONS

voblex
gimmick
bushwhacker
spinfin

Flies

Plugs

Plug-
spoons

Jigs

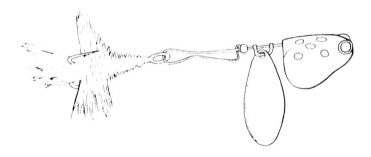

about a bar or axis, to which it may be attached at one end only, or along the whole of its length.

And our definition of a spoon:
a spoon shaped blade, usually with a treble attached at the tail end and a swivel at the front end; it usually wobbles rather than spins, so that there is no linear axis.

Now all spoons do not wobble, as many anglers mistakenly think. In our experiments in flume tanks we found that some famous spoons, Toby's for example, actually spin strongly under certain current or retrieve conditions, so that some spoons act like and are akin to other kinds of lures, undoubtedly spinners, which never wobble. At the other extreme we have spoons such as the Piker which always wobble under normal fishing conditions. We could refer to these as wobbled baits, but that is a title we prefer to use for natural fish baits that are retrieved with a wobble: *spun* natural baits are treated at length elsewhere in the book. So to conclude this short account of definitions, we leave you with the above two definitions and a realisation that spinners and spoons form a continuous spectrum, the ends of which are linked by spoons that spin.

The main types of spinners (plug-like spinners; bar-spoons; fly-spoons; mackerel spinners; minnows and wagtails) and spoons (Toby's; Copper and Silver; Jim Vincent and Piker) are described and illustrated below. The flow diagram relates the various types, including the borderline types which are discussed later.

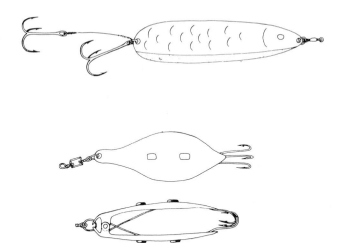

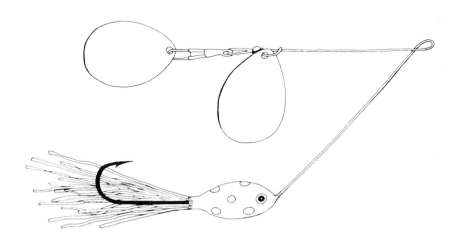

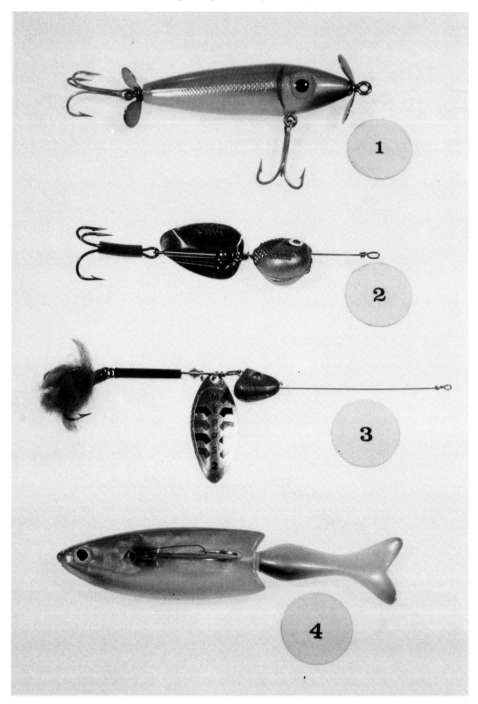

PLUG SPINNERS.   *1. Sinner Spinner   2. The Voblex   3. Mepps Adour*
4. Heddon Commando.

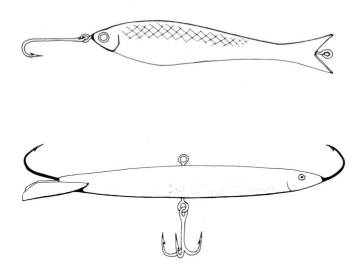

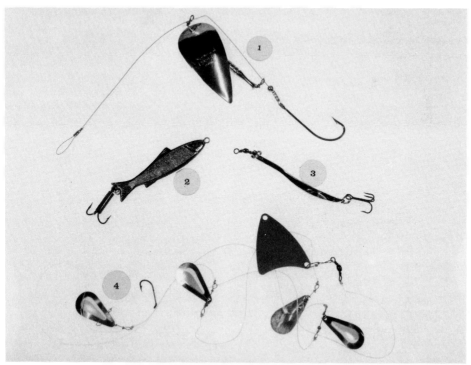

PERKS. *1. Normark Vibro   2. Shakespeare Troller   3. Shakespeare Condor Bar 4. Abu Konvoj.*

Feathered jigs and poppers, underated and underused by anglers in the UK, but very successful for several species.

CHAPTER FOUR

Good Spinners and Spoons in the Basic Patterns

In the earlier sections on definitions and variety it can be seen that we have placed *Bar-spoons* in a very central position parallel with what we call the *Copper and Silvers*. Bar-spoon is obviously a slight misnomer, very entrenched in angling literature, for bar-spoons are spinners and can be contrasted with the C & S *spoons* which largely wobble. The two types form the basic core of the spinning man's lure box.

Bar-spoons are deadly, and include many types well known to British anglers, such as Veltic, Ondex, Vibro and Mepps to arrange them in order of increasing weight for any one size of blade. Immediately a retrieve is begun the blades revolve, bite deeply into the water and produce a strong vibration. The *Vibro, once made by Normark, causes the top rod of any reasonably light spinning rod to bend and judder, but with all these spinners there is real *feel* on the retrieve. If everything goes slack whilst reeling in, two things can have happened: either the lure has picked up weed, or a fish has taken the lure and continued swimming towards you in a classic slack line bite. Both situations should be treated in the same manner, namely with a sweeping strike. In the case of the weeded lure the strike may dislodge the weed, or else start the blade spinning again in spite of the encumbrance: and fish *will* occasionally take a lure trailing weed from the hooks. If it's a slack line bite then the sweeping strike may connect with the fish.

Making bar-spoons is easy, as can be seen from the figures, but here we want to explain the basically similar nature of the various types. Firstly there is a swivel at the head of the lure. Attached to this is a bar, which gives the name bar-spoon, and this runs along the axis to be attached by various means to a treble hook at the rear of the lure. There are two additions to this axial arrangement. One is the crux of the whole lure, namely a spoon-shaped blade attached at one end so that it spins *very freely and loosely* about the axis. The second additive is weight, usually placed behind the blade and in front of the treble hook. Various bar-spoons have plenty of weight (Mepps,

*These were still available in 1986 from Simpson's of Turnford or Ashpole's of Islington.

33

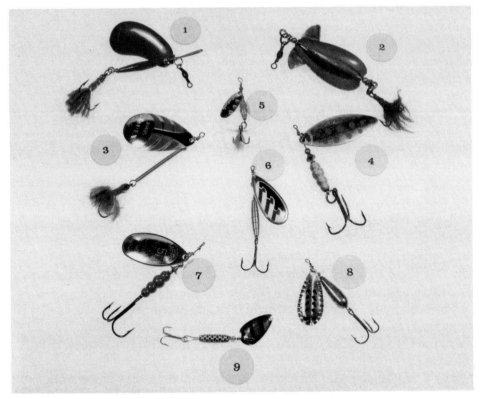

BAR-SPOONS.   *1. Kidney Spoon   2. Colorado Spinner   3. Ondex   4. Mepps Aglia (leaf)   5. Abu Colibri   6. T.A.F.F.   7. Mepps Aglia   8. Abu Droppen 9. Shakespeare Kilko.*

Shakespeare and Intrepid bar-spoons), others have much less (Veltic and Ondex). Light bar-spoons can be fished in very shallow and weedy water, and are essentially short range lures, whereas the heavier ones cast much further and can be fished deep quite easily. All can be retrieved very slowly, and in general the slower the better. Also, as a generalisation, we have found a steady retrieve to be more successful than a variable and jerky one. Both these remarks should be taken only as a rough guide, for trout sometimes need a very quickly drawn spinner; whilst a bar-spoon fished sink and draw style can be quite killing, that is by raising the rod top thus pulling the vibrating bar-spoon upwards, and then dropping the tip sharply so that the spoon flashes and flutters downwards.

Further additions to the basic bar-spoon pattern take the form of feather or wool to the tail treble, and various colourations or indentations of the blade. The value of these particular additions is discussed in the appropriate places in the text below.

An addition which really adds up to a slightly different kind of lure is achieved by placing a head *in front* of the blade. In the most well known form, the Voblex, the head is of rubber; in others it may be of heavier material and strongly attached to the bar axis so that it behaves as a built-in anti-kink device. Spinners like the Voblex are really part way to being plugs: they have plenty of weight, cast like bullets, and are really top-class spinners.

Fly-spoons, too, are in the basic bar-spoon pattern. The axes in these are usually wire or a string of swivels, the blade revolves in the usual way, but is sometimes attached so that it flutters rather than spins, and the treble hook at the rear is almost always replaced by a single hook carrying a fly often of recognised pattern such as a Silver Doctor. Generally speaking, fly-spoons are smaller than the average bar-spoon, and lighter, and are intended for delicate short range fishing with light lines. They are excellent for many species of fish but were intended for trout in low water conditions. We have fished them for small brownies and seatrout on moorland streams with considerable success, and here it must be remembered that each retrieve may be no more than a few yards each cast.

At this point we should contrast the spoon-like blade of these bar-spoons and fly-spoons with the Copper and Silvers. Generally, the blade on a bar-spoon is of shallower curvature than that of wobbling spoons proper, and they are never concavo-convex so far as we know. In the Vibro the unattached end of the blade is pointed, a factor which contributes largely to the tremendous vibration set up by this bar-spoon during the retrieve. Some bigger fly-spoons have quite a convex blade with a three-faceted surface, but these are rather unusual and may well be out of production. In the kidney spoon, a classic bar-spoon with a leaded axis, the blade is kidney-shaped, and the rotation is distinctly slower and more intermittent than in any of the types mentioned above.

All the spinners discussed so far are the basic bar-spoon type, but what is in effect a much more drastic change than any yet considered is to attach the spinning blade along the whole of its length, but in a fashion that still enables it to spin about a straight axis. The result can take two forms: one with a still recognisable blade such as the famous mackerel spinner and the second where the 'blade' is roughly shaped like a fish as in wagtails, quill and other minnows. These are still spinners in the strictest sense with a straight axis through a spinning body. Mackerel spinners borrowed, as the name suggests, from sea-fishing circles, we rate as one of the best and cheapest on the market, particularly for pike in shallow, weedy waters where we have taken literally thousands of fish. They are not that easy to make, but fortunately are very cheap. Quill minnows are easy enough to make, and in trout fishing hill country, such as the Lake District, Wales and Scotland, many village shops sell them made by the local expert. The photograph gives some idea of their hook-bristling appearance. As a rule they are nicely painted, with eyes on, as are the wooden and metal minnows, but all this detail may be wasted on fish, as we suggest below. The *general* colour is probably important but not the detail. All these forms of artificial minnows are tried and proven baits for trout and salmon but are very effective indeed for perch, pike and chub.

The Colorado spoon is a famous *spinner*, often denigrated by the modern pike angler, probably unjustly in our experience. The spoon-like blade is attached at both ends to the axial bar which is also leaded. But more important are two fins at the front of the spoon: these are set in opposite senses so that the blade as a whole spins strongly. It would be interesting to know the origins of this spinner, relative to the Copper and Silver spoons which we discuss in the following paragraph.

The next main category to think about is the Copper and Silvers. We use this title merely in the sense that it is central to that part of the figure, and that the simple dessert-spoon-shaped lure is one of the oldest in angling history. Perhaps the classic version has about a three inch spoon, of relatively heavy metal, and is copper coloured on the inside and silver on the outside – hence the title name we have chosen. All the spoons in this section

FLY-SPINNERS & SPOONS.   *1. The Roachtickle   2. Mepps Mouche Noire   3. Fly-spoon – with fly   4. Abu Fly   5. Plain Fly-spoon.*

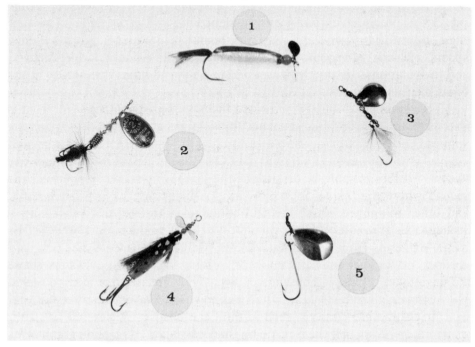

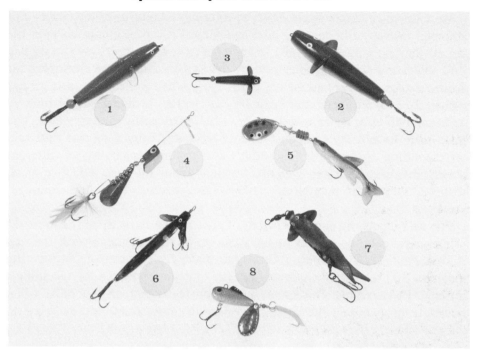

1. *Wooden Devon*   2. *Plastic Devon*   3. *Metal Devon*   4. *Morrum Spinner (Abu)*
5. *Mepps Mino*   6. *Quill Minnow*   7. *Wagtail*   8. *Abu Spin-up.*

do not usually spin about an axis but wobble upon a variously erratic course. The piker, for example, may deviate from a straight line by as much as twelve inches even on a steady retrieve.

Spoons like the C & S with their egg-shaped outline, and dessert-spoon convexity were the first spoons we made ourselves from the family cutlery, and are still the mainstay of Irish pike trollers. Probably most youngsters do this at some time or other, and having conned the old man into drilling a hole at each end, add a split ring and swivel at the narrow end and a split ring and treble hook at the fat end – and there you have a perfectly satisfactory, highly efficient spoon which rarely fails to work. The convexity combined with weight are the two variables which decide whether a spoon of this type will wobble well, and it may be necessary to get to work with a round-headed hammer to effect some changes of shape.

If we take this shape as the basic and classic spoon shape, there are various ways we can effect changes. Simplest, of course, is to change the colour. The standard Irish trolling spoon is copper-coloured on the inside and silver on the convex outside, but they can be copper all over, silver all over, red inside, or any combination of stripes and spots that the angler fancies. We shall return to this matter of colour when dealing with making your own spoons.

37

More drastic changes are effected by altering the outline of the spoon. For example, instead of being short and egg-shaped it can be elongated as in the case of the Jim Vincent spoons. In light metal (or wood, as was the *original* J.V. spoon and similar spoons used by the Red Indians) these are superb for fishing shallow broads and meres, particularly when trolled or trailed behind a boat. In heavier metal they can be cast better, avoiding the planing so common with light spoons, and can be fished more easily in deep water. The basic Jim Vincent style spoons, that is elongate, convex on one side and correspondingly concave on the other, and coming in all sorts of different brands, colours, sizes and weights, are just about the most effective of all artificial lures. It is possible to have weight, size or colour for almost all situations.

The next change to consider is that of altering the actual spoon shape itself by making it concavo-convex, usually convex on the outside towards the rear of the spoon. In the Gresvig Crocodile made by Paravan of Norway the spoon is still essentially convex on the outside, whereas in Gladding's Intrepid Flasha range the spoon is *flat* but S-shaped or sigmoidal when viewed from its edge. The latter range has flectolite added to the outside to

SPOONS. *1. Piker   2. Salamander   3. Abu Toby   4. Plain Copper Spoon.*

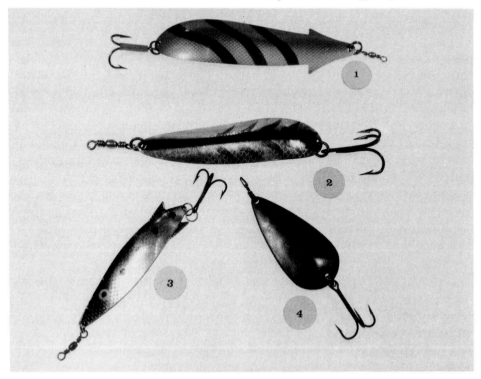

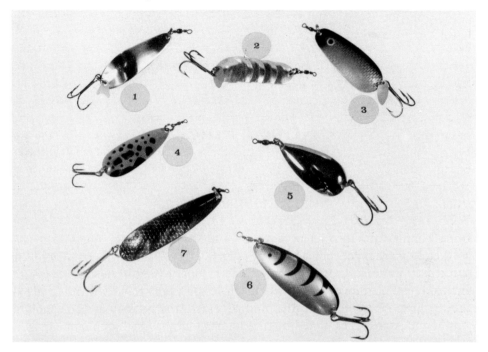

SPOONS.   *1. Shakespeare De Luxe   2. Abu Atom   3. Abu Mortblank   4. Shakespeare Jim Vincent   5. Plain Silver Spoon   6. Norwegian Paravan   7. Shakespeare Catcher.*

give numerous reflecting surfaces. Toby spoons are about half-way between Flashas and Crocodiles in their overall convexity, are similarly concavo-convex along their length, but have in addition two tiny stabiliser-like fins near the rear of the spoon, which are directed slightly outwards rather than inwards. Each of these spoons has a slightly differing action, they are heavier than the basic C & S and Jim Vincent patterns, and cast rather better. Under certain conditions they have a tendency to *spin* about a slightly wobbly axis.

Probably anyone reading this part of our book will be itching to say that all this is very well but spoons are very easy to make in all different shapes and sizes. This is true, and we hope we've catered for this instinct later, but the home handyman will find that most of his efforts classify quite naturally into the basic types we have just described, and which commercial lure makers have been producing for many years. You can add all sorts of things, extra trebles, trailing trebles (Commando spoons), plastic tags, garish colours, fur and feather, and the bulk still fall into the Toby, C & S, and Jim Vincent patterns.

CHAPTER FIVE

Good Plugs

NORMARK VIBRO RAPALA

Omri Thomas of Vibro let us have a set of these a few years ago. We have not yet lost a single one, and we dread doing so, for their scratched and tattered appearance bears witness to the savagery they have suffered at the teeth of pike. Little perch will hang on to the tail treble with their usual gentle pluck, but pike *maul* this plug. Even so, the hooks and hook-mounts on our plugs are still good, but the dorsal ridge has little remaining of the original dark colour.

Floating Rapalas of the 160 mm length, in silver or gold, we found superbly efficient on the Sixteen Foot River in the Fens. They can be flicked easily under the far bank and on a rapid initial retrieve will dive not too deeply to catch on the marginal ledge, but sufficiently steeply to get well down by the time they are halfway across. Considerable lengths of the Sixteen Foot are over nine feet deep and the 160 mm Rapalas will reach at least six feet down even on the shortest traverse at right-angles to the bank. Unlike many other of our favourite lures, such as Snipers, Rapalas do not, on our waters, take many perch and they are more successful with pike than anything else. Although we have fished them in amongst some big brown and sea trout they have never succeeded, and yet on the big Irish loughs they have on occasions been deadly with big trout (not to us, we hasten to add).

Returning to the use of Rapalas on the Sixteen Foot and other fenland drains, it is an excellent idea to flick them along the bank in front of you before moving on to the next swim. This not only produces plenty of activity of small pike which dart out of the marginal soft weeds, but the activity of playing small pike commonly stirs the bigger ones into action.

Rapalas can also be worked slowly and shallowly; at least, the floating models can. The sinkers like the Countdown series are equally as good as floaters, and it is simply necessary to get used to the sinking rate and diving rate for each one that you use. It is no good letting the plug sink right to the bottom before beginning a retrieve.

Normark produce one other Rapala range, the Rapala jigs, which is well worthy of mention. These have a similar shape to the rest of the range but are fitted with single hooks at the head and tail, and a treble hook on the belly. They can be worked off bridges as well as boats, though we hesitate to suggest that they be used in waters where there is no bank access to private fishing!

CREEK CHUB MOUSE

Several firms make floating and diving mice, in a variety of colours from grey to tiger-striped! The Creek Chub floater which dives to about two feet on retrieve is a superb lure. In all probability those made by other firms are just as good, but it happens that we latched on to Creek Chub's version in the tiger-stripes and have never looked back. Our first version had a 70 mm body plus a further 50 mm of stiff yellow tail, a black and yellow-striped body and a red throat. It casts extremely well, since although rather light it has a compact aero-dynamic shape: casts of forty yards plus are easy with a back-wind.

This plug is extremely buoyant and it needs fairly quick retrieve to get it down to two feet or so. The slow wobble is superbly effective. We first used it on a relatively deep featureless drain in Lincolnshire and found several small pike with it, and have subsequently used it extensively in the Fens both on the drains and gravel pits. It seems to come into its own in the same type of water as the Gudebrod Sniper, namely, shallow with a fair bit of sunken weed across which to retrieve. For deeper water it is better to go for a deep-diving mouse such as Tiny Tim or Mitie Mouse. Of course, the great delight in using a mouse is in using it near or on the surface, where you can kid yourself that you have persuaded the pike to chase a mouse.

NORMAN'S FLASHAD

A lot of Norman's lures are good but, whilst the top-water Chugger-flash is quite famous, the Flashads seem to have been overlooked by most plug fiends. This is another shallow running, wobbling plug, and it looks somewhat like a bream in profile and is fittingly flat like a bream. The diving vane is broad, and the plug has a very slow wobble. On one fenland drain Barrie has had fish after fish on it, and the only drawback seems to be that the position of the trebles relative to the stiff, flat body gives the pike a

41

fair leverage for unhooking itself – and quite a few do manage this feat. In fact, of all the plugs we have used, we have had a bigger percentage of fish come off with this one than any others: it also gets more takes than most other plugs. Heddon's Punkin Seed is a similar plug, but a sinker, and with a faster wobble. The two make a good pair.

HEDDON'S RIVER RUNT SPOOK

As far as British anglers are concerned this plug, and the various copies of it made by other firms, has been around a long time. In fact we can remember Bernard Venables listing it and illustrating it in books such as *Fish and Fishing*, and they were for a long time one of the few North American plugs widely available to Britain's anglers.

It is a floater, and with a shallow, wobbling dive down to a couple of feet or so. Bearing in mind the general tendency that today's plug fishermen have to use plugs that are too big, a general reversion to the River Runt Spook would do no harm at all. They can be dropped in the water with a little plop and the angler can quietly search the near bank and around the edges of weed beds. The trouble with big plugs is that on many occasions the splash of them hitting the water frightens all the fish within a twenty yard radius: since the cast tends to be much longer than twenty yards this probably explains why a big lure often travels at least this distance before anything shows an interest in it. The River Runt Spook is often snapped within seconds of hitting the surface.

Heddon also produces slightly different versions such as the Midget and the Midget Digit. The former is a real beauty for close-range light-tackle work: it is a slow sinker, has a 2¼-inch body (60mm), and the colour we prefer is black with a silver-striped body and yellow eyes. It is also one of the best *hooking* plugs that we have ever come across, probably because the body is not much larger than the hooks. On some waters it proved excellent with perch, and like all black lures seems particularly good at night. Both the Midget and the standard come in a deep diving version, that is, with a big, almost horizontally-set diving vane carrying the trace attachment link.

ABU'S HI-LO RANGE

We have, perhaps, always regarded Abu tackle with mixed feelings, based as it was originally on Scandinavian angling, but among the many superlative

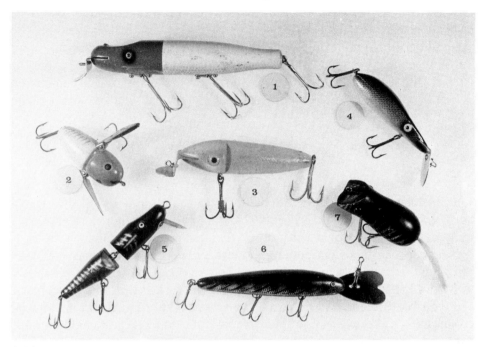

A SELECTION OF OUR FAVOURITE PIKE LURES. *As you can see, they are well-worn.* 1. *Creek Chub Pikie* 2. *Crazy Crawler* 3. *Sniper* 4. *Cello-Dip* 5. *Jointed Creek Chub Pikie* 6. *Norman's Deep Runner* 7. *Creek Chub Mouse.*

items they produce, and which we describe elsewhere in this book, is the Hi-Lo range of plastic plugs. No plug angler can afford to be without several of these. One of our favourites and one of the most successful of all plugs, particularly in the larger-size ranges, is the Hi-Lo M in the 40 g, 150 mm size. Four colours are available, and a really successful one is that with a golden back and sides, with a greenish head and green outlines to the scales; the stripes and dorsal ridge are black and the belly silvery. The Hi-Lo range has an adjustable diving lip: set it at a low angle to the horizontal and the lure dives very steeply; set it slightly backwards from the vertical and the lure either dives very shallowly or pops on the surface depending upon the rate of retrieves.

When fishing the big Hi-Lo in rough conditions there is a tendency for the diving vane to alter its position, and this can be irritating at times. Of course, the older the plug the greater is this tendency. The treble hooks are attached each by a *pair* of screws into the plastic body, but the chances of one pulling out are about nil: it has *never* happened to the authors, although we have found an occasional screw that works loose.

Pike of all sizes take even the jumbo-sized 150 mm Hi-Lo and the terrific vibratory wobble can, on some days, be far more effective than any plug or lure in the box. We have taken as many as eighteen pike in one day, *in the depths of winter*, using either this plug or a home-made wooden version of the same thing. It is not our intention to detract from Abu's product in any way, but it *is* possible to make yourselves wooden copies of the big Hi-Lo but, of course, with a non-adjustable vane, and these work really well. By making a few yourself it is possible to extend the somewhat limited colour-range available.

SHAKESPEARE'S BIG 'S'

John Hennes, the Shakespeare rep., thrust a brand-new Big 'S' into Ken's hot hand when they met early in 1974. Ken closed his fingers over it, and refused to let go – it looked just about the 'fishiest' lure he had ever seen.

Not only has this plug some great sweeping lines, it has a tremendous finish, and is available in a wide variety of colours. The one Ken possessed was in a blue and silver bream-type colour, and in fact this plug looks like a very pregnant bream. There has been a great deal of thought throughout its construction. The trebles are fine wire, and not too heavy, a common fault with many plugs. Instead of the usual screw-fitting for the trebles the eye is an integral part of the casting, and would take one hell of a lot of twisting before they would give. Split-rings hold the hooks well clear of any levering hold against the body itself.

This is one of the plugs with an in-built sonic vibrator – a lump of lead that rattles inside the body for the benefit of the old-fashioned thinkers. We have mixed feelings on their ability to attract, though. The only way to make them rattle and magnify the noise under water is by a very fast retrieve, and this is not that sort of lure. Occasional fast spurts, yes, but an erratic, swinging swoop with occasional stops can make this lure unbeatable.

Ken fished it first on the fickle North Met. Pit at Cheshunt, with success, and followed this with excellent chub from Penton Hook – the slack water, at the back of the island. Speaking to Peter Grundle (who is as great at freshwater fishing as he is at sea-fishing) we discovered another Big 'S' admirer; he (Peter) had taken six pike the day previous; nothing staggering, but good fish that moved on a day when nothing moved to other offerings.

SINNER SPINNER

Whether the Sinner is a plug or spinner is hard to say. Probably it does fit into the plug category because the blades at nose and tail do not attract by vision, being fitted merely to create vibration and disturbance, or an alteration in water pressure that definitely attracts.

One of the small baits, we needed to put some work on ours before it was ready for service. The belly treble, mounted just behind the head on the cigar-shaped body could be turned via its screw-fitting, and we removed it, set it with Araldite, and replaced it. The screw-fitting at nose and tail had a very long shank and seemed secure enough – but we left it turned back half a turn so that the small metal propellers could revolve more easily. We also put more of a twist in the vanes of the blades themselves, and found that this made a world of difference in its action.

As a surface attracter this plug certainly sends out the message. The faster it is retrieved, the harder the vanes turn and the slight 'scream' caused by the water disturbance rises in pitch. But the steady retrieve is not its only capability. Cast and allowed to rest on the surface, then worked back in a series of jerks with a long pause between each move, and the rod tip swung back strike-wise, it produces an action that has scored for us with pike, perch and chub.

Plugs from Woolco. Great value for money, and they offer an extension of some of our favourites in others colours.

MR THIRTEEN

Ken fancied the large, wood edition of this plug for some time before he invested in one. Eventually he chose the Red Head with frog-scale finish in 3⅝-inch size. Everything about the plug looked fine; although the belly trebles were fastened in with a flange and small grub-screws they were tight, and the finish, as with all Shakepeare items, was first-rate.

Came the next day of piking and Jack Simpson, who was with Ken, decided to have a throw around the big private pit they were fishing. He dived into the plug box, selected the Thirteen, and started work. After two or three casts Jack let out a yell of laughter, and Ken looked up to see his plug floating away across the pit. Jack reeled in, and realised that the trace was complete and the snap on the clip-ring firmly closed. Watching Ken's mis-spent gelt floating away, Jack then proclaimed that if it wasn't so bloody cold he would have stripped and gone in after it. Considering that the plug had been purchased from his shop, Ken wasn't exactly thrilled.

Fortunately the wind took it across the pit and it was retrieved. The fault lay with the eye, which had not been closed tightly. Two seconds' work with the pliers cured the problem and Jack fished on. It was a day of high wind and biting cold, where nothing took either live, deadbait, or sinking plug. Jack had three good 'grabs' at the Thirteen though, but they were half-hearted, just short of a full-blooded clang that could set the hooks.

Some weeks later a Yellow Coach Dog finish was taken into service and this has proved a first-rate surface lure with both of us. The manufacturers describe this as a floater/shallow diver, but our success has been when fished as a 'popper' on the surface, especially over those large, flat and featureless areas that every pit possesses. By reeling slowly, then raising the rod tip *vertically* the plug will pop and skip across the surface like nothing else we've tried. The change to a yellow colour has, for us at least, been an improvement from the results position, and so ensured a place for this in the 'necessary' side of the box.

ABU'S SNOKY

Abu's Snoky looks like something out of 1984; the pointed beak, hump back and long wedge-shape nose caused us to rechristen this plug 'The Concord'. But it looks more like a fish in the water than many of the lures in our boxes, and that may be what really counts.

When first we saw it there were serious misgivings as to its strength. The two halves of the body casting are welded together around the whole of the outer edge, and at first sight the hook-mountings appear to be glued in with it. Closer inspection showed that they are fastened internally though, and a word with Tony Perrin confirmed that they won't pull out. Certainly the eleven pound. pike that Ken has taken on his didn't leave any signs of strain.

This is another of the 'sonic' types with an in-built rattle. Earlier, we have commented that a hard retrieve is usually needed to make this type of attracter work – but this plug is an exception to the rule. Allowed to sink to its fishing depth, the gyrations this plug can produce must make the weight rattle, even on the slowest retrieve. Because the trace attachment is so far back towards the tail there is a very pronounced nose-down action which, when worked with a sink-and-draw motion raised mud clouds off the bottom, looking rather like a 'high' gudgeon freaking out. The gold finish we found especially attractive, and rather like an ornamental goldfish when the light hits the glitter scale effect.

MR MURDER

Mr Murder *sounds* the right name for a plug – and as every murderer is a one-off, so is this little widger. We say little, because that's the only size we've been able to obtain through our tackle sources – but Gudebrod plugs have always been difficult to get; probably because they *are* such good lures.

This deep sinker is a complete tail-over-head revolution. It looks like a very deep-set minnow, although ours has a perch type finish on it. The trace-fastening eye is just above the nose itself, and the diving vane is fixed just under the tail.

With this rather natty arrangement you quickly discover that there is a tendency for the plug to 'lift' hard on the retrieve, and not sink as most plugs do. So again this is a slow retrieve, sink-and-draw model that has, by virtue of its slim body, a fairly straight run that is killing for perch. We have had this lure so well taken that both sets of trebles, tail and belly, have been hooked well into the mouth.

A grand plug, one of our 'musts' in the perch and chub range, with only one possible doubt – the tail vane tends to provide a lever hold against the end treble, and could possibly cause a hook to free itself. But it hasn't happened to us yet.

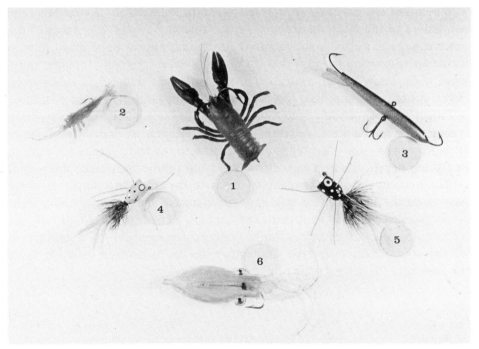

NEAR PLUGS.   *We are no longer experimenting with these: they work.   1. Crayfish 2. Shrimp   3. Rapala Ice Jig   4 & 5. Bass poppers   6. Sea squid.*

PLUGS WE DREAM ABOUT

Among the many things, we hope, apparent in this book will be the two facts that anglers collect plugs in vast numbers, and that many plugs are savagely adorned with treble hooks. If the hooks are to do their job properly they will be sharp and oft-sharpened so that they stick into almost anything with which they come into contact, including you and your clothes. If you carry many plugs to your fishing you'll need a big box to carry them in, or else you might just as well transport an armful of Prickly Pear cacti. You see the contradiction we are working towards, namely, that one of the joys of plug fishing is travelling light, and yet it seems necessary to carry a big box of plugs if we are to get the best results in the way of fish. Add to this the occasional encumbrance of a landing net, and you can forget 'travelling light'.

Or can you? Would it not be possible to get rid of the huge boxes and yet avoid periodic acupuncture during the course of a day? We have a dream which we hope will one day be taken up by the manufacturers. Something along the following lines is needed – assuming acceptance of the basic principle that treble hooks and plug bodies travel separately! This would mean that the bodies could be piled into a canvas bag, or into roomy pockets of the type in Barbour jackets, whilst the treble hooks, all mixed up, oiled, in quantity, and in a variety of sizes, could be held in a suitable box or tough bag.

Elsewhere in this book we have illustrated and described plug boxes and treble hook guards, but the advantage of this dream of ours is that the bulk and danger to the roving angler would be more or less removed. The disadvantage at present is that there are no suitable safety-pin type clips for rapidly adding and removing trebles to the plug body. What is needed is something like the illustration in which the clip is deeply set in the body of the plug, but until we obtain suitable clips in various sizes it remains a dream. However, we have already made some, using standard link swivels with safety-pin clips as well as some using safety-pins in various sizes. The disadvantage of both is that the clips project too far below the plug body.

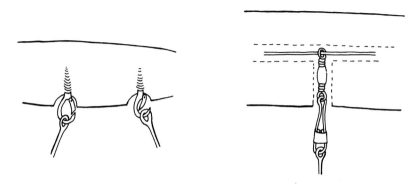

From the maker's viewpoint we should think it financially advantageous to dispense with treble hooks in the make-up of the plug, and just sell the body itself with simple clip inserts. Alternatively, the makers of plugs and hooks could get together and put very simple loops on the plugs and *clips* in place of the eyes on the treble hooks. In the meantime no doubt we'll go on buying expensive lure boxes, getting stuck on trebles, and extending our angling vocabulary with suitable expletives.

We should add, however, that Abu have made a considerable step in the right direction with their Kynoch plugs. These are about four inches long, one piece, and having an integrated link swivel, split-ring, and treble hook which goes diagonally through the head. The hook-cum-swivel is easily removed and the body can be carried loosely in the pocket. Another clear advantage is that when a fish is hooked it tends to 'blow' the body of the plug along the trace, thus giving itself no leverage at all: unhooking becomes easier for the same reason. On the models we have seen the link swivel is of the poor type, and what is really needed is a safety-pin swivel. If Abu can make a first-class plug of this type then they, or a competitor, could begin a range of dream plugs.

Perhaps this would be an appropriate place to append advice to those unfortunate enough to stick a treble hook in themselves. If the hooks are big, then go to a doctor with the lure attached (or unclip it if our dream comes true!). If the hook is small, rip it out with as little forethought as possible unless you think it is stuck in a particularly dangerous or unusually painful place. We've done this twice, on one occasion pushing back a little bit of flesh before washing and treating: it is far preferable to waiting for hours for the doctor to do the same thing.

In a serious attempt to solve the lure carrying problem alluded to, BR designed the lure hold-all illustrated. In it each lure is kept quite separate from others, and there is no tangling. In addition to the lures the other acoutrements of lure fishers also fit in the bag, such as camera, balance, forceps, food, drink, and anorak. On unrolling it whilst fishing the *first* thing you see is the lure roll, on the assumption that other items will be needed less frequently during the day.

CHAPTER SIX

Top Ten

It is inevitable that with the enormous range of lures available everyone will have a few favourites. And it is likely that each person's list of favourites will be different from that of the next person. We have tried to be just a little more objective with our combined list, picking those that really are consistently good in the UK – lures which we would not contemplate going fishing without. Furthermore, we have tried to rate them 1–10. Thus the Buzzer we rate as the best of all lures, and the Crazy Crawler creeps in at number ten, the only truly top surface lure in the list. Note that we list four plugs, three spoons and three spinners; and that the top three are respectively a spinner, a spoon and a plug, which is perhaps the exact opposite of the order you would receive from many anglers. At number ten the Crazy Crawler only just makes it. Were we picking a football team the Toby would be next on the list! And the bar-spoon series (Mepps, Veltic etc. etc.) good though they are, are excluded because the Buzzer totally eclipses them.

BLAKEMORE'S BUZZER

It should be pointed out that this tandem lure, part fluttering spoon, part jig, so alien to anglers in the UK, is actually made by different firms under different names. Thus Heddon's Climax is the same thing, as is Northlands Reed Runner. Perhaps the fact that so many firms make the same lure is a reflection of its efficacy. Of all the lures that we have used over the years it is, simply, the best. During 1985 we found that we took about three times as many fish on Buzzers as on any other lure, mostly pike, it should be emphasised. The Buzzer has a leaded jig on the lower part of the tandem, usually equipped with a weed-beating, inturned single hook, and a fluttering spoon, usually copper coloured, on the upper bar. Observations with small

51

pike shows that whilst the spoon may act as an attractor, the fish actually home in on and grab the skirted jig.

Buzzers cast extremely well and yet can be fished within inches of the surface or at great depth. The lure can be retrieved steadily or fished with an incredible sink and draw motion. If a single hook is used it can be fished successfully in amongst snags and weeds. But we do feel that the single fails to hook big pike on occasion, probably because the powerful jaws are able to clamp the lure flat between the upper and lower jaw edges. We often add a trailing treble so that it hangs just within the ambit of the rubber skirt. Attached with a link swivel it is easily removed to enable one to fish snaggy swims.

RENOSKY LASER SPOONS

These spoons are, like the Buzzer, very unusual in the eyes of UK beholders. For a start they are fish shaped, with fins, and a print of a fish on the reverse side. The print is fully durable and can be one of a variety of species including rainbow trout and perch. The one we have had real success with has a shiner on the reverse side, a bleak like species. Two points arise with respect to this spoon: as a silver spoon it is as good as any other silver spoon we have tried; and the fishy side results in other species than pike falling for it. It is, for example, the *only* spoon that we have used consistently for zander fishing. Like the buzzer the laser Shiner casts a long way, and can be retrieved either very shallowly or very deeply. The silver-cum-fish appearance undoubtedly gives two attraction points as far as zander are concerned. The pike probably do not distinguish as finely, but they take it well anyway.

CREEK CHUB PIKIE

This is probably the most consistently successful plug in the business, a surface diver. It comes in various sizes and colours, but the pike-coloured, single jointed form, some 4–5 inches in length is perhaps the best of all. The perch-coloured form runs it a close second, and we note that Gordon Burton lists such a lure as one of his best plugs in the PAC journal 'Pikelines' no. 30. You can get deep divers in the Creek Chub range, but it's the surface floating, shallow divers that we prefer. Pikies retrieve in a fairly straight line, with a little wobble, but erratic action can be induced as required by use of the rod tip, and a really fast wobble can be imparted by a fast, deepish retrieve.

BLAKEMORE'S TROUBLE SHOOTER

This is Blakemore's equivalent of the Big 'S' widely used by UK anglers. We rate the Blakemore version, with its slightly fatter belly, as slightly better than the Big 'S'. It also takes other fish than pike, notably perch and chub. We have never been convinced that the sonic boom of this lure has the slightest effect on fish catching and, indeed, we feel the same about the Big 'S'. The real killing aspect of the Troubleshooter is its high speed wobble which it takes on at the slightest pull. It also dives well and deeply, or can be fished quite shallowly. Once again the pike and perch colours are good but there is also a red one (which we informally call Red Robin) which is highly effective at times. The size of the version we prefer is about three inches in body length and we rate it as the best small plug ever designed, the Creek Chub Pikie being essentially a bigger plug.

NORWICH COPPER SPOON

This is the first British lure that we have listed, and we rate it as number five behind four US lures. We define Norwich (or Copper and Silver) spoons elsewhere in the volume, but essentially it is the traditional egg-shaped, English spoon, widely used in Norfolk, and indeed in Eire on the large loughs. Many times they have been manufactured at home from household spoons, but are nonetheless effective for that. Once again they come in many sizes but we opt for the three inch blade for pike fishing, stepping down a little for other species, perhaps to about one inch length. The copper colour (copper sheet or paint) is the best we feel, though some waters respond well to brass, others to silver or silver and red. If the copper is well buffed or polished it has the typical pink suffusion or bloom of copper and it is in this state that the spoon seems to us to be at its most effective.

In terms of casting ability it is midway between a Toby, which casts well, and a Vincent, which doesn't. In terms of retrieve a three inch blade will wobble unless retrieved very hard, when it *may* spin. The wobble gives a series of pulsing flashes from the convex side, and a duller, more complex pulse from the concave side. A pike can see a spoon from one side only! Whilst this is often forgotten by most anglers it is important because an upstream cast may show one side of the lure to the fish, and a downstream cast the other side. So with all spoons we constantly cast back along the length we have recently covered. Nowhere is this more important than in fishing the three inch Norwich Spoon.

GUDEBROD'S SNIPER

Our third plug is the four inch bright yellow or perch pattern, and is still one of the best plugs ever made. It is a pity that Gudebrod do not still make it. It has, on shallow weedy waters, an irresistable slow, shallow side-to-side wobble. It takes a variety of species and Barrie's best brown trout, of sixteen pounds, fell to this plug. That was on Loch Lomond, but the lure is just as effective with pike and perch on the Fenland drains. All lures have some drawbacks, and this one's is that it leaks eventually and needs to be dried out and any holes plugged (!) with Araldite. It casts extremely well and with practice can be retrieved as shallowly as three inches or as deeply as three to four feet.

THE MACKEREL SPINNER

Oh! what a neglected lure. Of course, sea anglers use them for mackerel, not with any great thought but because they happen, by tradition, to be available in sea resort tackle shops. Inland they are not commonly for sale, but you will note that of spinners we rate only the Buzzer lures above it. Mackerel spinners are superb in freshwater, taking many species. The sizes 1–2 inches seem to be best, and they cast very well especially if fished on lines of 7–8 lb. b.s. On the retrieve they can be fished in the surface film almost, and very very slowly, but they work very effectively at any depth. Red wool can be added to the treble hook but this should be done sparingly – a worm-like trail, rather than a fuzzy bundle. This is then most effective for perch, which will often snip-snip at the wool until they take a firm hold.

THE VIBRO SPINNER

The tragedy is that this lure is no longer with us, having met its commercial end during one of the 'low' periods of spinning enthusiasm. We still have a few ourselves and, as we pointed out elsewhere in the volume, they can still be found in some shops. They work well in all sizes, but for our repertoire of lures we prefer the large sizes. They are, as their name implies, the most vibratory of all lures, giving so much resistance on the retrieve that it feels one is landing a small boat. They are very very consistent takers of big pike and big perch, and we have caught hundreds of good perch on the tiny ¾ inch size. If the 'vibe' stops, you strike hard: weed can cause them to stop whirring, but so can a fish.

JIM VINCENT SPOON

These we prefer in copper, but silver, brass and so on have their uses. In terms of technique we prefer to use them for casting from boats or for trolling, because only in the heavier metal sizes do they cast well. Often they tend to plane on the wind and both distance and accuracy are lost. But under many conditions they score well, particularly on deep, clear waters at dawn and dusk, and on shallow waters disturbed by a big wind. This latter feature probably led to their use on the Norfolk Broads by the man who lends his name to the spoon, but they originated in North America and were found to be in use by the Red Indian peoples for (northern) pike and muskies. Originally they were carved in wood, presumably heavy (?) and presumably painted. There *is* some scope for inventiveness here because a very slow sinking spoon would be a Godsend on many waters. Perhaps a lead strip along one edge....

THE CRAZY CRAWLER

Its name says it all! We have described this often enough as the laugh-a-minute lure, and one never quite gets used to its flip-flop, flip-flop progress across a calm surface. On a quiet day in the countryside, the water flat calm, the noise of its progress seems so incongruous. Perhaps this is what the predator feels – its peace is disturbed. The last fish we had on one, in November 1985, weighed 18¼ lbs and it launched itself on the CC, mouth agape, in about two feet of water on a tiny Fenland drain, completely swamping the banks with the huge bow wave. Perch take the CC readily, especially the smaller version coloured like a bumble bee. In fact our experiences suggest that the smaller bumble bee version is a little more effective than the traditional red and white, two inch bodied one, although this latter is the only one we possess at present. The CC is not a lure to try when all else fails. Try it as a matter of course, because on some days they go quite mad on it and refuse anything else. Nor should you be misled into thinking of it only as a calm water lure, even though that is when one enjoys using it most. It works just as effectively on a big swell.

CHAPTER SEVEN

Roll Your Own: Making and Maintaining Plugs

HOME-MADE PLUGS

The problem here is knowing where to start – not where to start when making a plug, but knowing where to start telling you! We could write a book on this subject alone, so great is the choice of materials and design and the chance for individual inventiveness. It is this last point, the scope for enterprise, that really makes plug-making a pleasure. And when your home-made lure succeeds, as it will, it is difficult to describe the excitement. The very first four inch, single piece floater that Barrie made caught a 4lb 12oz pike from the Glucose factory lake at Rawcliffe in the West Riding: that was years ago, but you notice how the weight is remembered, and he can recall the swim quite clearly.

That plug was very similar to Abu's Hi-Lo Bo, but there is certainly no need to copy other designs. Think out your own theory, and then try to make a plug that works. Take, for instance, the Waddle-Arse. This is a big, two-jointed, wooden plug not unlike a Creek Chub jointed Pikie but with rear section completely free of attached hooks. The idea was that the tail section would waddle more freely without the weight of the hooks, and that the plug could be retrieved half-on and half-under the surface as shown in the illustration. It works perfectly. Had the rear hooks on this plug been

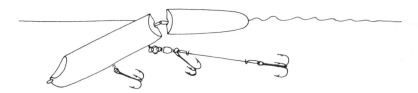

attached to the rear section their extra weight would have slowed down the rather fantastic waddle. A further advantage is that the trailing hooks take a clean hook-hold and are difficult to lever out as the pike leaps and rolls.

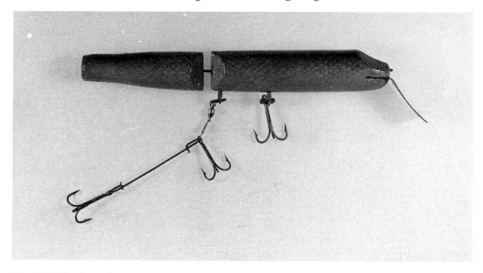

The Waddle-Arse plug.

Of course, one mistake was to make it so big. A good principle to get hold of when making plugs is to make them small rather than too large: it increases the chance of a small fish taking them thus giving you the confidence that they actually do work. But the Waddle-Arse is a winner.

How was it constructed? The figure depicts the stage-by-stage building of the Waddle-Arse plug. Step one is to choose the wood, in this case a length of one inch diameter dowel rod or broom handle in soft wood. Try to choose a piece with a fine and parallel grain, and then cut the two joints of the plug to about ⅛-inch longer than you intend them to be. The next step is the only difficult one in the whole operation: drill a hole about ⅛-inch diameter along the length of the head joint. We use a specially-made long bit and do the drilling on a lathe: this bit will drill a hole up to five inches long and if everything is centred correctly the bit comes out of the back of the joint in a dead central position. If using an ordinary hand drill or electric drill, the joint being held in a vice, it is better to drill in from both ends. The holes *usually* meet in the middle even if the junction is a little scruffy. It can always be cleaned out with a steel knitting needle.

The holes through the joint take the wire which will connect the joints and also hold the hooks. Having marked the positions of intended trebles on the belly of the head joint, drill short holes through to connect with the long central hole. When this has been accomplished, treat the inside of all holes to a liberal soaking with a water-proofing agent such as sanding sealer, and allow it to soak in and dry.

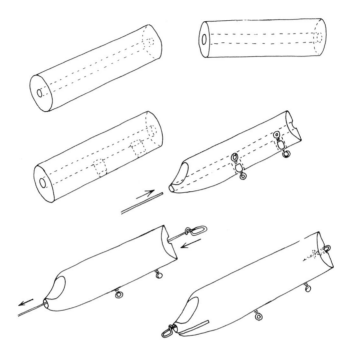

Shaping the body is quite enjoyable. We use a coarse rasp and finish off with sand-paper of varying grades. It is possible to do some shaping with a knife or saw, in particular the chamfered edges where the two joints connect and which give the joints more freedom of movement. Make a saw cut at the head of the plug in the position you intend to place the diving vane.

The plug is now ready to take the wire and hook mounts. Push a large tightly-fitting swivel into the hole on the belly, so that a wire can pass along the central hole and through the eyes of the swivels. This *can* be tricky because the swivel eyes sometimes refuse to lie at right-angles to the length of the central hole! But it can be done.

The wire to use is stainless steel music-wire in the appropriate thickness. Ours is available in one pound rolls from most large ironmongers or metal workers. Having threaded a piece of wire successfully through the front joint, cut it so that about two inches sticks out at either end. Using pliers, fold over one inch at one end and pull the narrow loop well into the joint. Then do a similar loop on the other end and, using pliers, slowly push the wire back again until a small loop shows at both ends. That at the head end is for attachment of the trace, whilst that at the rear end is for attachment of the second joint. When doing a normal double-jointed plug, as opposed to the Waddle-Arse, you then repeat this procedure for the second joint.

Ancient lures against an ancient backcloth.

It is necessary to seal the holes around the wire loops to keep out water: plastic wood or Araldite can be used. The front of the rear section then has a ring-headed screw placed in the position shown in the figures, and a split-ring is used to connect the front and rear sections.

Attach the trebles by means of good split-rings. The advantage of attaching the trebles and diving vane before painting is that the balance of the plug can be tested in water and any corrections to the shape made with a rasp. The trebles can be left on during painting or not as required. Coloured hooks sometimes look rather nice.

On the subject of painting we intend offering no advice, save to say that scruffily-painted plugs often work as well as superbly finished jobs. Perhaps it *is* just worth adding that scale finishes can be achieved by spraying through a galvanised wire gauze screen. The whole can be finished off in a coat of polyurethane to give the skin some hardness, but with pike, for example, the paint doesn't last long anyway.

The diving vane is another tricky piece of work. We cut the slit in the head so that it will be a tight fit for the thickness of metal chosen for the vane. The vane will probably have to be cut to shape with tin-snips. It can be glued in position, or several vanes of different shape can be used with one plug, each having a different effect upon the action. In the latter case we rely on the tight fit to keep the vanes in place.

Some of Barrie's home-made plugs.

Buzzers.

Choice of hook-size is as important as the diving vane to the action of the plug, and it is as well to try several before making a final choice. Our experience is that you always need larger hooks than you expected or hoped for!

Clearly, the above system of hook attachment is pretty robust: the weakest parts are probably the split-rings, seemingly a necessary evil. It *is* possible instead of the big swivels, to insert link swivels, but the hooks still tend to hang too far away from the body of the plug. However, a much quicker if less safe way of hook attachment is possible. The body is shaped before any attempt is made to plan for hook positions. When the body is ready the hook positions are worked into the wood. All that is needed after this is a split-ring through the ring-head. Well, since it is so easy, what is wrong with the method? The main problem is that positioning the ring-headed screws tends to unbalance the plug and great care is needed, as well as occasional abandonment of a body with too many screw holes! Also, after a session or two in use there is an increasing risk of the screw pulling out as the wood rots along the length of the thread. However, if you are clever at positioning the screws then it is a quick method of finishing off plugs.

In the good (?) old days the Flap-jack type of plug was easy to make from the handle of a toothbrush. The bristle end was cut off, and the handle dipped into boiling water, which made it pliable and capable of bending into the banana or other shapes. Once shape was achieved, the plug was then cut to size, holes were drilled, split-rings and trebles fitted, and the job was complete.

Unfortunately, modern handles are made of brittle plastic and no matter how you heat them, they invariably snap when you try the bending exercise – or they catch fire. But it is still possible to find sheet perspex and other soft plastics that can be cut and moulded to produce some fascinating divers.

From the above it will be apparent that great variations of body-size and shape and colour are possible. But we have assumed that a diving floater is needed and that the body material is wood. In order to make a sinking plug you can insert lead into the belly of the plug, but this is certainly a tricky and skilful operation; it is easier to make floaters than sinkers. The great inventiveness of anglers really comes to the fore at this stage of thinking because it is possible to make plugs of plastic, rubber, fur and hair, latex-coated foam, as well as many different kinds of wood. The number of possible combinations is immense and it really would be silly of us to try to give account of numerous plugs made of differing materials. We feel we have outlined the fundamental points in the description of the Waddle-Arse construction, but the number of short cuts and alternative arrangements make the mind boggle. We shall mention specially constructed plugs at appropriate places elsewhere in the text.

PLUG MAINTENANCE

The best way of cutting down on maintenance is to spend a few extra minutes at the tackle shop. Every product has the odd dud that slips through, and although they are few and far between along the plug shelves, it does happen. Don't just accept the plug – examine it from head to tail, looking for tell-tale pin-holes that could be the forerunner of leaks. Look at the diving vane if one is fitted, and make sure that it is fitted squarely to the body. The photograph shows two identical plugs with one incorrectly fitted vane that rendered the plug useless.

Hook attachments should be a tight fit and trebles should swing freely from them. Even a treble hook without a barb has been known to appear on a plug before now – and if the body mount is one of the moulded type, replacement could be impossible. Finally, check for cracks on a cellulose finish. Once this occurs it is a short time before water causes the cellulose to lift further, and flake off.

On the workshop side a pair of tin-snips, long-nosed pliers, split-rings, spare trebles and eye mounts, some Alasticum and Araldite glue will see you through most repairs. A little thin oil can ease a few tight situations and help to cut back on future work.

The pin-hole problem is one we have outlined elsewhere in the book, and it happens to the best of plugs at times. Before sealing the hole with glue,

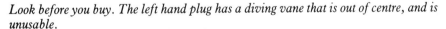

Look before you buy. The left hand plug has a diving vane that is out of centre, and is unusable.

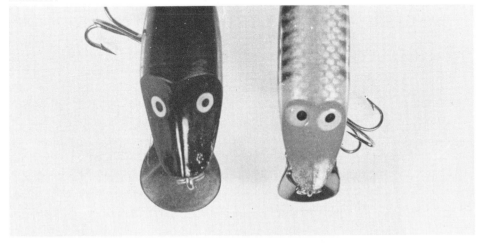

remember to shake out any water already in the body, and dry it. A touch of paint when the glue is dried off, and the job is complete. If, on test, the screws holding hooks to a plug appear loose – and this can be found on new or old models – they are best undone, smeared with a little Araldite, and then re-set. Of course, it may present problems if ever the hook has to be replaced, but at least it won't lose a fish whilst working.

Painting, or touching-up can be time-consuming unless you are an artist. One short cut is to use pressure-spray cans of cellulose that come in umpteen colours. Mask out with Sellotape that which you do not want covered, and remember to remove the hooks before starting, unless you want to colour them. With a little practice the colours can be 'blended' where they meet. Above all, do remember that because the plug may look a little secondhand and amateur in its finish, it doesn't mean that the fish won't accept it.

CHAPTER EIGHT

Spinner Making

Spoons are rather easier to make than bar-spoons, mackerel spinners or minnows, so we shall begin with and concentrate upon them. It should be said at the outset that neither of us are good handymen, and anglers who are should be able to make most of the types of spoons and spinners that are produced commercially. There is great scope for inventiveness, both artistic and scientific, in the making of artificial lures, and with today's materials available we feel there are many new types waiting for an active mind and skilful hands: or if not new basic types, at least new faces on old lures.

Let's begin with the household dessert spoon. Although this is often talked about, it is unusual to see anglers using a home-made Copper and Silver style spoon. Yet they are easy to construct and highly efficient. In the first place many dessert spoons have the correct egg-shaped outline with the correct convexity, and it is easy to find them in different qualities or weights of metal. Firstly, saw off the handle with a hacksaw, then use a file to round off that end of the spoon. Alternatively, the next step can be done first, namely, drilling a hole at each end of the spoon: if you do this drilling first you can hang on to the spoon handle whilst doing so. Make the holes with a diameter of about 2–3 mm, but not too far from the ends: the nearest edge of each hole should be about 2 mm from the end of the finished spoon. If this last distance is made any greater it is almost impossible to fit split rings without straining them.

Split rings are a problem. Quite simply, look for strength and smallness. Those where the wire has a flattened cross-section and a little kink or two where the ends meet tend to be weak: these should only be used on small spinners and in the smaller sizes. Having obtained good split rings, attach one to each hole of the spoon. Then to the narrow end (opposite the 'handle' end) add a swivel, and to the broad end a treble hook. In the case of really large spoons it's a good idea to add a treble to the front end too, and it doesn't seem to impair the action of the lure unduly. The only remaining problem is to colour it. A whole suite of perfectly good spoons can be made in this fashion.

Barrie's work-bench, with some spinner-making tools and materials.

But in general it is necessary to cut the spoon blades you need from sheet metal, simply because you may wish to make long Jim Vincents, concavo-convex spoons and so on. Almost all metals are useful at times. What you must do is keep a sharp eye open for bits of metal everywhere – tin trays, reflectors from car lamps, bumpers, and many other everyday discarded items can be used. Alternatively, it is possible to buy quite small sheets of different metals of varying weights.

First, you need to get a really good shape cut out in cardboard so that you can place it on the metal sheet and pencil around it. We always get someone to cut ours with the right equipment, since labouring away with a hacksaw can be really hard work and not very accurate. Having got the right outline it is necessary to file down any bumps or rough edges, before attempting to shape the curve of the blade. For this purpose you need a round-headed hammer or two, and a large block of wood such as a cross-section of tree about two feet across. A shoemaker's last is also useful. The effect of the hammering is to produce a bumpy or scale-like finish which is no bad thing on a spoon. When first trying to hammer out a flat piece of metal into a convex spoon of the Jim Vincent style, it is easy to become enthusiastic and quickly ruin its shape. Begin tentatively until you see how that particular piece of metal is responding to the hammer. In time you will find that it is quite easy to make a shallowly convex spoon, or a deeply convex one, or a concavo-convex one.

Marking the metal prior to cutting with tinsnips, using an earlier made blade as a template.

Beating the spinner to obtain curve.

Perhaps the most common mistake made by beginners at this game is to use metal that is too thin, simply because it can be cut very easily with tin-snips. Tin-snips are useful, and they come in different strengths and sizes, but it is advisable to find someone with good metalwork equipment who will cut out your shapes for you. Having got your shape ready, and having hammered it to the required convexity, all that is needed are the finishing touches that you made to the C & S spoon discussed above.

Bar-spoons are a little bit more tricky. You'll need the same equipment as for spoons, but in addition a good pair of long-nosed pliers with rounded jaws; metal wire for the axial wire; dress eyes (from pairs of hook and eyes) for attaching blades to the bar; beads, and bodies (or weights) for the bar.

The first step is to prepare the blade itself in the same way as for spoons, but remember that the metal can be much lighter and in this case is easily cut with snips. Drill a hole at *one* end in exactly the same way as with spoons, but do *not* thread the blade on the bar wire. If you do this the blade is too close to the bar and to any body or weight that you place on it, and it does not rotate efficiently. Instead, modify a dress eye as shown in the figure or use a commercial clevice, put the blade on this, and then thread the dress eyes on to the bar. This means the whole blade attachment swings much more loosely although, of course, quite securely.

The tricky bit with bar-spoons comes just before you add the blade to the bar. It is necessary to bend the bar wire into a ring at the front end and to do this use either the long-nosed pliers, or a thin metal rod firmly clamped in a vice. You need a neat round ring, and whilst this is easy to achieve with soft wire such a ring is useless in a spinner since it bends the first time you cast it into a piece of bridgework. The wire needed is stainless steel piano or music wire in various grades. Sizes 24 and 26 are two useful thicknesses. It is tough stuff, and you're sure to suffer a lacerated finger or two before the evening is out.

Having constructed a loop as shown, slide a bead along the bar so that it is flush up to the loop, then add the blade itself, then another bead; at which point you must decide whether to have a body of beads, plastic tube, swan shots, barrel lead, dowel rod, or what-have-you. When you have the body in place, add another bead, and finally make a loop at the end on which to add a split-ring and treble hook. Do not jam the whole lot up too tight so that the dress eye cannot rotate. In our experience the body is best glued in position so that wear, tear and breakage is not caused by the assembly forever sliding up and down the bar.

The first bar-spoons that Ray Webb and Barrie made for use on Hornsea Mere looked extremely crude, worked like a bomb, and on the first trip to Hornsea took a blind pike of three pounds, which surely proves that the vibrations were right! At this stage it is possible to experiment with bar

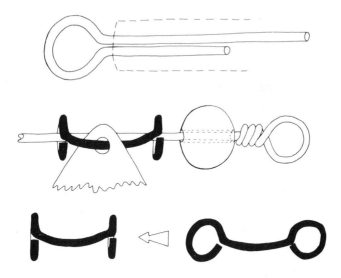

length, blade shapes, body weights and so on. The only thing to watch is that the bigger you make them the more difficult it is to make them work well. For the larger sizes we copy the proprietary brands such as Vibro. Incidentally a number of firms, Tom Saville's included, make a whole range of spinner-maker's accessories including the eyelets and beads, so that by being inventive and shopping around as well, the would-be spinning enthusiast is well catered for.

It is not our intention to give a blow-by-blow account of making all sorts of spinners, since our two descriptions cover a great range of lures once the basic principles are mastered, but we shall briefly give a pointer or two towards some of the other types of spinner. Quill minnows, for example, are best made by actually buying one of the type that you fancy, or which is very good on your waters, and then copying it at home. You'll need cable wire, bird quills in various diameters, treble hooks, whipping thread and varnish. Traditionally, tapered shank trebles are used in quill minnows and these are certainly less cumbersome than eyed trebles which will suffice for the rest of home spinner making, but put a loop of wire round the join of the bends as well as tying along the shank.

Mackerel spinners are difficult unless you have access to facilities for brazing a tube along the centre of the blade. This tube *can* be Araldited into position, but the life of the spinner is shorter. The rest of a mackerel spinner is easy once you have this problem mastered. Wagtails need very little comment since today there is a wide range of rubber and plastic tubing

A selection of materials obtainable from Tom Saville's tackle shop at Nottingham.

available. Apart from this you'll need cabled wire, beads etc., and some thin metal from which to make the spinning vanes at the head end. The only difficulty is fixing these vanes to a rigid head at the front of the lure. Again Araldite, the universal cure-all, stick-all, is necessary. Wooden minnows and metal minnows can be made if you use wood- and metal-turning lathes and drilling equipment, but wooden minnows can, at a pinch be made without this equipment.

PART TWO
TECHNIQUES

CHAPTER NINE

Casting

In casting, more can be learned by watching than by reading. This chapter is therefore devoted to illustrations, explanatory captions and minimal text. Barrie posed for the photographs very nicely.

The first four photographs illustrate the use of the heavier type of double-handed rod referred to. With practice, accurate casts can be made over considerable distances.

CASTING WITH A TWO-HANDED ROD. *The grip, arms spread shoulder width, middle finger of the right hand controlling the line from the reel.*

Commencement of the two-handed cast. Feet comfortably spread, the angler facing the direction of the cast.

Power. Both left and right arm work in a sweep to bring the rod over the angler's shoulder. The line is released at the centre of the stroke.

Follow-through. The rod is held in this position until the plug touches the water.

THE OVERHEAD CAST WITH A SINGLE-HANDED ROD. *From a position of one o'clock the rod is brought vertically over the angler's shoulder, driving the plug out. The line is released at the eleven o'clock position.*

Follow-through. With the rod held above the water-level, the angler can watch the reel and check the accuracy of the cast at the same time.

CASTING FROM THE LEFT-HAND-SIDE SWING. *Useful for tight corners. The picture shows the commencement of the cast.*

Swing-through and the line release.

Follow-through, watching both the reel and the plug.

CATAPULT CAST. *Ideal for small holes in tree-lined banks etc. Maximum tension is followed by the release of the plug and line.*

The moment of release.

Casting in winter can be cold. It is a total fallacy, though often enough repeated in texts, that lure fishing in winter keeps you warm. It has exactly the opposite effect except when actually walking between swims. The hands suffer greatly. We have found that some gloves, especially those of a cheap plastic/leather (waterproof), and with a lining can be used very successfully. Because weed and other vegetation has died down the occasional miscast is less important than in the summer months. One pair of these gloves cost less than £5 in 1986, and will last through the three coldest months without wearing out (that is assuming that an angler spins at least once a week).

CHAPTER TEN

Landing and Handling Fish

One day someone will perfect the ideal landing net. Of course, they will patent it and make a fortune – for nowhere in the field of angling is there more room for improvement than with this single, essential item. Brief specifications of this wonder net are unknown as yet. But Ken would suggest that they could read as follows:

'Folding into a pocket-handkerchief size, and completely crushable. When needed this item opens on touch, and becomes immediately taut with a sinking net at least three feet deep. The sides are rigid, enabling a thirty pound pike to be safely lifted, and the handle is always long enough to cope with the steepest bank an angler is likely to encounter. The whole thing is immediately self-drying, smell- and rot-proof, and folds back to its original pocket-handkerchief size by perceptory powers at the will of the angler.'

All right, so that was supposed humour. But it highlights the problems of landing nets to perfection, starting with size. Size is weight, weight is loss of mobility, which in turn leads to fewer fish. It is possible to own an assortment of different sized nets – but of course the big pike always comes when you have anticipated small perch, and vice versa. So it is probably better to aim for the middle-of-the-road size, concentrating on construction and medium weight.

First, shape. A large round frame is ideal, but cumbersome. It can be purchased with four hinges, or made with three, so that it may be folded after use – but there is a tendency for the hinges to pinch the netting material, cutting and opening the top row of meshes so that the net itself will not hang fully from the frame.

One way round that problem is to fasten the top meshes by half-hitches to brass or plastic rings, which in turn fit on to the rim. But they will rattle at every step, and this can be a confounded nuisance. Alternatively Elastoplast can be wrapped on the join. It lasts about three seasons.

Triangular frames are easier to fold, but the base of the triangle can present problems. If this is solid metal, there will also be two joints that can pinch the net material. Also, the netting tends to fall from the frame when it is collapsed, and in doing it will prevent the arms from opening properly.

The base section formed from leather thonging of cord is one answer, but it also has a disadvantage in that if you are trying to 'scoop' a big fish into the net (especially if the net is small) or land a fish from a strong weedbed, the soft base will collapse and the fish stands an excellent chance of escaping. A superb modern invention, micromesh, causes two serious problems for the spinning man: hooks get *deeply* tangled; and currents can bell the net dangerously.

Weigh up the pros and cons for yourself. We favour one of the triangular non-collapsing frames when wading for chub etc. or a collapsible net with a plastic-coated steel wire base that is held exceptionally rigid by tensioning on both arms for pike. Barrie has a very large round frame at all times – and the reference is to his net! It can be towed through undergrowth much better than a triangular net.

Solid metal, light alloy or fibre-glass are the materials used for frames, and each has some advantage. From a boat, where record-breakers can be expected and weight is of no real consequence, then solid metal is ideal. But for the chap who is walking the banks it is definitely 'out', and alloy has an edge in these circumstances. Remember, too, that there is alloy and alloy; some frames on sale at the moment are rubbish. One decent lift for a good fish and they are buckled. Solid alloy is the answer, and square or oblong in section rather than round.

Specimen-hunting groups have come up with a superb frame over the last few years (Springbow). The idea is that hollow fibre-glass tubing is used as side-arms, and these are wedged under pressure into the handle of the net. By bending along the sides they tension a protected steel wire across the base, producing a 'bowed' shape which is a cross between round and actual triangle, very large, and with great strength. Unfortunately, the design does not appear suitable for adaptation as a collapsible model, but there could be a fortune awaiting the person who perfects it.

For wading or walking a collapsible net is a boon. Providing that the knuckle and locking mechanism where the frame hinges at the joint with the handle is completely fool-proof, all will be well. But there are some weird and wonderful creations on the market, not all of which are trouble-free. There is a lot to be said for a plain flip-over joint that is made from good gauge brass. Beware the push-button, spring-operated wonder gadget. The more mechanism there is, the more there is to jam, buckle and generally frustrate the angler. The means of attaching a net to the angler is also important. Look for the compromise between a hook or clip so strong that it breaks the finger-nails each time it is replaced on the belt or bag, and one that is so loose that the net falls off while walking along the bank. When this happens the angler will be unaware of the calamity – until crisis hour, and a fish has to be netted.

Often the hook or attachment on the net is suitable but the ring fastening on belt or bag is at fault. Trial and error are the only thing, and a little ingenuity with a pair of pliers can work wonders. From personal experience – beware elastic as a means of attachment. Usually the net gets caught on shrubbery at the waterside, and when the angler turns to find out why his progress is being impeded, the net releases itself and travels at a rate of knots towards his body. Nasty, dangerous and painful.

Finally, there is the handle. For a wading net there is no great problem, except to say that we prefer something thick that we can get a good grip on, and that if possible it should have a hollow, or wooden piece, so that something will float if it drops into the water. The angler himself could do with something similar!

A present-day gimmick seems to be the telescopic handle on a wading net, propelled forward by spring action when a button is pushed, or opened by the angler extending the handle manually. It is difficult to see what is behind the idea – after all, when you are wading you should be close enough to manage a fish without requiring an extension.

Even more important is the fact that a telescopic handle is susceptible to strain so a heavy fish lifted with the net extended can damage the sliding parts to the point that they will no longer move. We are for the simple life, and happy with a medium-length strong, floating handle when wading.

For those who really need a long handle – which includes the bank angler not wading, or the chap who likes to combine both wading staff and landing net, a length of fibre-glass tubing is probably ideal. It is light, will float, and is strong enough to probe a pool you might want to wade. If you are an angling heavyweight who needs have something to push and lever with – then we suggest the proper implement for the job; a good wading staff.

There is a compromise for the angler who wants both hands free with a long-handled landing net. Here, by a leather thong and dog clip, the net is hung across the back and carried without interference to angling activities. When a fish has to be netted, the hand drops down to the side where the net is, slips the release spring, and the net drops down practically into the hand.

Our personal opinion is that this system is not only safer than relying on a collapsing net, but also allows a fair-sized rigid rim to be used. Beware the handle that is too long though, for it will interfere with an overhead cast – with painful results to the angler's head.

As to net material, well, present-day material trends are towards the micromesh. No doubt about it, wear and tear on fish scales are saved by this

Springbow net from Don's of Edmonton. Ideal in every way for that big fish.

soft material, and every angler seeking fish he knows will have to be returned should use one. But micromesh removes more slime than does the older material; and it tangles hooks almost inextricably at times, during which period of time they can be a danger to the netted fish. Despite the conservationist rally, based upon ignorance, old fashioned net material is kinder on fish when lure fishing.

Fishing for the pot is different, and it doesn't matter whether the net is cord, stranded nylon, or micromesh under these circumstances. What is vitally important is that the net should sink, and a small-bore lead bullet stitched into the base of a landing net will make sure this does happen.

Two final thoughts before leaving the subject of netting. Remember that the net itself is replaceable. Some of the slime-stiffened, mesh-broken smelly objects that one sees are neither practical nor necessary. Ken recently spoke to someone in a fishing pub about the smell from his net. The immediate reply was that it gave 'character'. Ken's suggestion that perhaps he should wear a Davy Crockett hat was not well received. Last, but by no means least: when the chips are down, the fish is beaten and being pulled towards the angler ready for landing – then, at that moment, the best thing in the world is a really deep net – at least three feet from rim to base.

Ancient lures against an ancient backdrop: Kidneys, Colorados, and Norwich spoons.

How to use the net? Well, everyone knows that. Haven't angling books for years been churning out the 'sink the net and draw the fish over it' doctrine? There is no doubt that is the correct way, but only if the fish will fit into the net itself, and the water is absolutely still.

Running water requires some thought. That lead bullet stitched into the bottom of the net will be great for holding the bag down where there is only a moderate current. But as the force of water increases, so the tendency arises for the net to be washed back out through the rim. From here disaster is inevitable, and there is only one way to prevent it happening. First, play your fish to an absolute standstill, then face upstream, and enter the net at an angle of forty-five degrees into the water, so that the current drives the netting straight out behind the rim. Then draw the fish upstream to the limit of the rod-length, and allow him to drift down into the net itself. Beware of the pull on micromesh.

It all sounds rather complicated, but keep in mind the fact that the net must be streamed out behind the frame and that, gently handled, a completely beaten fish is a very viable proposition, and you won't go far wrong. It would be no exaggeration to state that three-quarters of all fish netted are not played out, and therein lies the cause of the failure rate at the netting stage of all, not just small, fish. Nevertheless there may be good reasons for rapid netting. All is a compromise.

Ken has a colleague who has a different approach. Whenever he stops to use his rod he drops the net pointing out from the bank into the water at his feet. Then, when it is settled on the bottom, his fishes. Once a fish requires landing he has only to pick up the net as the fish is brought over it, and providing he moves quickly enough, the net will remain behind the frame during the netting. Disadvantages? Yes, of course, if the bank shelves steeply then the net slips off into deep water. Also, we don't much like stooping very low with a fish on a short line; this is how breaks are made. Finally, consider the wearisome return journey to collect the net you forgot. But for what it is worth, there is one idea.

So much for the still and running water approach. Now, what about the fish that is too large for the net? Well, it's either heads or tails. Once one end or the other is into the frame you can only hope that the bag of the net will be enough to contain at least the bigger portion of weight so that the whole thing can be safely lifted.

Which end? Well, for us it is the tail end into the net every time. Yes, we can hear the howls of the experts enlarging on the theme that with the tail a fish can expend leverage, and possibly jump free. But let Ken tell you this story.

A young angler was salmon fishing on the Towy in Wales. The lure – a River Runt with trebles at belly and tail. It had rained, and on the fifth cast

Quick release for the landing net with a dog-lead clip.

83

the angler ever made in salmon fishing he was into a real old-fashioned rod-bender that jumped – but you have read all that sort of stuff before.

Finally the angler (perhaps we would be nearer the truth to have said 'young impecunious angler') went for the net. It was woefully inadequate and even allowing for the exaggeration of a first fish, there was a good half of the body that would never fit. So accordingly, and in defence to the good books and pundits, the angler sank the net, and drew the fish head first over the rim.

But even as it slid halfway the treble at the plug's belly caught in the netting and as if by telepathy the fish lunged. Yes, you can guess the rest. That caught treble was the lever needed and away went Ken's first salmon. He is not ashamed to say that he sat down on the ground and cried!

In the net is half the battle, out on to the bank is the other. Let's face it, no landing net is designed to withstand a dead weight lift of twenty pound or so. Or if it is, there will be two men and a boy walking after the angler carrying it. Which reminds us of the incident witnessed on the Royalty, where two anglers were seen driving the end of an eight-foot collapsible landing net handle against the road bridge. One of the two had landed an eight pound barbel with the handle fully extended, by lifting the shaft at its extreme end. The result was obvious; there was such a bow in the shaft that eventually, despite hammering, the two lads were obliged to drive back to London with the thing sticking out of the window.

Once that big 'un is in the net, lay the rod down on the bank, in the water, or tuck the butt into the top of your wader. Then go hand over hand down the shaft, and grip both sides of the rim or net with each hand. Then lift, and walk well back before you put the weight down – it's amazing how far a fish can 'bounce'. And put it down on a soft surface, holding it firmly until it quiets.

GAFFS

If we had a large salmon played out, or the new British record pike under our rod tip, and considering the subsequent rage and exasperation if either were lost then – and under those circumstances only – might we reach for a gaff. In other words, we don't like them, and at best consider their use a necessary evil.

This, of course, may be taken by many as a sign of either sensitivity or senility; but it's not just the dislike of drawing cold steel into a fish – it is the fact that so many fish are gaffed where there is no need whatsoever. In fact the gaff, to many anglers, is a status symbol. Large gaffs sometimes hang

Under this bush on Leland Water the pike often take immediately after the splash of the lure.

from very small bodies, and at the slightest sign of a fish, irrespective of size, out it comes and in it goes.

What are the essentials of a good gaff? Strength first and foremost. Those that are cheap, finish up being repaired first. Think of the strain on a gaff used to lift a twenty-five pound lead weight with a 'straight' lift, and you will understand a little of the wear put on to its various parts. Now bear in mind that in the excitement of the moment few people really give a straight lift – and you can really appreciate the strain put not only on the hook, but also the shaft of the instrument itself.

Steel and brass are the only materials that can take that sort of use, definitely not alloy. Weight and strength are synonymous in this case. A good gaff extends to 3½ feet, in two or three telescopic extensions, the handle being of solid construction and the top solid steel. Pike gaffs should be as illustrated since the intention is *not* to stab the fish but to lift it clear of the water in good condition. The V-shape lessens the chances of the pike levering itself off the bend. With salmon a V-shape would be useless, since very little penetration of the flank would be made.

Looking at gaffs as a whole, our complaints lie in the protective sheath that so often fails to cover the point when it is collapsed, and with the hand grip, for we have yet to find a collapsible gaff that has a leather loop for wrist

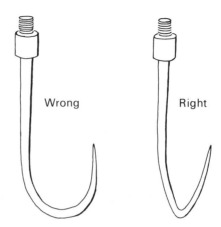

Wrong   Right

security. We are aware that such a loop could be added by the individual, but feel that it would be better incorporated in the construction stage.

The traditional gaff head whipped to a strong pole is fine for the gillie, but cumbersome and a menace when carried by the roving fisherman. No matter how one tries to retain it, by the end of the day the cork protective covering on the point is missing, with painful results.

Where to gaff (the fish, that is) leaves a choice of chin or mid-way along the body. Most books refer to the 'point of balance' when gaffing salmon – but in the general excitement of this final act, most people badly misjudge. Ken has vivid recollections of poaching a large salmon at night when the point of balance was misjudged, and as the fish came out of the water it 'whipped', with the result that the poacher concerned took a full toss into the river.

A sharp point, the point of the chin, a straight lift – and the job is done – providing that the fish is properly played out.

TAILERS

Not often remembered, and usually associated with game fishing, the tailer is a sophisticated form of the rabbit snare on a pole used by keepers for ridding waters of pike. The principle is that the open wire loop is slid over the tail, and then the pole is jerked up and back towards the angler, so that the wire tightens around the wrist behind the tail, lifting the fish from the water.

They are fine for big salmon, and with sensible use do not inflict as much damage as a gaff. The main disadvantage is that the pole and loop are clumsy

B.R. with improvised storage on his jeans – can be dangerous.

Spinning and Plug Fishing

and heavy to carry around, and of course the pike has little or no wrist on which to get a grip. Weighing it up with the pros and cons we feel happier with the net or gaff.

BEACHING AND HANDING A FISH

If you are caught without the means of landing (and should it happen, it serves you right!) then your only resort will be to beach the fish if there is a convenient place, or to try and lift him out by hand.

To be successful, beaching requires the fish to be played until he is more tired than usual. When this point is reached, walk or climb round to the point where you intend to do the landing. Lift the fish so that his head is out of the water, and then, without giving line from the reel, walk backwards, drawing the fish firmly, quickly and very smoothly back with you.

As he hits the beach there will usually be a kick, and this helps to get the carcass just that little further up from the water's edge. Then it is a question of drop the rod, run forward and grab and may the Lord have mercy on your fingers should it be a big pike: it's not the teeth you should worry about, but flying trebles.

Handing a fish – lifting it out of the water by the tail – is quite a practical proposition at any time. Barrie showed Ken how it should be done with one of his (Ken's) best gloves some time ago. Unfortunately he left the glove under the dashboard of his van for a couple of days, and when the door was opened the smell was a trifle over-powering.

Use a woollen or soft leather glove, play the fish to a standstill, grasp the tail at the wrist or the jaw of a pike and lift, or rather drag if there is any size to the fish. Ken would, however, suggest a small plastic bag if the glove is to be carried as a regular feature. Pike up to round about double figures can be grasped at the back of the head with the left hand, but when much heavier than this great strength is required and it is far better to beach the fish if possible. When plug fishing *any* handling technique must be done with great care, for a sudden lunge on the part of a pike can drive a treble hook deep into the angler's hand.

CHAPTER ELEVEN

Techniques of Spinning

The techniques of spinning are as varied as in any other branch of angling, if not more so. Spinners can be pulled fast through the surface waves, bouncing from wave to wave; retrieved slow and deep; held static, but spinning, in fast currents; and Barrie has actually had two pike, small ones, take a spinner in the air some 4–5 inches above the surface of the water, although he wouldn't recommend this as a regularly producing technique! The idea in spinning is to have spinners or methods to cover as many contingencies as possible: there's no point in having a box of mackerel spinners if you are fishing the river Shannon, for example, where a few big Copper and Silvers would be better, coupled with a powerful two-handed rod and fifteen pound b.s. line.

On the other hand we do not subscribe to the view that you can do almost anything with a spinner that can be done with a natural bait. There are many occasions when natural baits, whether spun, wobbled or static, will outscore a lure. And in general, spinning is less effective in winter than in summer. For the salmon family this is, of course, no problem, but in pike, perch, zander and chub fishing it is as well to remember that when the water temperature gets really low a small natural bait is more likely to effect their capture.

That then is the first major point of this section, that spinning in the warmer months is not only more pleasant, it is usually more effective. This is not to say that we do no spinning in winter. On the contrary, in fact, but we choose the conditions carefully, and the waters carefully. In every area of the country you will find waters which, sometimes for no obvious reason, respond well to artificials in winter.

The other aspect of *when* to spin is what time of the day or night. The answer is any time, whatever you are fishing for. Pike, for example, home in quite happily to a vibrating spinner or wobbling plug in pitch darkness, just as small brownies will do on a mountain stream. As we pointed out elsewhere, vibrations are probably all-important in lure location by the fish.

Personally, we do not mind fishing in the heat of a summer's day, provided it is the kind of leisurely affair that one indulges in after a morning's tench fishing. But in general the dawn, dusk, and night periods tend to be best, just as they are for so much fishing.

When spinning at night it is well to have a small Billy Lane stop knot, tied in nylon, on your line about ten feet above the lure: this gives a little click as it enters your top ring and tells you that your lure is ten feet away from the bank or rod tip. In addition, you must be careful to have at the top of the trace something that is big enough to be stopped by the top ring of the rod. The last thing you want to happen is to have the trace swivel or spinner link swivel enter the end eye of the rod: you can stop it with a swan shot, or bead, or some types of anti-kink vanes.

Another useful trick is to have a stop of sorts at the *other* end of the line, which tells you how far you have cast. In this case it is not possible, or at least not sensible, to use a Billy Lane stop knot since this tends to cause tangles when buried on the spool. But having decided how far you wish to cast, say thirty yards, pull off that amount of line, then add a thin rubber band to the spool, and finally reel back on the thirty yards of line. On casting, the whole lot pulls up short when thirty yards of line are out. This is useful when the casts are made regularly across and down a river that is, say, thirty-five yards wide. On occasions when there is just enough visibility, you soon get used to making casts of variable length and direction. Otherwise night spinning is as easy as during the day, and is merely a matter of knowing where everything is. Netting a fish is usually a matter of netting the splashes, and things can occasionally go a little awry here, but if you can get the fish sliding bankwards after judging the distance of the splashes the problems are few. It is possible to tape a small torch on the handle of the net, just about a foot above the net rim. Switching on a torch can affect your own night vision for a few minutes, but a little light at the actual moment of netting can be helpful. Night spinning is exciting, and more than in any other aspect of the sport the take seems to come thumping out of nowhere. You develop a sense of feel and touch that you didn't realise you had, almost to the extent that you get from worming mountain streams for brownies in the dark.

So far we have considered when to spin, and the general effects of weather and temperature, but another important matter is *where* to spin. Here there are really no restrictions other than those placed by club rules. Large reservoirs and huge rivers like the Shannon or the Great Ouse Relief Channel can be imposing, and the natural tendency is to use big lures and powerful tackle, partly in order to cover the water and partly to give you the feeling that at least the fish has *seen* it. But in fact, light spinning on big waters can be extremely productive at times, and the only things wrong with

A range of pike flies for lead-cored line work.

big waters are the air of monotony that they manage to convey, and your own sense of feeling very puny while flicking out a tiny Mepps spinner into a vast emptiness.

Almost all waters can be spun through, including snaggy and weedy water, and before going on to some general matters concerning what one might term standard spinning technique, we shall say a word or two about that special situation of fishing in the weed or snags. The problem is twofold really: firstly, the link swivel or top trace swivel gets caught in soft blanket or silk weed, as do the trebles; secondly, the hooks themselves easily foul coarser weed, logs and so on. The first of these problems is almost insoluble since blanket weed will clog anything, but other weeds and snags can be defeated to some extent by using weed guards on the treble hooks. These are easily constructed from SWG wire of the appropriate grade (in this case no. 28 SWG) and such a spinner can be retrieved through sunken trees and water lilies with little fear of snagging up. After a few outings the weed guards become strained and need to be reset or replaced by new ones. Weed guards of this type can be used on any trebles, and if not too rigid will not impede the striking qualities of the lure. It is, however, a nuisance to kit out all the trebles on a big plug.

Another idea is a Russian spoon consisting of two lightly sprung blades. On a take, the blades are pushed together exposing the hooks simultaneously. Barrie first used these lures on a Peterborough brick pit where he and Fred Wagstaffe fished them without loss through huge sunken trees and masses of branches. As spoons, they are not as effective at attracting fish since their action is rather lifeless, but it should not be beyond the imagination of inventive anglers to produce a home-made lure on the same principle, which does work well.

A third way of beating weeds is to use a lure such as the Bushwhacker. These are a sort of combined spoon/spinner/fly and they fish really well through lily beds, branches, and even *Potamogeton* beds. As with all lures, they give up the ghost in really soft weed.

Many anglers are realising that great sport can be had by looking for fish *in* weedbeds as opposed to fishing the fringes, and it may be that other weed-defeating ideas will come out in the future. In the meantime, apart from the above ideas, various commercially made lures have excellent built-in weed guards. The use of big single hooks may increase for such fishing, since it is easier to build a good weed guard for one hook than to make three for a treble hook.

Homing in now to general spinning technique, we shall assume that, as already recommended, you will have the appropriate tackle for your water. On that assumption we'll go on to think about the following topics: still waters from the bank; rivers from the bank; and still waters from a boat –

Author's workbench with an assortment of lures and tackle.

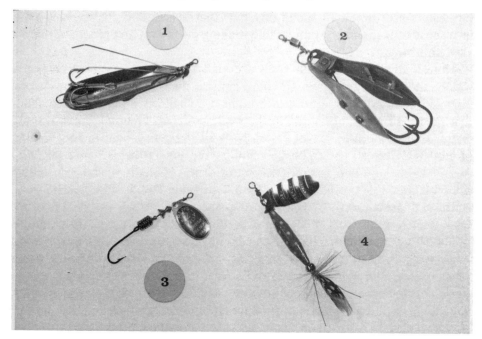

WEEDLESS SPINNERS. *1. Abu Flamingo   2. Russian Double spoon   3. Mepps Aglia – single hook   4. Abu Reflex Vass.*

digressing at times to interpose related matters of tackle or technique. At an early stage the angler will decide on a wire trace or not, and for pike and zander there really should be no question: as thin and as dark a trace as possible is the ideal, in a breaking strain not dissimilar to that of the reel line. For other species the reel line can be tied directly to the spinner eye or to a link swivel to facilitate changing of lures during the day. In the last instance you need to be confident of your knot for a day's spinning.

This brings us to the question of using an anti-kink vane. We discuss the various types below, and it really boils down to whether the angler is prepared to risk kinks in his line. Personally we do not like encumbrances on the line, and a bit of light spinning with a Veltic or mackerel spinner does not really need an anti-kink device. On the other hand, in a big river like the Great Ouse, particularly if there is a strong flow on, you need both weight to get the bait down and an anti-kink device which actually works well. There is always a temptation to fish too light when spinning, but in heavy water conditions our advice is to make a bold decision, use plenty of weight, perhaps in the form of a half moon lead, and make sure the spinner is fishing deep and well. It soon becomes apparent if you have chosen too much weight, whereas the opposite isn't always obvious. Clearly, a combined weight-cum-anti-kink device is ideal. To sum up, if the line isn't becoming twisted (and to test for this simply drop the spinner on the ground to take out the line tautness) then keep spinning; if it does twist up add an anti-kink vane, preferably in the form of lead if you can.

These general remarks apply as much to fishing still waters from the bank as they do to rivers, particularly if the water is deep, and particularly with certain spinners which have a tendency to give kink trouble. At this point then, you will have your tackle assembled and be ready to cast. In a shallow lake with weed up to just below the surface it is often necessary to begin the retrieve immediately, attempting of course to work the bait into any pockets, and to choose spinners that come in slow and shallow, such as mackerel spinners, small Vibros, one inch minnows, Veltics and so on or plugs which work close to the surface. In deeper water it is necessary to count the bait to the bottom on the first cast in order to ascertain relative depth. With many spinners you will know from experience just how many feet per second they sink, so your counting will give you the actual depth. On the next cast begin the retrieve at the depth you wish to fish.

There are two ways to conduct a count-down. One is to hold the lure on a tight line, in which case you are in direct contact the moment the retrieve begins; the second is to allow the spinner to sink under its own weight on a free line, in which case the retrieve causes the spinner to leave the bottom at a high angle before direct contact is made. Both methods are satisfactory as long as you realise what you are doing. When the bottom is snaggy, the second method is probably better, for there is slightly less chance for the hooks to get caught up.

The actual retrieve has been debated for years, but as a generalisation or a starter at least, as slow and as deep a recovery as possible is best. Sometimes it is necessary to retrieve fast, and sometimes shallow but begin with deep and slow. Personally we prefer a steady retrieve particularly when perch fishing, but there are times when working the rod top from side to side or up and down, or even fishing sink-and-draw, produces takes that the steady recovery didn't. The main trouble with a lively retrieve is that the fish may miss. Both pike and perch are bad shots in our view, and pike in particular may well rely almost entirely on vibrations rather than vision, especially in the split second before the take.

On most still waters it pays to try a cast or two along the bank, as well as a few casts standing well back from the bank. Because anglers may have baited up for roach it could be that pike and perch have moved in very close to the bank where the spinning man would normally stand. After fishing in this way, give the swim a fair old coverage, trying for depth and distance as well as areas marginal to weedbeds, if not *in* the weedbeds. We have always felt very strongly against the common advice to fish as round a clock face, each cast going a few degrees to one side of the last. It makes for boring and mechanical fishing. We much prefer to work out or guess where the fish might lie and then really concentrate on giving it to them. Once spinning becomes mechanical it is so easy to miss bites and lose lures, and the whole joy goes out of it even if neither of these probabilities materialises.

In river fishing the natural tendency is to fish across and downstream; and it is generally more common to use lead to get the bait down, and anti-kink vanes to avoid line twist. However, although most anglers seem to fish downstream it is neither necessary nor always desirable. When casting upstream there are several definite consequences. In the first place the lure comes back at you much more quickly, and although it obviously reaches the fish at the same speed (!) the fish actually has plenty of time to see the lure because as a rule it will be facing into the current. The angler also approaches his quarry from behind, and the main risk of frightening fish, given that the angler as usual avoids his shadow falling on the water, results from fish very close to the angler darting upstream and transmitting alarm ahead. When fishing downstream a frightened fish often darts away upstream going *away* from the fish you are after.

When fishing in Barmston Drain in Hull city reaches, where there is considerable flow, Barrie found that pike fell much more readily to a spoon fished upstream than to one fished either downstream or across and down. In fact three times as many pike fell to the former method. We have found that the same obtains with other fish and on many other waters and would recommend that although upstream spinning is often hard work, needing twice as many casts, it should be given a real trial on small to medium rivers up to about the size of the middle reaches of the Great Ouse. With larger, deeper rivers upstream spinning may become just too difficult, but it is always worth a try to see what happens.

Across and downstream spinning should never become a mechanical process. Try to search out holes, give the lure a different line or different speed, and as in all fishing employ the craft as delicately and quietly as you can. We have sometimes had the feeling that footfalls on the riverside, as opposed to the lakeside, are less important: but still we fish quietly.

Avoidance of snags is always a problem, since the angler often tries to fish very close to them. This is understandable, as fish often shelter in the snags. One place where anglers commonly get fouled up is just before the lure reaches the rod, at about the point where the river bottom (or, indeed, lake bottom) begins to slope upwards. Not only does debris collect here, but the angler often fails to raise his rod top gradually as the lure nears home. Raising the rod top means that with a steady retrieve the spinner or plug will continue parallel to and above the bottom contours, rather than ploughing into them close to the bank. A couple of casts is all that is needed to work out the best retrieve for the slope of the bank.

If you do get snagged up avoid savage pulling of any kind, but work your way downstream and try to tease the lure gently off the obstruction. It is possible to float proprietary tackle-freers down the line, or even to convert a bottle for that purpose: these are attached to the line so that they are free sliding, and are then allowed to float well downstream of the spinner before being pulled again from the upstream end. It has the same effect, sometimes more efficiently, of walking downstream and pulling. You cannot use the same technique if you snag during upstream spinning, but you can walk upstream of the snag and pull from there.

There are many tricks to be learnt about spinning rivers, and new ones will come to the thinking angler. For example, it is sometimes possible to float a light spinner into position by placing it on a piece of wood and floating it downstream. If you are positioned on the inside of a bend it is occasionally possible to float your lure almost across and round the bend before retrieving, thus getting a longer retrieve than would have been possible by normal casting.

As with most spinning, we feel that the speed of retrieve should be steady rather than jerky, and the pace judged relative to the type of fish expected. Fred Wagstaffe once told us that in his opinion a big pike could and would overhaul any lure, whatever its speed, if it was attracted to it. On the other hand we're sure that you could outpace and outmanoeuvre a river perch, and perhaps a chub wouldn't deign to follow unless the spinner passed through his manor. Trout will sometimes chase spinners for enormous distances and it is probably impossible to outpace them.

In boat fishing there are basically two methods: either the boat is anchored and the spinners cast from it and retrieved, or else the spinner, or plug spoon is trolled (trailed) behind. In the former case our remarks about bank fishing apply; in the latter some specialised techniques are an advantage. For example the boat rod rests help greatly in keeping the rod out of the boat but in reach of the fisherman. Without rests they have to be propped on the gunwhales on a bit of cloth to avoid damaging the rod. Takes when trolling are usually savage and the rod top whips round, and the fish usually hook themselves: here the main problem is stopping the progress of the boat before the rod or line snaps! Strong rods and lines are definitely more efficient, and frankly we would double up on all strengths for trailing lures.

An alternative technique is to use a weight attached to the boat by a thin rope, and by a clip to the top of the trace or further along the reel line, lowering the whole lot down to the desired fishing depth. The clip is designed to release the lure in the event of a take but the *line at the rod top goes slack*, at least momentarily, giving the angler a few seconds to think and act.

As a digression we would mention that some activities, now largely illegal in these islands, are still practised in the Soviet Union where the catch is

K.W.'s way of storing deadbait in the freezer: individually wrapped in newspaper and then rolled into a polythene bag.

invariably to be eaten. The rudder-like Otter Board is still used. Here the board works its way out at almost right-angles to the boat and then moves parallel to and maintains pace with the boat. Between the board and the boat are any number of spinners attached on short traces to the main line: a kind of highly mobile long lining. This method mostly succeeds with lake perch, trout and char, and is usually too shallowly fished for pike.

The same enterprising anglers use a similar system from the bank, either one man and his Otter Board, or two men (one on each bank) with a cord between them and numerous spinners. They either hold stationary position in a strong current, or walk along in a gentle one!

So far we haven't said anything about the anchored static (but spinning) spinner. This is a method used by salmon fishermen. A paternoster lead is attached by a link to a swivel some distance above the spinner. The tackle is cast into a swim of suitable depth and current, the lead takes a hold on the bottom, and the spinner streams out in the current: a kind of legered spinner! A deal of skill is needed not only in the actual fishing thereof, but in getting the right lead, and lure. Fished thus a pool can be very slowly covered. Surely here is an untried technique for pike rivers, although we have tried a vaguely similar method with plugs without much success.

CHAPTER TWELVE

Ultra-light spinning

Ultra-light spinning started several years ago for Ken on the river Towy, where he was early autumn fishing for sewin. Although the river was clearing after rain and seemed ideal in every respect for a fish or two, they had proved indifferent to the fly and the rod had been set aside until nightfall. Resting on a rock ledge above the Junction Pool Ken imagined he had the river to himself and was mildly surprised when another angler made his appearance on the opposite bank.

His rod looked very much like a cut-down split cane fly rod, to which was attached a small Altex fixed spool reel. The whole thing resembled a child's set-up and quite incapable of dealing with several pounds of fighting sewin – let alone the odd salmon that were also running. During the next fifteen minutes Ken witnessed some of the finest casting and spinning techniques that he has ever seen – either before or since. The small Mepps-type spinner seemed to twinkle in and out of every possible run and hold, resulting in a good fish taking where he (Ken) had been fishing unsuccesfully just a short time previously.

Any admiration that had been forthcoming for the spinning techniques was immediately eclipsed by the sheer skill displayed by the angler in playing that sewin, a four-pound fish that performed every trick in the calendar and one or two others besides. Although the line could not have been of greater breaking strain than two pounds, a break was avoided time after time by the angler who, when the moment of truth approached, merely altered the tension on the spool and gave the fish a nearly slack line. On the second time that this trick was used Ken realised he was watching a vintage performance – and suddenly also realised where he had seen the style described. It was straight from the pages of an Alexander Wanless book.

On his return from holiday Ken contacted Ron Coleby, the antique book seller near Lincoln, and thanks to his industry and interest managed to assemble a complete set of all the Wanless works. The words of that firey

Perch taken on the ultra-light outfit.

and pugnacious writer proved so challenging that it was immediately decided to emulate his 1920 style, and spin with ultra-light tackle.

Vic Gibson, the then rod maker at Dons of Edmonton's tackle shop, was enlisted to help find a modern equivalent of a Wanless wand. After days spent in discussion and many more in experimenting with various blanks, a Fibatube 7-foot No. 4 fly rod was selected which had three inches lopped from its tip, stiffening its action slightly.

In keeping with the Wanless tradition the solid cork handle, fifteen inches long, was smoothed parallel, leaving a dome at either end to stop the lightweight plastic Fuji reel fittings from sliding off. Rod rings presented a problem: Fuji rings were used for the end ring and for a single leg butt ring. But it was not possible to match any of the stand-off types of proprietary ring to fit as intermediates. Eventually Vic, with great patience, manufactured some himself from 28 gauge steel wire. Whipping them into place was another patient task, as they had to be tied on the sides of the blank instead of mounting flat with the normal foot fittings.

Finding a matching reel was another problem only solved when John Hennes, the Shakespeare rep., suggested his company's closed face match reel. Quite apart from a fast retrieve, the reel had big advantages in allowing a fish to be played from the handle, together with an adjustable drag situated on the side plate of the body – easily accessible should one suddenly want to let a fish run, à la Wanless. Matched with 2–4 lb. breaking strain Sylcast line, the whole outfit proved light as a feather, accurate as a rifle and, more important still, as resilient as a spring.

The beauty of a new type of rod is that it inspires one to try new techniques and methods. We (yes, Barrie liked the set-up and equipped himself with a similar outfit) soon found ourselves looking at a whole range of lightweight lures that we had previously decided to be too small for practical casting with our standard spinning rods.

As our new ultra-light so closely resembled a fly rod it was natural that our imagination should first turn to spinning reservoir lures. We had, for a long time, been using Muddler Minnows and Polystickles as a lure with a small fold-over lead, or swan shot pinched a foot or so above the hook to help achieve distance with a cast. Then, browsing through a 1920 Hardy Catalogue we spotted a coloured photo of salmon flies with spinning vanes mounted in front of the head.

A talk with Dennis Howell, the pro fly tier at Dons, resulted in the production of a large imitation roach, with weighted body and spinning vane at the head. We also prevailed on him to produce some tube flies tied as minnows and his imitation of a red-throat shown in that illustration turned out to be

1. Red-throat tube minnow   2. The 'bent' polystickle   3. Cohoki plug/spoon
4. Mackerel spinner.

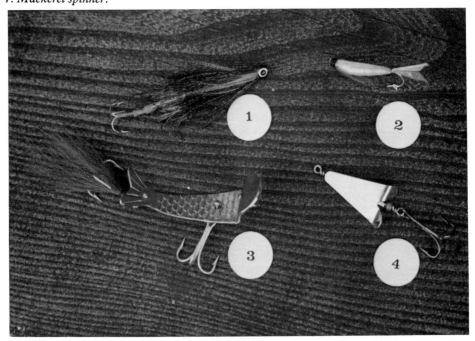

99

so life-like that we have asked him to experiment further with an identical model complete with spinning vanes, or a small bar spinner at the head.

The Polystickle has long been a tried favourite, as we mentioned earlier. But we fancied one that would have a definite wobble, as opposed to the normal straight retrieve. Dennis managed to find (?) some large bent-shank hooks and somehow tied a lure to these. The result, retrieved with a swan shot pinched a short way up the line, is a beautiful swooping wobble that has taken for us – as indeed have all flies we have described – some excellent chub.

Still in the fly category, we have now accumulated a fair selection of fly-spoons in different sizes and, of course, the Mepps fly spinners with an imitation Palmer tied on the long-shanked treble. Wooden and small metal Devon minnows, quill minnows (alas, no longer made from quill) and the new soft plastic minnows with nose-mounted bar spinners by Abu or Mepps are all musts in our tackle boxes.

But best of all with this little wand is the natural bait, the preserved minnows that are single treble mounted, and small sprats mounted on leaded spinning rigs. We have both discussed the success obtained by using the ultra-light in this way, and have arrived at the conclusion that one reason is probably because we are fishing with a completely home-made outfit – rod- and lure-wise at least – which gives one the confidence needed to really work for a fish.

Mind you, playing a fish to the bank, a good fish that is, can be no small achievement. As is so often the case one sets off to catch one species of fish and finishes up with another that is totally unsuited to the tackle you are using. This perversity on the part of fish is such that some of Ken's most exciting pike days have occurred with the ultra-light when he was really after perch or chub.

If you hit a good fish in running water then all that Wanless ever wrote on free-lining a fish into submission usually works, and works well. The moment a hard run is commenced then the tension is practically removed from the spool on the reel, and the fish allowed its wilful way with only a gentle reminder that there is a restriction. Wanless maintained that this gentle pressure was better than all the bullying in the world, and that it worried a fish into exhausting itself in half the time it took with heavy gear and brute force.

But what about the fish hooked in still water? Give him a free line and he will merely cruise off somewhere and sulk on the bottom – usually at some distance from the angler, and with so much line out that no amount of heaving will make the slightest impression.

Well, the cure for that situation can be obtained by looking at the photograph. From it you can see just how much spring there is in the little rod, and provided that the rod tip is kept as near to vertical as is possible,

The ultra-light rod in action.

then that spring will keep sudden and direct strain off the line and prevent a break in the majority of cases. Of course, there comes the moment of truth in this situation as in any other, when a fish just keeps going despite all the line pressure you dare give, and though the rod be bent nearly double. But that is a great part of the pleasure in angling, and if a break should occur, then reason with yourself that had it not been for the lightweight approach, then possibly the fish would not have been hooked in the first place.

Actually, that last statement sums up our whole approach to the ultra-light outfit. We use it when normally the conditions of weather or water would never let us consider spinning with any of our normal methods or when smallish fish are to be expected. Therefore we find we enjoy a few extra days spinning during the season with the minimum of discomfort from portly or cumbersome tackle. Just a little rod, a reel, and two small boxes of tiny lures or mounted minnows can provide a staggering day's sport. We do not approve of line-class fishing, that attempted export from the other side of the Atlantic. Here, our objective is to use the technique to catch fish, not to succeed in spite of the tackle, which is the objective of line-class angling.

CHAPTER THIRTEEN

Boat fishing

Wandering along the bankside casting a lure into likely holes between the weed beds, and carrying little but a net and pocketful of lures, is a delightful way of spending a morning, but boat fishing also has its charms. In terms of reaching swims not accessible from the bank it is often a highly practical way of fishing, even with a small boat on small waters.

It is not our intention to discuss the type of boat needed. The trouble is that most anglers have to make do with what is actually available and in most instances these craft are not specifically designed for anglers, let alone the man carrying several rods and hundreds of lures. Generally speaking, large lochs need a clinker-built boat upwards of twelve feet in length. Some modern fibre-glass boats are also good, but whether wood or glass we are relatively unhappy on big waters if we do not have a good outboard motor, chosen for the size of the boat, and a sound pair of oars.

Certain other items make for more enjoyable fishing. For example two good, heavy anchors (one at the bows and one in the stern) attached to more rope than you are likely to need, mean that you can anchor in almost any position relative to the snags or ledges you intend working. The rope should be thick, not clothes-line thickness, for with the latter it may be difficult to pull a heavy weight out of the mud. Another bad feature of boats, from the angler's point of view, is the pair of rowlocks. Rowlocks are almost universal, and whilst suitable for the *rowing* enthusiast, enabling him to make quite intricate manoeuvres, all they do for the angler is increase the risk of the oars being lost. Now the Irish are not noted for their efficiency in most matters, but on this question of oar attachment they are 'spot on': they have a block of wood on the side of each oar, and the block has a hole through it which fits over a pin sticking up on the gunwhale. Sophisticated versions have a locking nut which screws on to the top of the pin.

Using this system of oar attachment one can, in the even of a take whilst trolling, or in the event of spotting a big fish, drop the oars without a second thought and attend to the more important matter of fishing. It might be a good idea to outline the kind of real situation that arises. Suppose the angler is rowing gently towards the sunken tree around which he intends working his plugs, and having previously established the position of the tree, the suggested approach is as follows. First, approach downwind rowing gently and quietly, and if the wind is moderate cease rowing about ten to fifteen yards short of the distance from which you intend casting. Drop the oars and, without rocking the boat, move into the bows and drop the bow anchor gently overboard. Hold it on a tight line after it hits the bottom and allow the stern to swing round as shown in the drawing. Make the anchor rope fast, having judged the amount of line to let out in relation to the wind strength. Move gently to the stern, wait until the stern is pointing to the sunken tree, and then lower the second anchor. With the bows pointing into the wind in this way, and with two anchors firmly fixed, the angler can work the plugs past the snags in the knowledge that the boat is fairly static – or to

Plug fishing from a boat.
Barrie, with boat set out,
ready to go.

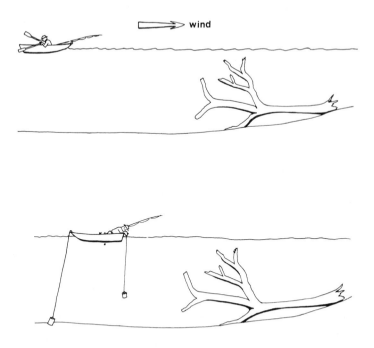

put it another way, the sunken tree will not move between casts! Most plugs, of course, do not have weed guards on them, nor are they easy to construct on plugs, so recourse to weed-guarded *spoons* is necessary if the angler wishes to fish *in* the tree.

This outlines one way of working the lures from a boat. Broadly speaking there are two other ways: casting from a slowly drifting boat, perhaps assisted by the use of drogues or an otterboard, and trolling. The former can be carried out under any conditions, a drogue slowing down the movement under strong winds and drift, but it is most pleasant under relatively calm water conditions. Fish can be approached very quietly, but perhaps there is a tendency to cover the area too rapidly.

For many years one was advised to sit down in the boat during casting, but our own experience is exactly the opposite: good accurate casts, long casts, and proper working of the lures can only be achieved in the standing position. Obviously, great care must be exercised, and it is advisable (whether standing or sitting) to wear a life-jacket. Life-jackets are not designed with anglers in mind; they make casting a little awkward at times, and there is a great temptation to remove them. Don't. We came across some at Ardingly Reservoir in 1985/6 that fit snugly beneath a Barbour jacket.

When trolling it is a help if two rods can be used as shown in the figure. The rods should be firmly held at the butt, and the best boats have a bar of wood for this purpose. Personally we feel that a couple of soft pads on the stern should be used to take the mid-section of the rod. This prevents damage to both rod and line. The anti-reverse mechanism should be *on*, since there is little point in having the handles spin round when a fish takes, or indeed in having the slipping clutch set very light. The fish may hook itself in its strike, but even so the angler needs to be pretty quick to the rods. Clearly, heavier line is needed for trolling like this and we would

Deep diving plugs and deep working spinners various, including the Vibro Sonic Bat (middle right).

105

Surface lures and shallow divers on the terrain close to which they often work well.

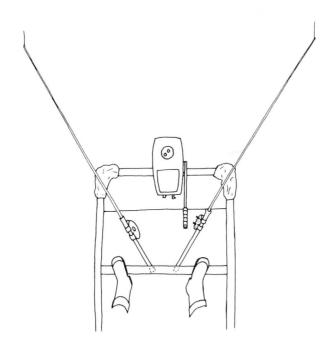

advise something like twenty pound breaking strain for pike fishing, for example. When fishing the same swim 'on the drift' one could probably manage quite well with 12–15 lb. line.

An improvement on the above system is to have one person rowing and the other watching the rods, even holding one of them. The main trouble with this method is that when a fish takes it is always *you* doing the rowing, never the other fellow! The echo sounder, mentioned later, is a boon whatever trolling system is being employed.

ELECTRIC MOTORS

There are few things better in this world than watching a fellow-angler rowing whilst you are fishing. There you sit, pretending to rig the tackle, whilst the other chap pulls the boat in ever-diminishing circles until finally you reach the place you didn't intend to fish. On a more serious note though, the boat with two in it is ideal. But there is a different situation entirely with the single-handed boat.

For a start you are rowing with your back to where you want to be looking, so in theory at least you are forever seeing where you should have been fishing; in practice you are acting the owl and trying to turn your head through 180 degrees. Nor is that all the problem, for having found the place you want to cover, you have then to ship oars, and in all probability turn round in the boat to face into the fishing area. And that, no matter how careful you are, means noise and disturbance.

So the answer is an outboard – not one of the petrol jobs. We were once lent one of the Shakespeare Electric Motors to try, and immediately realised this was the answer for the single-handed angler. Nothing could be simpler than this piece of machinery. It is light, can be mounted on to the stern, and clipped to the 12-volt battery of the car for power. With a little sensible use there is at least five hours running which will leave some life in the battery to start the car on the journey home.

The controls are simple enough – on and off. There are more sophisticated models available where the running speed, on/off controls etc. work from a foot pedal, leaving both hands free to fish. But we managed easily with the one lent us. Maximum speed is around three knots, and the whole engine is absolutely silent. No fuss, no mess, easy to start, and just a steady 'plod' to where you want to fish.

We didn't try it for trolling, but would imagine it would be useful in this capacity. We also discovered that if water conditions and wind pressure were bad then the engine could be turned through 180 degrees in its mounting, and the boat pulled instead of pushed – a better, more stable proposition where the bluff stern of the boat is made to meet the weather. One final good point – the price compares very favourably with the petrol alternative. In fact, one of these with an echo sounder and the plug man has just about every modern aid in the calendar.

What about landing fish? Gaffing is much easier from a boat than from the bank. In the first place one can get really close to the fish and more or less

A simple lay-out of plugs, all within easy reach of the angler.

above it. For sea-fishing and salmon fishing when the fish is probably going to be eaten, a short-handled, round-bend gaff is ideal. For pike fishing the same, but with a V-shaped bend for insertion under the tip of the jaw is ideal. Netting can be a problem if the net has a long handle; whilst the netting itself is a terrible nuisance if it is actually *in* the boat. It *always* gets tangled up with the plugs. Fortunately, Bill Keal came up with an ingenious system that we'd never heard of until some years ago. A triangular net is used, with the arms in the relaxed position, and it is hung over the side as shown. Before netting it is lifted clear of the rowlock or pin, the arms held open, and the fish slid into it. At this point the arms are *closed* and the whole bundle lifted aboard. The same procedure can be used less efficiently with a rigid, round-framed net.

Well, by now you are probably wondering what on earth to do with the hundreds of plugs you have, if the boat itself is full of all this paraphernalia. If we had a set of dream plugs and commodious pockets there would be no problems at all. As it is, one has to find a place for the plug boxes as well as the lures that are actually being used most often. The former should be placed under the seats if possible, and the latter can be thrown loosely into a Woolworth's toolbox (plastic) which is our usual system, or they can be hung on the gunwhale or on one of the strengthening struts. Better still, we

109

Artificial crayfish – inconspicuous but successful even where the fish have never seen a crayfish.

suppose, would be to design some kind of board upon which the plugs could hang, and which could be leant against the side of the boat. If this board is covered with modern cheap carpet the lures will not fall off.

All this sounds very complicated but in reality it isn't, and we would return to our theme at the beginning that lure fishing from a boat, particularly in clement weather, is a most delightful pastime. It is pleasant to cast plugs and watch them work right up to the boat, perhaps coming up from depth with a rampant pike in full pursuit, and it is equally pleasant to get a good fish or two this way. Some would say more than pleasant.

110

ECHO SOUNDERS

One of the most important requirements of the would-be plug enthusiast is an accurate knowledge of the depth of the water, not just where he happens to be fishing at the time but over as much of the water as possible, so that he knows where the ridges, ledges and deeps are in relation to his casts. We spent many years plumbing waters by the laborious, though not unenjoyable principle of casting out a sliding float above a lead weight that would sink it.

Several casts had to be made in each place, carefully adjusting the stop-knot for the sliding float between casts. It took a long time to obtain even a *rough* idea of the bottom contours.

To give you an example of the advantages of an echo sounder, we have just contoured in detail a river and lake complex in two hours, using a small boat and Seafarer Mk II sounder. Plumbing the depth from the same boat, using a line marked in feet, would have taken at least a full day's work and the picture obtained would have been approximate to say the least. From the bank, only a rough and incomplete picture could be built up, and that would have taken more than two days' work.

Of course, the plug fisherman has another rough and ready technique he can use on a swim-to-swim basis, namely, that of using a diving plug and retrieving it until it hits the bottom. By varying the length of the cast, and then the angle of the cast to the bank, an idea can be obtained of the variation in bottom conditions, position of weeds, sunken trees and other obstacles. It is a time-consuming method, extremely costly in terms of lost baits, and a most skilful way of finding snags!

Therefore, whether one intends bank fishing a water or not, a more or less complete picture built up from echo soundings is an enormous help. We've mentioned the Seafarer Mk II simply because this is the excellent tool we happen to have used. The machine is quite easy to use and consists basically of two parts; the main body which holds the battery and a dial on the front, and the transducer which hangs over the side of the boat. We usually place the body of the sounder on a piece of sacking in the bottom of the boat – in a safe position where nobody will kick it over or tread on it. The transducer is the particularly sensitive part of the equipment and under no circumstances should it be dropped or knocked. We attach ours as shown, tied to a lath of wood which protects the head of the transducer. But it can also be inserted in a piece of polythene tube. The main thing to remember is not to row into the shore in such a manner that the transducer knocks on rocks, logs, or the bottom generally. Always unclamp it as you come in to land.

The manufacturers of our particular echo sounder include instructions on how to read the dial, which we have summarised in the diagram. For lure fishing set the switch to 'feet', since it is unlikely, if not impossible, that you will be operating at depths over sixty feet. There is a fathom setting for deeper water, but even those anglers using lures at sea are unlikely to be fishing at great depths.

When over a hard, level bottom such as clean gravel, the neon indicator shows on the dial as a clean hard line (Fig. 1): a sensitivity switch allows one to 'focus' the echo. If a hard bottom is covered by a layer of mud then this shows as a layer of fuzziness on the *shallow* side of the hard line (Fig. 2). Thus the hard line may register at twenty feet, and if two feet of soft mud

Kwik-fish lures, imported by Graham Easton of T. G. Lures, at the top and top right, with traditional Pikies, Hellbender, Shadrack and Cisco.

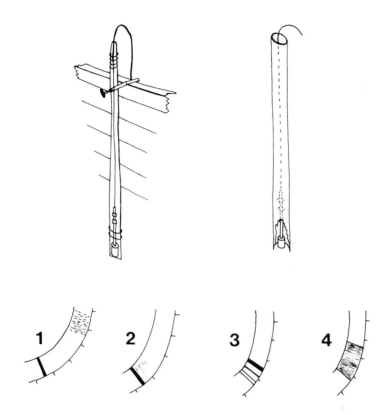

overlay the gravel then the neon will show a fuzzy mark between twenty and eighteen feet. Similarly, five feet of weed growth would show as fuzziness or intermitent flashes between twenty and fifteen feet. Shoals of perch, bream etc. will show up quite clearly, but in our experience the thinner branches of a sunken tree have a similar effect on the reading: in either case the position of the bottom and of the shoal or snag shows quite clearly.

Irregular rocky bottoms usually have a hard line approximating to the upper level of the rocks, with intermittent weaker flashes *below* it (Fig. 3). Slopes which are particularly steep show as a broad but clear band (Fig. 4). Some idea of the usefulness of the equipment can be gained from the fact that we recently discovered a steel hawser stretched underwater between two islands: naturally, it had claimed its share of tackle and lost fish.

In recent years more sophisticated sounders have come into use, such as the famous Lawrance range which prints out on paper an accurate cross section of the traverse and the position of shoals of fish and snags. They are a great pleasure to use although one does feel uncomfortable using such sophistication.

The plug angler afloat is placed, therefore, in a quite enviable position in that he can anchor his boat in a position adjacent to a good shelf, weed bed, or sunken tree and work his lures around them; or he can pick a good line along which to troll (or trail) his lures. In the last case, naturally, he can keep the echo sounder working so that he can 'follow the contour'. Since he will know the depth at which his lure is fishing, you can see that this is an extremely positive approach to trolling. After an unproductive run along a particular ledge with the lure, say, three feet off the bottom, a second run can be made with the lure at a different depth. The important point is that the angler has a really good idea of the depth at which his plug is working, and of the nature of the bottom below the bait.

Following the contour is not a very easy matter in some cases where great variations in depth take place, but in large lochs and rivers it is quite possible if reconnaissance mapping has been carried out beforehand. Even on small variable-contoured lakes short, accurate trolls can be carried out, although here the angler will probably revert to the 'anchor-and-cast' system.

CHAPTER FOURTEEN

Spun and Wobbled Natural Baits

Spun and wobbled deadbaits are undoubtedly the most neglected methods of fishing in the whole of the sport, particularly the former. Probably the aftermath of the Victorians has something to do with it – people immediately conjure up a picture of several hundredweights of ironmongery in the form of hooks, swivels and gimp wire, garnished with evil-smelling preserved baits that slop into and taint everything within view. But ideas have changed and methods with them, and those old evils are now dead as the Dodo.

There are several very good reasons for using a deadbait, the first of which is directly connected with size. Earlier in the book we lamented the passing of the really heavy spoon or spinner that could cover areas of water which the modern lightweights cannot reach or descend into. With a deadbait the most distant river bank is the limit, the only thing that could possibly govern the size of bait selected being the strength and ability of both the angler and his rod. In progressing upwards into light beachcasting tackle there is no real bar to size. Even on those enormous gravel pits where boats are forbidden, the angler armed with a large spun or wobbled deadbait and matching tackle is the only person who is equipped to fish water that others cannot – or will not – reach.

Cheapness is another concrete reason for using the deadbait. As we shall see later in this chapter, it is not necessary to use elaborate or expensive rigs, so the man with his deadbait can take financial risks by fishing weeded or snag-ridden areas where a brother angler, armed with his £2-a-throw spinner, cannot, or dare not fish.

But it is the versatility of the deadbait, its ease of control, the ultra slow wobble, part-wobble or spinning action which practically induces the bait to talk that produces fish when use of the artificial may fail.

Deep-freezing has made deadbait spinning child's play. We have both cultivated our local fishmongers who allow us to select the herrings, mackerel and sprats that we want and by bulk-buying and individually

Distance with ease,
using a wobbled deadbait.

freezing each fish we are able to stock twice a year or so with first-rate baits. We not only take care that our fish is fresh but also are careful to be selective in size and weight so that we don't damage our tackle with occasional block-busters that strain rods or snap the line during the cast.

Shock leaders, ten feet or so of nylon monofilament of a much greater breaking strain than the line attached to the rest of the reel, can obviate quite a lot of strain and prevent the dangerous accident of snapping off during a cast. Generally, however, these are not necessary. Believe us – a large dead fish loaded with umpteen large trebles flying through the air can be dangerous, both to the angler and the occasional spectator. There is also the tragic possibility of a water bird or stray household pet animal attempting to eat the lost bait. Rare though such an event must be, it is of such stuff that propaganda is made for the anti-anglers brigade.

We also freeze any sizeable freshwater fish that we can, their flesh being firmer and less likely to split during a cast than sea fish. But somehow we never seem able to put enough away, possibly because of our livebaiting demands.

There is no doubt that the toughest and most long-lasting bait for spinning is one that has been preserved, and for the benefit of those anglers who are already wrinkling up their noses with the imagined smell of formalin on reading these words, we set out our method of preserving that leaves no taint, no smell, and produces a first-rate bait in its natural colours.

Add a pint of water to a tablespoonful of forty per cent formaldehyde, obtainable from a chemist. Place the baits in this, and leave them for two days. At the end of this time they should be carefully washed in cold water, and the formaldehyde solution thrown away. Take care to wipe any greasy film from the baits, and then place them into a mixture of one part of sugar in four parts of water, using a wide-necked jar or open pan of some sort. After a few days exposed to the air in this, the taint of formaldehyde will have disappeared. They can now be packed into a Kilner jar, a fresh brew of four parts water to one of sugar poured over them, and the jar sealed. They will keep for as long as you want, and be as attractive to use as when they

Snags galore! Best dealt with by a spun deadbait for the pocket's sake.

117

were first killed. One word of warning – formaldehyde is poisonous. Be sure to wash everything that you use thoroughly, do not leave the mixture lying around within the reach of children, and make sure you wash your hands after every part of the operation.

The search for firm baits has led us to try some pretty odd things in our time, but one of the latest methods we have adopted is undoubtedly the best. We start by thoroughly drying any fish, whether from the deep-freeze, the fishmonger's slab or the preserving jar, with an old towel. When they are as dry as possible, we dip them into a medium-sized tin of clear cellulose varnish (Ronseal clear is one of our favourites) and then hang them up to dry. Those baits too large to fit completely into the tin we dunk as far as possible, and then paint them with a brush so that a thick skin of varnish dries from nose to tail.

We only do enough baits for one day's fishing in this way – they don't last any longer – and prepare them in the shed on the day before we fish. By adding yellow Dylon dye to the varnish we can turn out golden baits, or we may use any other colour that we feel we might need. In fact it is possible to make golden and natural coloured baits by part dipping or painting. The permutations are endless, and our finished baits are firm enough to withstand really hard usage.

Sealing sprats.

Mounting minnows with a darning needle.

Quite how our ancestors managed to tote deadbaits around before the marketing of Tupperware we do not know. We have several different sizes of these boxes that we pack baits into before leaving home, including a few ready mounted on whatever rig we are going to need. More especially do we do this where really large baits, which take time to mount, are to be used: the early casts made at the beginning of a day are often the most productive, so it is essential that precious minutes are not wasted.

As to the mounts we use – well, starting with the smallest and simplest, we have the treble-mounted minnow. There is a special tool that makes mounting this lightweight child's play; just a darning bodkin pushed into a wooden handle so that the eyed end is outwards. It takes seconds to slide this through the mouth and body of the minnow, then out through the vent. A short length of nylon with size 12 or smaller trebles (depending on bait size) ready tied on is then threaded through the bodkin eye and pulled back out through the mouth taking the line with it. Simple but very effective. Split shot can be pinched on to the cast loosely, and slid down into the mouth to provide any necessary weight to help control the retrieve. Cast from an ultra-light rod with a very fine line it makes just about the most killing bait we know for chub, perch, trout and, often, pike.

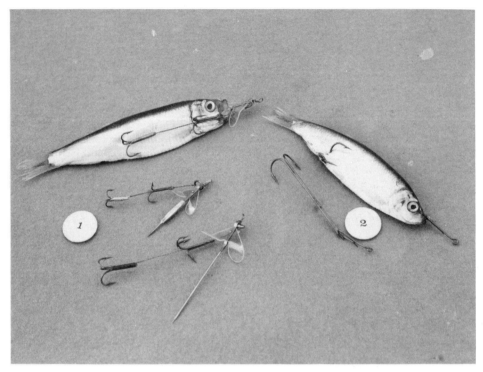

1. Mounted sprat – sprat and prawn tackle   2. Sprat mounted on two hook bait pin.

By the time one or two casts have been made with this rig the vent end of the minnow will have worked well down around the bend of the treble, causing it to swerve and wobble in large circles. If you want to keep its original wobbling action, that of small circles, then try using a single sliced hook instead of the treble. Pull the shank well up into the belly, and it will hold the bait firmly in place. The difference in action that this makes is quite considerable.

Bleak and sprats are superb spinners mounted on a sprat mount – leaded, with vanes and three trebles. Although they are moderately priced one can make them, using sheet plastic for the vanes, a baiting needle and barrel lead for the body pin and cabled Alasticum with suitable trebles. For fishing shallow water where weight would possibly be a disadvantage, use a prawn mount, which is identical in every way except that there is no lead weight on the body pin. Quite often we have seen sprats mounted on both these rigs by anglers who insist on putting a kink in the body of the bait. This merely destroys the spinning action imparted by the vanes, and produces a wobble. Mount the bait absolutely straight for a perfect spin, and remove the vanes completely and mount with the body curved if you are seeking a wobble action.

Probably the quickest and cheapest way of mounting a wobbling sprat is with the double hook steel pin, shown in the photographs. These cost a few pence each, can be pushed through the body and clipped on to the eye mount, then attached to the line or trace. It isn't always necessary to push the pin from vent to mouth – if the pin is pushed out just behind the gill then the set angle will make the bait take on a first-rate wide sweeping curve that we have found irresistible to pike. If there is any disadvantage in this method it is that lead for weighting must be placed on the cast and not inside the fish. This may seem a very small point, but the difference between cast and body weighting is reflected in any action which the angler may attempt to induce into the bait by raising or lowering the rod, or shifting the angle of retrieve from one side of the body to the other. This is immediately transferred to the lead on the cast, as opposed to the bait, when the lead is carried externally.

When it comes to rigs for larger deadbaits such as herrings, large roach etc., there is a lot to be said for the Jardine snap tackle for a mount when one is casting over short distances. The end treble is pushed well below the dorsal fin, pulling the tail back to produce a wobble action. The second

DEADBAIT TACKLES.   *1 & 2. Plastic immitation minnows   3. Double-hook baiting pin   4. Sport spinner   5. Prawn spinner   6. Archer flight.*

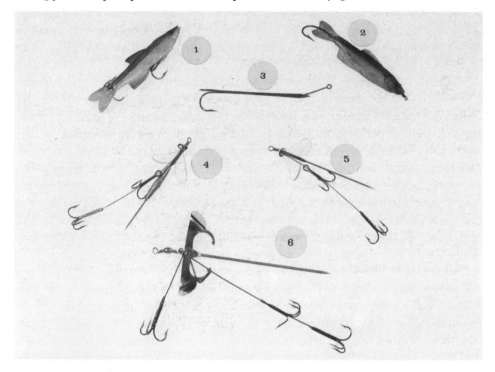

treble should be pointed into the shoulder, behind the gill cover. The end of the trace is slid under the gill and out through the mouth so that strain during both cast and retrieve travels through the bait, not to the outside hooks. Two or three turns of fine nylon round the shoulder of the bait will also help to hold it on to the hooks, and a small barrel lead can be slid down the trace into the mouth to provide body weight.

For long-distance casting the bait must be mounted so that it holds together, and cannot break apart either during the cast, on impact with the water, or during the retrieve. It is still possible to obtain Archer Deadbait spinning mounts and as a spinning rig this takes a lot of beating. Both metal vanes open outwards, the body pin is pushed through the mouth, and head of the bait slid between the jaws. Both vanes are then closed and the headand body hooks are fastened into place. Our photo shows one set of trebles – those on the other side of the body being hidden.

We add any extra weight that may be needed to the body pin by means of barrel leads or, if we want to cover shallow water, air is injected into the stomach or back with a hypodermic syringe. Incidentally, if we are going to use the air treatment we take care to push the body pin upwards into the flesh below the backbone so that the stomach will remain unpunctured.

For large baits that are to be wobbled we find nothing to beat the single big treble threaded from vent to mouth. During the threading it is an advantage if you pass the baiting needle out through the flank for about an inch or so, then back into the centre of the body. This helps to create a shallow curve in the bait during the retrieve and also helps to keep it from collapsing back on the rear treble.

Actually, this collapsing problem where the points on the end treble finish up buried into the vent of the bait can prevent the hooks getting a good grip when a strike is made. We have both lost fish because of it, and at the moment are experimenting with small buttons or washers threaded on the Alasticum immediately above the eye of the treble before it is mounted, to act as a buffer between it and the flesh. Our early results have been good, and our hooking ratio to strikes made has shown a distinct improvement. Other anglers use a split polythene tube of about ¾-inch length, convex side outwards.

Of course, there are many more rigs that one can use for mounting natural baits for both spinning or wobbling – Fred Buller's book *Pike* shows an excellent selection – but we have described only those that we use. They are all very simple, and it is this simplicity that has endeared them to us. The more trebles and Alasticum that attaches to a rig, the greater the difficulty in mounting the bait. Not only that, but we are entirely unconvinced that pure numbers of hooks are any better at holding a fish, or even increasing one's chances of hooking them when the strike is made. But, as we stated at the beginning of this chapter, this is an under-exploited section of the spinner's craft, and it is wide open to experiment. There is no doubt that the perfect rig or mount has yet to be invented.

Our earlier mention of flexibility when retrieving a natural bait deserves a little enlargement. We notice that most spinning enthusiasts who take to using dead fish still imagine that they are towing a lump of metal through the water, and whether it is because they subconsciously fear that by slowing the bait it will not spin correctly or, worse, will catch on the bottom, they continue to retrieve at far too fast a rate. Quite apart from its natural attraction, the whole idea of using a dead fish as a lure is because any buoyancy that it possesses will keep it fishing when other baits collapse and sink. It is impossible to retrieve a wobbled bait too slowly – in fact, we occasionally stop and deliberately allow any we are using to drop to the bottom, often taking a fish as the bait slides slowly downwards. At its slowest, wobbled deadbaiting is only one step removed from static deadbaiting.

Retrieving a spun deadbait demands a slow even retrieve that should be practised in the water at one's feet until the slowest movement consistent with the bait's turning is established. Beware of sudden snatching at any

MOUNTED HERRINGS. *1. Archer rig   2. Adapted Jardine-snap   3. Single treble, body threaded.*

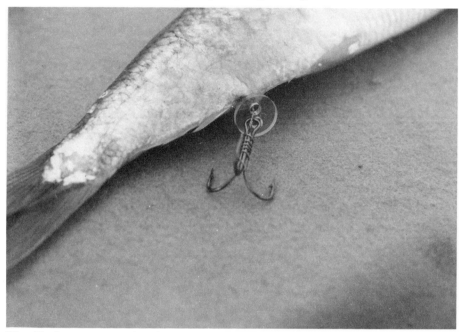

The shirt-button stopper, keeping the treble from jamming into the body of the deadbait.

time, regardless of whether you are spinning or wobbling. This can only tear hooks out of the flesh, or worse, cause the skin of the bait to break up. Of course, there's no reason why a change of pace should not be made; just avoid snatching.

Finally, we would like to remove all reservations that exist in anglers' minds that natural baits can only be fished for pike, and only then on large waters. Spun sprats and minnows are acknowledged as killing baits for salmon and trout respectively, whilst a spun bleak is the bait *par excellence* for Thames trout. Perch and chub are very partial to all of these baits, particularly minnow at any time of the year. As for the size of water one fishes – well, even in the smallest brook a dead fish is more easily controlled than a metal spinner or spoon, capable, with careful weighting, of working into tight corners where the artificial just cannot begin to function. Add to this our previous point of cheapness and the case for a working natural bait makes a great deal of sense. The actual techniques of retrieving spun and wobbled deadbaits will be dealt with in the sections appropriate to the relevant species. Suffice it to say for the present that with spun deadbaits, which are usually smaller than wobbled deadbaits, the strike is instant: with small wobbled deadbaits this can also apply, but in general the angler should steel himself to treat each tiny pluck as a good take and then stop retrieving and wait for the fish to move off with the bait.

PART THREE

CHAPTER FIFTEEN

Rods

If you walk into a well-stocked fishing tackle shop and turn towards the rod racks, you can be sure of entering the valley of indecision. There they stand; long rods, short rods, thick and thin rods, cork handles, composition handles, plastic wrapped – each with a tag showing bare details of what the rod is, and how much it costs.

Naturally the salesman will take over, display his goods and try to suit you, but try as he may, and honest as he may be, he can only fit you with what he thinks is the best rod for the type of fishing you have described to him.

Now a fishing rod is a very personal 'thing'. If you go to a gunmaker and buy a good grade gun the stock and fittings of the weapon will be measured, tailored and designed to fit your body. This naturally makes for increased accuracy and comfort. Roughly the same thing should apply with a fishing rod. A rod which does not 'fit' the individual will not cast accurately – and can be guaranteed to become a ton-weight of discomfort by the end of the day.

Before you select a rod for spinning remember there are some basic principles which run something like this:

1. A rod is an extension of the angler's arm;
2. it assists in making a successful cast;
3. it assists in retrieving a bait to the angler's satisfaction;
4. it helps drive the hook home, and
5. it helps play a hooked fish.

With those thoughts in mind let's try to understand something of what goes to make a good rod.

One of the great games in a schoolboy's life is 'Whangee'. It involves a length of cane or stick, to the end of which is impaled an apple or ball of mud. A good heavy switch of the cane and away goes the missile at the required rate of knots. Wonderful for long-range window breaking, but of course it doesn't take long to realise that the furthermost windows can only be reached by using the longest practical piece of cane.

1

2

3

4

5

6

Look at the first figure. Here the cane is a few feet long, and because of this it will only throw a very limited distance; but short though the distance may be the missile will land accurately. Fig. 2 shows a cane considerably longer in action. This will throw a missile a long way indeed – but not with the degree of accuracy shown by the short cane.

Now substitute a rod for the cane, and a lure for the missile. The short rod will cover a short distance – with accuracy. This is the ideal rod for use in tight conditions such as casting on small rivers, streams, under trees or from a boat. The long rod will place a bait some considerable distance, but with less accuracy. Large lakes, big rivers, and gravel pits are ideal for this style of rod where systematic searching of the water will be undertaken. These situations are shown in the photographs.

Now have a look at our schoolboy again. In Fig. 3 he is using a thick piece of cane, and the missile has not travelled very far, nor very accurately. This is because there has been little or no spring from the cane. Again, in Fig. 4 he is using a very thin, springy cane, and has not achieved distance or accuracy with it – the spring is just not enough.

Taking this one stage further Figs 5 and 6 show the same effect achieved by either too large, or too small a missile on the cane. The photographs

Wagtails and slotted minnows, and the man who started the fixed spool reel represented here by his reel, the Illingworth.

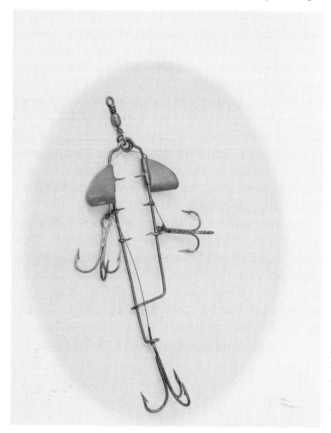

Deadbait spinner rig. The spikes are used to grip the deadbait. They can still be bought as old stock in ancient out-of-the-way tackle shops.

translate the diagrams into a fishing reality, and prove another principle – that weight of lure and strength of line must balance if a successful cast is to be made.

To help this 'balance' a fishing rod is tapered from butt to tip and the degree of taper and where it is placed can influence the punch that will go behind the cast. A long, slow, taper the length of the rod will 'spring' a plug over a considerable distance. A taper commencing near the rod tip will flick a plug over a short distance – with accuracy.

At one time much was written and heard of the reverse taper rod. In brief, this means that the rod tapers from the tip outwards to the reel fitting, then, through a long handle, it tapers back again to the butt cap. In theory, extra energy is stored during the build-up of the cast, to be unleashed at the moment of release. In practice that is so, but there is a tendency for the rod to continue to curve downwards after the cast, causing friction and deflecting the bait from its intended path. We feel that the added advantage of the reverse taper is grand for beach casters, where one could then use a rather lighter than usual rod, but of no enormous significance in a spinning rod.

The stepped-up rod, usually one which has received an extra wrapping of glass fibre cloth or carbon equivalent during the manufacturing stage, is stiffer than the ordinary rod, and capable of harder work and handling heavier baits. It is an excellent weapon where heavy deadbaits or big lures have to be flung over long distances.

Now let's go back to the rod rack at the tackle shop and narrow the selection of a rod down to the type that will suit our fishing. For chub, perch and light pike work with short casting and small plugs and spinners we will need something in the 5½- to 6½-foot range. Such a rod will probably be described as 'single-handed'. You can be assured that the action, or taper, will have been designed by the manufacturer to give excellent results – providing you don't try to overload it with a heavy lure or line.

For heavier lures and heavier lines a rod in the 6½- to 8½-foot class will be the type to look for, and for the real long distance, heavyweight work then nine to eleven feet will be nearer the length required. Most rods in the former category can be single- or double-handed, those beyond that length will be double-handed only.

The single- or double-handed tag refers of course to the length of handle. Largely it is a matter of personal choice, but there are some pros and cons that should be considered where the manufacturer offers a choice. Single-

Whilst long rods for lure fishing are not always necessary, as in this situation, they are useful when there is much marginal rush growth.

131

handed handles are usual on short rods and cast very accurately in punchy fashion – because no co-ordination is needed between the two hands. They are lighter, leading to less fatigue at the end of the day, and by being lighter give a much better sensation of 'sport' during the playing of a fish.

Double-handed rods are usually long, and can, as we have seen from our diagrams, cast further and will guide a fish more easily than the single-handed effort during the actual playing. One final word on the double-handed rod. If this is your choice, Ken would advise you to make sure that there is a large rubber button fitted to the butt end. The natural tendency to tuck the rod into hip or groin during a day's work can have a painful effect without this protection.

Let us now allow our imagination to run riot a few minutes, and try to envisage some average spinning waters. Think first of a large river. To reach the area where a fish might lie, which is often against a far bank, is going to require a fairly hefty bait and a strong line to carry it. Also the river may be

A big lure such as this needs a powerful rod for proper, balanced casting.

Out of balance. The plug is too big for the rod.

Still out of balance. A powerful rod and tiny plug.

fairly full, perhaps even in flood, in which case it may be necessary to add weight to the bait by some means or other to get it well down below the surface.

Now think big in another direction, and imagine a large lake, reservoir or loch. If it contains really big fish we may want to use a big bait. If boats are not allowed then we may want to cast that bait over very long distances to reach 'fishy' areas, or if a boat *is* allowed, then we may want to get a bait thirty or so feet below the surface to reach them. Again, we are thinking of heavy or big baits, added weight, and a strong line.

Now let us think about those other waters we imagined where distance was not the object, but accuracy and delicacy the major factor. Obviously the long rod with its slow taper would be unnecessary, in fact the light line and small lure would produce such an imbalance that casting of any sort would be nearly impossible.

This is where the short rod, between six and eight feet, is a necessity. Because it is small, it can be used single-handed, which in itself allows for better co-ordination of movement when the cast is made, and so improves accuracy. The action, or taper, should be fast, most of the spring taking place between the tip and mid-section of the rod itself. Used with a light line the bait can be accurately flicked over a short distance with the minimum of fatigue. In contrast to the long rod the bait is fired *at* the target.

Has this flight of fancy produced anything useful? We think so. It acknowledges that weight of lure and strength of line are of prime importance in spinning. It also shows that size and strength of water are equally important, and in perspective proves that these facts dictate any sort of rod we may use. In short, water governs the weight, weight governs the line, and the rod is an accessory to spinning – never the reverse.

The handle on a spinning rod is something accepted without comment by the majority of anglers, but we reckon that this is the most intimate part of the instrument. Comfort here will influence not only casting, but to a lesser degree one's whole concentration during the day.

Cork has been the usual handle material, and there is no doubt that good quality solid cork is warm, comfortable, clean and long lasting. We are emphatic that the circumference of the corks should suit our hands, long experience having taught us that thin handles lead to sloppy casting and over-thick grips become tiring. For most adult males a diameter of about one inch or a fraction less (2.5 cm) is about right. We also dislike sudden ridges or tapers up and down the corks, and abhor short two-handed rod handles that make us pigeon-chested when gripping them with both hands spread in the casting position. Sheet cork handles are usually thin cork wound round a wooden or other former.

There has been a tendency in recent years to move away from cork as a material for handles. Ribbed plastic is one alternative, but with what advantage it is hard to see. And now we have Duplon seemingly becoming universal even though it is not as strong as cork. Cork is warm to the touch (desperately important on a cold day) and cleans in a few minutes. There is also less likelihood of the rod slipping through wet hands. But whatever material you decide on, do make sure that the handle is not too thick. Ken can recall one rod with this vice that left his hand looking like a carpenter's G-cramp for days after an outing.

Winch fittings to hold the reel in place deserve some thought. Most of the major proprietary rods designed for lure fishing have a locking device which ensures that the reel, once mounted, cannot work free. Usually the fitting is recessed into the handle so that there is a crank, or offset, which gives a straight run for the line between reel and first rod ring. Not all rods have this refinement, and where the winch fittings are mounted on the conventional straight handle, the locking type can often be fitted.

Locking is usually achieved by a screw movement of one or both fittings locking down on the flange of the reel, preventing movement through the constant vibration of casting and winding. Ken has a 'thing' about ordinary winch fittings that push together, and maintains that more bad language is used annually by anglers who have a reel fall from the rod at a crucial moment than bears thinking about.

The position of the reel fittings depend on the rod length. Usually it is well up the rod (towards the top of the handle) to help balance the reel. But that does not mean that the point of balance of a rod must be at the reel fitting. Usually it is slightly above the handle. Balance at the reel fitting tends to lose the 'feel' of a rod at the tip – an important item as we shall see later.

One last type of reel fitting is worth considering, and this is the whip-on locking fittings. Certainly nothing could be lighter and the position can always be moved, albeit with a little trouble. Where lightness – and that is the theme of this section – is required, then this fitting with leather hand-grips takes first place.

Fuji marketed an entirely new concept in handles with their Fujispeed Grip. Made from plastic, with an imitation leather finish, the Fujispeed Grip does away with reel mountings in any form. The handle unscrews into two parts, the reel is inserted, and then the halves are screwed together again. Simple, safe and foolproof. There are numbers of collets which fit inside the handle end, enabling any diameter of blank to be fitted. Ken has only seen one in the single-handed size, but feels it to be a warm, comfortable winner.

It is generally accepted that handles on spinning rods should be parallel for fixed spool reels, and cranked for multipliers. But there is much to recommend a cranked handle with a closed face reel, because it tends to iron out the kink between line exit on the reel and the first rod ring. Again, a matter of preference and, of course, deciding on what type of fishing one intends to do before selecting the rod.

Ferrules deserve thought and attention. Split cane, solid fibre-glass and some hollow fibre-glass rods have metal ferrules. Make sure that the female part is reinforced at the end, otherwise it will split. Also check that they are of the splint-end variety, whipped to the rod for extra security. Metal ferrules should be greased (candle or bees' wax are ideal) and not oiled, and a plug fitted into the female ferrule (when the rod is not in use) is provided to keep grit and dirt, which encourage wear, from collecting.

Hollow fibre-glass and carbon rods usually fit together with a spigot. This needs no attention, other than making sure that the small gap is maintained between the rod sections when both joints are mounted. It is left to allow for wear, and when it disappears it is time to cut back with a fine file the female section at the end of the spigot so that the joint will again become a tight fit. Spigot fittings benefit from a little candle grease – it cuts down wear and makes the joint less prone to slipping.

ROD RINGS

For lure fishing of all kinds you need rod rings that will not groove, wear or crack easily. Barrie has used a carp rod, made up by Davenport and Fordham's, for eighteen years and the rings are quite ungrooved after thousands of hours of fishing, including a great deal of spinning and plugging. These rings are of seamless stainless steel, extremely hard, and are probably 'diamite', one of the hardest of all rod ring materials. It is certainly better to pay a high price for good rings than to buy the cheapest ones which are usually soft and will barely last half a season without wear. If in doubt, consult a good tackle dealer or one of the better tackle suppliers.

Apart from stainles steel or chrome-hardened unlined rings, it is possible to buy lined rings either for the end ring only or throughout the length of the rod. The linings can be ceramic, such as Sintax or Regalox, or they can be Aqualite, a rather more glassy and more brittle material. We have rods fitted throughout with these rings and although wear and tear is minimal (Regalox does groove) the rods have a heavy feel and a softer action than they would have with lighter rings. For trolling they are probably excellent, but for casting continuously you really need lightweight rings except at the tip ring and butt ring, which can be lined.

To be quite fair to those advocating lined rings throughout it must be admitted that the range of ring sizes produced by the manufacturers is usually much greater than the range you see in the shops: it is nearly always possible to get smaller and lighter editions of those on display in many tackle shops. If the stainless steel rings are *really* good, it is possible to dispense even with lined butt end rings.

For lure fishing other considerations than type of ring metal are necessary. For example, should the rings be High Bells Life (that is, well off the rod) or Full-open Bridge rings (that is, close to the rod)? Unless very fine line plugging for perch is being done, in which case high rings facilitate casting during wet weather, the low rings are better and lessen the chances of a loop of line taking round the ring supports during a full-blooded cast in confined circumstances. In the late 1970s Fuji and other firms began marketing a superb range of lightweight, lined rings which more or less make wire rings obsolete. Had these been available when we built the ultra light spinning rods we would have been saved a lot of hassle. (Some of these modern rings do wear fly lines a bit heavily, it seems, but that need not concern us here.)

It has been common for many years to have a large diameter butt ring, the idea being that it allowed the flapping early coils coming off a fixed spool to level out without friction. However, it has been shown in recent years, by Don Neish we believe, that a *small* diameter butt ring probably increases the length of the casts with *thin* lines. Apparently the slapping action from each coil of line unravelling off the reel and hitting the rod acts as a brake when large rings are used.

Spacing of the rings along the rod is not particularly difficult, and any tackle-making shopkeeper will give advice here. (In Cambridge, Barrie runs to Percy Anderson or Les Beacroft for help, whilst Ken has only to ring Jack Simpson.) The only points to remember are to place the rings with Sellotape first before binding and to avoid an arrangement which, when the rod is

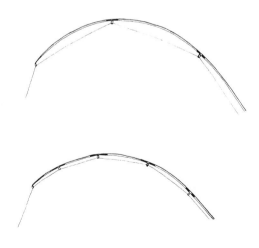

bent, looks like the first example shown in the figure. Try to strike a medium between too few rings, or the too many which will soften the rod action. There has been a tendency during the 1980s to reduce the number of rod rings in specimen hunting – in extreme cases to a tip ring only! This may facilitate casting but it *greatly* increases friction whilst playing a big fish, as the illustration implies.

ROD MATERIALS

Something left until last has been the choice of rod materials. There are several choices – hollow fibre-glass, solid fibre-glass, split cane and carbon and each has its own devotees.

Solid glass-fibre is heavy, 'cold', and appears to lack sensitivity. It is the sort of stuff one associates with open boats and shark fishing. But this is not entirely the case, and provided one keeps to the small rod – six feet and under – it is only slightly different from its hollow counterpart. It is becoming of historical interest only. Its main advantage lies in its enormous strength, and it really comes into its own when fishing tight, well-snagged areas where a tug-of-war to release tackle may ensue. The biggest disservice the tackle industry perpetrates with solid fibre-glass is fitting ferules that would appear to have been cut from an oil pipeline. These are one or two makes with light but strong reinforced ferrules, and these are the ones to choose from.

Hollow fibre-glass and the word indestructible are synonymous in many anglers' minds. Fibre-glass blanks are only as tough as the manufacturers decide – and the best ever made will not stand slamming in car doors, stepping on, and other forms of maltreatment seen beside the water. Light, tough blanks are expensive and trouble-free, although repeated snatching at tackle to effect a retrieve from snags can, and does, produce a bend, or 'set' as it is called.

Fibre-glass may be rot-proof, but the silk whippings that hold rod rings etc. in place are not, and a thin coat of copal varnish every year goes a long way towards keeping a rod ready for instant use.

Hollow tubes are usually joined by means of a spigot, hollow in itself or solid, shedding weight and providing extra toughness at an acknowledged weak point of the rod. Some are now made with carbon-reinforced sections, compensating for wear and adding even more strength. Beware of bad fitting during the manufacturing stage though, and carefully check the rod by putting the joints together and feeling for 'sloppiness' before actually buying.

The left-hand wind RYOBI Multiplier, which prevents 'cross hands boogie'.

This section would not be complete without mention of carbon fibre rods which are replacing glass on the rod stands. We now have extensive experience of carbon rods of all kinds, including spinning, and will not go back to buying new glass rods. Much greater precision in design seems to have been built into carbon blanks and one can find them with *exactly* the action you seek. Some can even be jumped upon with no ill effect (e.g. Ugly Sticks).

Split cane is making a massive come-back in the United States of America as a rod material – but tends to remain an 'out' in this country, mainly because of its expense. Rather a strange situation when you appreciate that Britain produces the best split cane rods in the world.

Make no mistake, a rod built from split cane is warm, light, responsive to the hand – but an absolute swine to keep if it is to last. Modern cassion glues have obviated the old habit of the sections that form the rod becoming unstuck, through either over/under heat or over/under moisture conditions.

But the problem of 'set' can rear its ugly head in a split cane rod at an early stage, no matter how well you dry and handle it between outings. Basically this is a problem of strain, and a busy plug caster's rod is well and truly thrashed from this quarter throughout the season. If you are dead set

139

An 'antique' catch. 1910 Hardy Victor rod, Silex reel, Silk line, Pubjab steel trace and Hardy Wye Phantom. Taken on the River Lea.

(pardon the pun) on the stuff, then be prepared to strip and turn the rod rings every two or three years. This produces at least a temporary straightening.

Having said all that, Ken admits to owning a seven foot split cane old faithful that has more years than he has sense, and looks like a dog's back leg. Every year it is put aside for the rubbish bin – and solemnly retrieved for yet another day. The excuse for its redemption? It may be useful on some small water or other.

By design, this chapter contains a large amount of very elementary knowledge. We have deliberately included it because the rod is a prime piece of equipment, around which all remaining tackle must fit and balance. It is generally the item of tackle most taken for granted by anglers, and the idea that any old rod will double-up for a bit of live – and deadbaiting, plus some spinning or plug work, still largely exists. Not always is this the fault of the fisherman – tackle dealers advertise 'Sea or Pike Rods', extolling the adaptability of a rod that will do everything beside a gravel pit, or from the pier!

Take it from us: lure fishing is a specialised form of fishing and it requires a specialised rod. Think carefully, and re-read this chapter before making your choice. And remember that in lure fishing you spend more time holding the rod, actually 'living' with it, than you do in almost all other forms of angling.

CHAPTER SIXTEEN

Reels

FIXED SPOOL AND CENTRE-PIN REELS

Very few anglers these days own centre-pin reels that are good enough to cast a lure directly from the reel, but probably there are still a few people around, ourselves included, who began fishing and particularly plug fishing, with a centre-pin. Barrie used, among others, a bakelite centre-pin called the Aerialite made by Allcock's. Now, you cannot cast plugs directly from the reel, but you can pull off loops of line from the rod rings and, if the artificial lure is a heavy wooden plug, cast quite a long way. So plug fishing and cheap centre-pins went together when Barrie was a boy.

Ken remembers the Adaptacast coming on to the market. This was a twin set of reel saddles, joined in the centre, that allowed the reel to be turned out of the parallel-to-handle position into the cross position, exactly like the fixed spool reel.

In fact the principles were the same. With the reel full to the brim with line, it was turned into the cross position, the cast made, and line pulled freely over the lip. After the cast it was turned back, and the angler could retrieve in the normal way. The disadvantage was line kink, which increased as each successive cast was made. Unfortunately, you couldn't reverse the drum to eradicate the kink action. Mind you, the Malloch reel made just after the First World War allowed ... but that is history, and proves that there is not much new under the sun in the world of angling.

The centre-pin can, of course, be used in connection with plugs when trolling is the technique, and here one has the added pleasure of *playing* a fish on a centre-pin. It would be a good point here to mention some of the better centre-pins on the market: the Match Aerial, Rapidex, Trudex and Trentman are among the good ones, but it is possible that some of these have now been taken off the market because of the real competition from fixed spool reels. With each of these reels the angler *can*, with practice, learn the Nottingham cast. But Barrie's Rapidex, for example, is just that little bit sluggish to get much distance.

There is a tremendous, almost bewildering choice of fixed spool reels available. And unlike, say, ten years ago, many of these are really good reels. Thanks to the efforts of some anglers, notably Richard Walker and Eric Hodgson, firms include a roller in the pick-up which considerably alleviates the problems of resistance. As far as we know, Intrepids were the first people to put on a roller pick-up: they had a cheap but good reel called the Elite. This is not to say that there are not plenty of other reels on the market, and that they will not better those already mentioned in some respects: Daiwa and the Abu range of closed-face reels immediately come to mind.

A short while back we mentioned left-hand wind. What is the significance of this? Quite simply, if you are a right-handed person you need a left-handed reel. This is because the right hand is used for the most important jobs of the day – holding the rod, making the cast with a one-handed rod, or *guiding* the cast with a two-handed rod. The split second the plug hits the water the left hand can, whilst the right gets the rod in position, flick on the pick-up and begin turning the handle if necessary.

Consider the alternative for a right-handed angler: he makes the cast with his right hand; transfers the rod to his left hand after the cast; then with his right hand begins the retrieve. The *important* hand is involved with the easy task of turning the handle whilst the weak hand is guiding the plug and

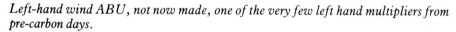

Left-hand wind ABU, not now made, one of the very few left hand multipliers from pre-carbon days.

Here's looking at you: plug versus pike!

playing the fish! Quite crazy. Of course, most multiplying reels are for left-handed anglers. But Ryobi Masterline do some very good left hand wind multipliers for lure fishermen, and today most fixed spool reels come either left or right hand wind, or both. Ryobi even make an ambidextrous multiplier.

It is not our intention to decribe in great detail all facets of casting lures with a fixed spool reel but there are certain points worth making. For example it is *most* important not to underfill or overfill the reel spool. If the angler has access to bulk spools of reel line then the job of filling the spool is easy: simply reel on the line until it is level with the lip of the spool, neither underfilling nor overfilling. If, when practising a cast or two on the lawn, you find the line jumps off at the slightest provocation, then snip off about twenty feet of line and you should then have it about right

The other line twisting, cutting, cursing fiddle is when line slips between the spool and its housing, to disappear in a maze of turns around the central spindle. Fortunately, several companies have produced the skirted reel, an extension of the spool which fits back over and not into the housing, making this problem almost obsolete.

If you have no access to a bulk spool then the procedure for loading a spool is as follows:
1. Reel on one hundred metres of line directly on the spool.
2. The line should fall somewhat short of the lip when it is all on.
3. Reel on some backing line, or wool, until the level of the spool lip is just reached.
4. Take it all off again and replace with the wool or backing underneath.
5. The reel line *should* now come just up to the lip of the spool.

Obviously bulk spools are better, as they are for all fishing. When casting, pick up the line on the index finger of the right hand (if you are right-handed) which should be holding the rod on the reel seating and be positioned, therefore, directly over the reel if the rod is held horizontally. Take off the pick-up. The next job is to throw the lure with the rod end, at which time the force of the throw will flick the line off the finger with no effort at all on the part of the angler. The other method of holding the line, by gripping it against the cork of the rod handle with the index finger, is a far less precise way of casting, and it is far easier to accidently hang on to the line too long with the result that it whizzes round your head like an angry wasp. Barrie once did this whilst wearing a bobble hat and the lure whistled round and round the bobble almost severing it from the hat before whipping it off his head. The resultant language was as colourful as the hat and as spikey as the trebles on the plug in use at the time.

When the lure hits the water the pick-up is engaged, but the critical thing is to check with a quick glance that this action has not imparted a loop into the line. To reel the line on to a spool which has a loop sticking out not only causes slight kinks and bends in the monofilament but seriously impedes the next cast, both for length and accuracy.

If you *do* introduce a loop unknowingly, then try a long cast into open water to free it: *never* try a tricky cast under trees.

How do you set up the fixed spool reel for retrieve and playing? There are two ways: one is to set the slipping clutch at something less than the breaking strain of the line and then drop the index finger on the spool when a take occurs; the other is to have the clutch wound up tight, whack the fish *hard* on a take, and only give line by letting the reel handle turn backwards. Most people do the former, which is probably why we do the latter.

If you use the method by which the reel handles are allowed to turn backwards, always make sure the anti-reverse mechanism is off! This is no more laborious than checking the clutch-setting, and both can be altered accidently anyway.

Barrie punching a deadbait on a gravel pit.

This basically is what you do when using a fixed spool reel for lure fishing, but the actual precision of casting, and the accuracy, only comes with practice. It is easier to practice with plugs than with any other tackle since their very weight takes the hard work out of long casts, and their size facilitates observation of the whole cast and retrieve.

There are other wrinkles, do's and dont's. For example, try to avoid the embarrassment of casting with the pick-up on. If you do this the plug hits the water in front of you with an almighty splash, and all the heads on the water look in your direction whilst you try to pretend that a fish has just risen, or chased a mallard etc.etc.

Don't reel the trace swivel up through the end ring of the rod! It makes the next cast rather lethal at times. If the weather is rough and windy it is quite possible to do this without hearing the click as the swivel goes through the end eye. Not only is the next cast dangerous, but the lining of the eye itself may be damaged. One way is to use a large swivel on the top of the trace, but in general we prefer small swivels for other reasons.

When spinning in the dark it may be necessary to put swan shot at the top of the trace so that this stops as it hits the end ring. The earlier mentioned problem of loops is all the more critical at night and it may be that here the fixed spool reel should be abandoned in favour of the closed-faced reel, even though the latter is not so good for playing heavy fish.

Despite our list of problems which can arise with fixed spool reels, we like them, and for the considerable chunk of our middle to light range of spinning use nothing else, our ownership including those by Mitchell, Abu, Intrepid and, more recently, skirted reels by Diawa, Ryobi and Shakespeare. But always remember that these reels are not miracle machines and we make a point of stripping, examining, cleaning and oiling the several makes two or three times a year. Prevention is better than all the curses let loose over a lost fish.

CLOSED FACE REELS

You either like or hate closed face reels – and there seems to be no middle course. At 'face' value they iron out all the loose line problems that plague lure fishing in windy days when every second or third cast is aborted by the line winding either round the reel back or handle.

Casting and line control certainly couldn't be simpler. One has only to press the button at the back of the reel, and the line hangs automatically held against thumb pressure, waiting for the cast to begin. Once the forward swing is at its peak one has only to release the thumb and out goes the line. Winding the handle immediately collects the line again, ready for the retrieve.

One further advantage of the closed face reel is that pushing the release button during the cast immediately stops the line. This is not only an immense advantage if you see that £2 of plug is heading for the reeds on the opposite bank – it assists also in preventing extra line pulled from the reel during the cast from lying on the surface, needing frantic handle-winding before the plug can be made to move.

In other words, once the plug is close to where it was intended to land, drop your thumb to the release button, and the plug, continuing in flight, will hit the water with no slack line behind it. Of course, some practice is necessary, but Ken has found this immensely useful in using surface lures for chub, where 'plop' and immediate action in a tight corner would be the only way of beating a well-hidden fish.

So much for the good side of closed face reels. Now, on the debit side. The main problem is line going through a rapid succession of angles. Think about it. There you are, stuck into a good fish, with the rod well back – and the line at the rod tip already at an angle of nearly ninety degrees. Following the line down through the rings (more resistance) it disappears through the closed face line guard, and turns immediately sharp left, through another angle of nearly ninety degrees. It then loops over the pick-up (ninety degrees) and then on to the spool itself, about another ninety degrees.

Now think of the other types of reel in turn. With the multiplier and centre-pin there is 90 degrees at the rod tip as the line comes through, then it more or less runs straight on to the drum. Result? Little or no friction. With fixed spool reels the line has the initial 90 degree angle at the tip, and another ninety degree over the pick-up. But friction here can be reduced by a roller type bush on the bale arm.

So bad does friction become with the closed face job, that an element of risk creeps in without notice. Barrie first discovered and discussed it with Ken, who then realised that it had become one of his many habits. Imagine that big fish again. You hold tight, pump up with the rod, and eventually are leaning back like a strap-hanger on the Underground. At that point you have to wind down to the fish in order to pump again, and because line friction is so great, you tend to drop the rod point a little in advance of the winding – giving just little slack line to the fish. The rest is easy to imagine.

Another bad point with the closed face reel is that the spool itself has for some reason or other – probably weight ratio – to be very slim. This in turn leads to less line being carried, and shorter casting. We have already pointed out in the section on fixed spool reels the friction trap created by a spool insufficiently filled. Therefore, if the spool is narrow it empties quickly, and friction sets in almost immediately the cast commences.

There are several models on the market to choose from, but two merit comment. They are the Abu range, and those from the stable of Heddon.

Closed face reel, the Heddon 150: grand for tight corners.

Both 'handle' well, but one gets the impression that perhaps the Heddon range is especially designed for plug casting alone, and not as a double-up for general coarse fishing. Both models have a side-operating knob for applying drag, but Abu here have a more sophisticated setting that is very positive.

The main difference between the two lies in the pick-up mechanism itself. Abu favour the floating pin type, whilst the Heddon pick-up is a circular piece of metal with a succession of small shallow grooves cut around the face, over one of which line will catch. We don't think there is much to choose between either method – each involves a certain amount of 'snatch', but not enough to provoke breaks. Probably the biggest difference lies in the price.

For easy fishing and very accurate casting the closed face reel is hard to beat. There is a certain care-free style about it that certainly attracts many anglers. But neither of us feel that we would like to tackle a real record-breaking heavy fish behind one.

The J.C. Higgins Spin-Casting reel is a closed face reel which gets around the problem of deep, narrow spools, just mentioned in connection with usual closed face reels, by having a series of steps in the spool so that a relatively small amount of line is held on each step. This reel is unusual in several other respects: the cast is made with a finger on the button at the rear of the reel, which has the effect of trapping the line; the stepped spool is at the *back* of the flier housing, not at the front as with most other fixed spool and closed face reels. Sears, Roebuck and Co. made this reel and we hope they still do, for it seems to combine the advantages, for light spinning anyway, of both the fixed spool and closed face types.

For all the dials and levers on the multiplying reel, it remains a basic centre-pin that is geared for a faster re-wind (the revolutions of the spool are 'multiplied' as the handle is turned) with an added advantage in its ability to be thrown out of gear, overcoming inertia on the spool when a cast is made. They are ideal reels for the angler using using a medium- to heavy-weight lure over middle to long distances. For really bad weather conditions – pouring rain, and especially during high winds – they are superb, and for handling big fish they are theoretically and mechanically perfect.

Having written all those glossy words, it must be said that there is a large proportion of the angling community that dislike or are frightened of them, although anglers rarely admit to the latter reason. Most of the dislike stems from the constant fear of over-running with an immediate bird's nest; a condition brought about either by lack of mechanical knowledge and care, or misunderstanding of the manufacturer's instructions regarding balance of accompanying tackle.

On the mechanical side it must be said that one need not have a degree in engineering to cope with everyday running and use. The parts affecting a reel's efficiency centre round end bearings (ball-bearings in better class reels) set in both end plates. Leading directly from one spindle will be a form of governing mechanism, usually fibre blocks that are thrown out by centrifugal force to act as a brake as the bait nears the water at the end of its

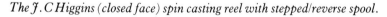

The J.C Higgins (closed face) spin casting reel with stepped/reverse spool.

*That springtime wonder,
a bird's nest caused by
bad reel adjustment.*

trajectory. A manual brake is also fitted in the form of a drag, which keeps the spool revolving in sympathy with the weight of the bait used during a cast. Finally, there is a lever or push button that disengages the spool from the retrieving gears, used before the cast is made.

Correct adjustment of those parts we have listed, plus attention to the general instructions that accompany the reel, will guarantee trouble-free casting. Perhaps the easiest way of explaining our thoughts on this is to take an imaginary reel from its case, and go through the pre-casting routine, starting with lubrication. Most manufacturers recommend or sell an oil of the correct viscosity. Use that, and that only, leaving the extra fine and super oils to the casting experts who are looking for added distance at a competition. Don't flood the reel; by doing so you will impair the efficiency of drag and braking parts, besides splattering line on the spool with oil, which won't improve it.

Make sure that the line itself is not below or above the breaking strain recommended by the manufacturer. Light lines will not run efficiently; heavy lines produce unwanted and damaging strain. Whether you use mono-filament or braided nylon is a matter of choice, providing your selection is not a line that is prone to excessive stretching. Many anglers have trouble in matching the line on the spool with the position of the line spreader (where one is fitted) on the front of the reel. The answer is to tie a small swivel on to the end of the line after each outing, and then wind this up to the prongs of the spreading mechanism itself. This stops the line from running right on to the spool, and subsequent misalignment when it is re-threaded.

Correct filling of the spool is important. When underfilled there is an inefficiency because the rate of retrieve is slowed down. When overfilled the line binds against the insides of the end plates, and causes unnecessary friction. Also, take care not to wind on too tightly; coils of line will cling if you do, again causing drag.

Following that pre-casting attention, comes the cast itself. This can be resolved into one simple drill that need be done at the commencement of fishing only; ever after this drill, the reel will be 'set', and should need no further attention through the day.

First, adjust the spindle so that there is a minimum of end play. There is a natural tendency among anglers to think that if there is plenty of play, there can be no friction and that the bait must travel further; as also the anglers who use both spindle adjustments for a brake. The minimum of play is the setting to work for. Then set the drag to zero, and release the spool. Now the drag is adjusted so that the weight runs slowly and just – but only just – stops.

Give a jerk with the rod tip, and the bait should drop about three feet before coming to a stop again. This is the governing mechanism taking over, bringing the spool to a natural halt. Wind back until the customary two feet or so of line hangs below the rod tip, release the spool, and you are ready to cast.

The governing mechanisms on the latest magnetic reels operate similarly in practice, but they do have a 'Mug's scale' of 1–10 marked on the side: only progress through the loosening grades as you become competent with each type of lure.

Knowing that the mechanism of the reel is properly adjusted, concentrate on the cast, and avoid releasing the drum too early during the swing. If you do this, the drum speed will build up to such an extent that an over-run is more than possible. Let the line follow through – and the reel should come to a halt as tha bait hits the water.

For those that think this is a tall order, let me state that Ken has seen Johnnie Logan at the London School of Casting use this method and

Showing just how large and crude home-made spoons can be – but they really need larger trebles.

immediately after the cast, lean his rod against a seat. Without any braking from his thumb the spool stopped without overrun the moment the bait hit the water. With practice, of course, it is possible to avoid setting the drag entirely, and to control the spool solely by pressure from the thumb – but practice is the operative word.

Quite often abortive casting with the multiplier is the result of damage to the reel itself, caused by thoughtless brute force on the angler's part. Imagine a plug well and truly snagged, and the natural reaction by many anglers. They reel down tight on the line, screw the slipping clutch up hard – and lean back. Result? Well, strain on the spool is transferred to the fine spindle ends, and this causes distortion. Ever after that when a cast is made the drum will not run truly – and the angler's springtime wonder, a bird's nest, must result.

Even if the spindle ends are not damaged, tightly wound monofilament is capable of distortion and even the fracturing of a plastic drum. In fact some anglers wind a fair layer of braided line on to the spool first, so that it can act as a cushion against this strangling effect of monofilament.

So whenever you are snagged, remember the procedure. Wind up to the line, lay the rod down, and take two or three turns of line round your well-protected forearm. Now you can pull to your heart's content without straining the reel or, for that matter the rod, in any way.

Looking over the market in this country there is no doubt that it has a very strong bias towards Abu multipliers – and certainly they have a superb range of models to choose from. In particular we like the left-hand wind model they used to make – there seems little point, as already mentioned, in constantly changing hands whilst fishing. Also the high-speed model deserves mention; there are many occasions when a little burst of speed can produce some extra special action to a plug. Ryobi Masterline now do better left-hand wind models.

Heddon, Phluger and Penn freshwater multiplying reels are rarely seen, which is a great pity. They have some grand engineering, but perhaps lack the 'follow up' in servicing arrangements that could be necessary with such delicate mechanism. Certainly, secondhand models that come on to the market are snapped up in double quick time, and command a high price. If you're really on a budget, then have a look at the nearest Woolworth's stores. They have two models that are heavy in weight, but certainly light in price.

The bony skull of a pike requires a balanced set of equipment, particularly lures and rods.

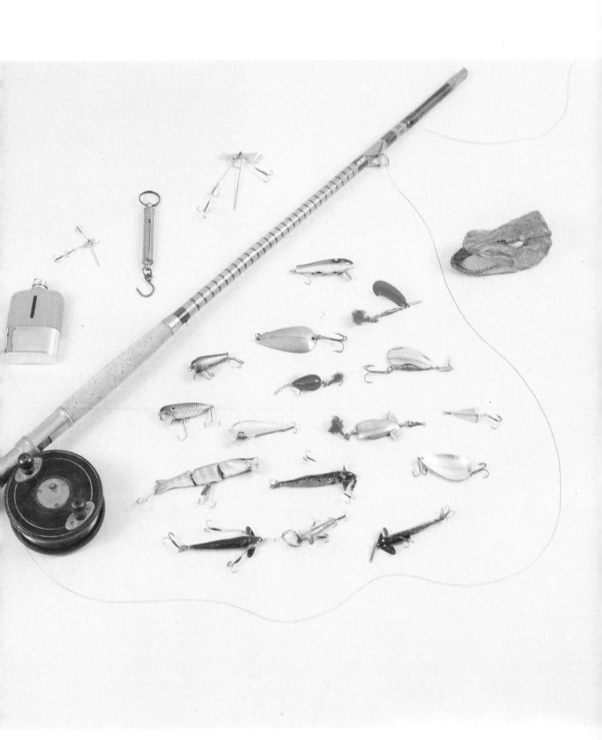

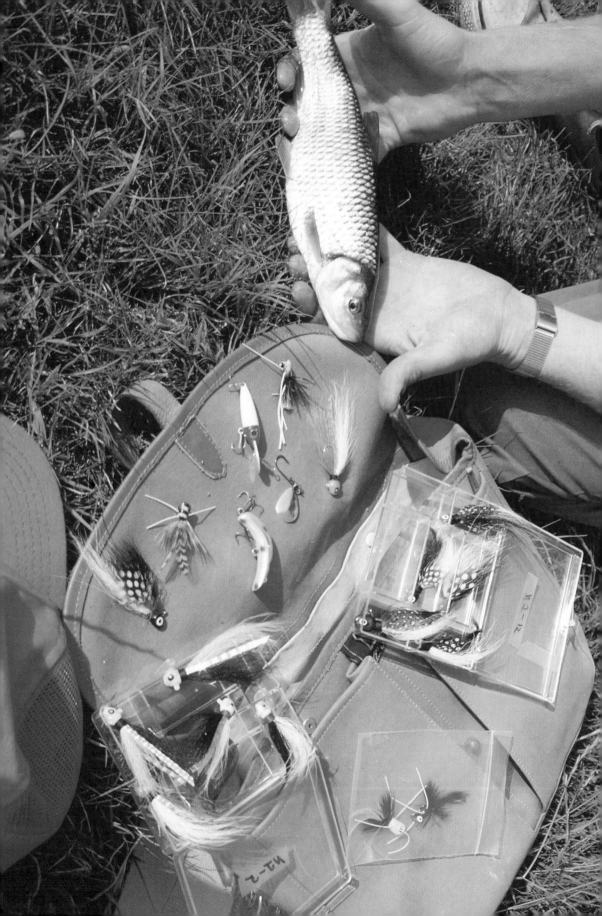

CHAPTER SEVENTEEN

Lines

MONOFILAMENT

If you are considering spinning as a full-time sport then we suggest you read this chapter twice. If you are already well advanced in the craft, then we ask you to forget your Tooty Fruity Never Fail Nylon that you swear by, read with an open mind what follows and then reconsider your favourite again.

Did you hear the story of the spin-fisherman who decided to buy a 5 lb b.s. line? When he used it, he tied a bad knot, losing forty per cent of its strength. At his first cast the line naturally became wet – and another fifteen per cent of its strength was lost. Because he had a cracked rod ring the line frayed, and lost a further twenty per cent strength. By exposing it to the sun, stretching it when he became snagged, and keeping it in a warm cupboard it lost another thirty per cent. Next time he took his reel out of its case he found the line had disintegrated into a pile of dust!

Far-fetched? A little – but not as far as you would think. Nylon may be better than horse hair, silk, flax, gutta percha, and all the other old-fashioned trouble-makers, but it is not a miracle material, and one needs to use a little thought before blindly purchasing it.

Let's start with two cast-iron, irrefutable facts. The *first* knot you tie in a nylon line reduces its strength by about ten to fifteen per cent if it is a good knot; up to thirty per cent or more if it is bad, or badly tied. We use the double clinch knot, or half blood knot, and take our time tying it. Before we ease it up tight (as opposed to pulling it or jerking it) we moisten the loose knot in our mouths so that it won't 'strangle', and further reduce the line circumference. Tie more than one knot, and down sinks the strength of the line again – unless all the knots are as good or better than the first, in which case the theoretical loss (after the first knot) is nil.

Our other fact is that all nylon line, on becoming wet, loses up to fifteen per cent of strength immediately. Which rather makes a mockery of our five pound line that we purchased – its actual breaking strain in use would be about four pound. Of course, it is difficult to guard against ultra violet rays when one is fishing, but it is possible to use a little sense in purchasing line, and if it has been standing out in a showcase near a window, then look elsewhere.

Cracked rod rings we have dealt with in a previous section, likewise the problem of line angles on a reel, all of which produce friction, which in turn generates heat that destroys the properties of monofilament. But pulling and stretching a line? Obviously one cannot use a line without some strain. It is just a question of reducing it where possible, and being prepared to scrap lines at regular intervals and respool afresh.

Which make is best? We plump for pliable, low glint lines and among those that we use are Maxima, Sylcast and Platil. Although it is possible to further reduce glint by staining and dyeing, it may detract from the original strength and we prefer to leave the line in its original colour.

BRAIDED LINES

On the credit side, braided lines made from nylon or dacron are softer and more pliable than monofilament, and less prone to lose strength when wet. They knot easily (but still, of course, lose strength) and are practically uninfluenced by the stretch factor that weakens most monofilament lines.

On the debit side they are not as long-lasting as monofilament and more prone to abrasions. There is a certain tendency to cling when wound round a drum, and by virtue of thickness alone create more friction when leaving the reel, lessening the distance that can be covered. Our main dislike is that they are very visible in clear water conditions, so much so that a nylon trace of some sort must be adopted for general use. As we have discovered, this means knots (in the plural) and subsequent risk of loss of overall strength again. To sum up, braided lines are in a class of their own for trolling, but for us it is monofilament with all our general spinning work.

Lead-cored lines are expensive but excellent for certain kinds of trolling, in which plugs can be used as well as other lures. With the speed of the boat constant, and a certain length of the marked line out behind the boat, the depth at which the lure is working can be known exactly: in general, a lead-cored line gets the line to the right depth more easily than other lines, and without the addition of action-killing lead weights. Lead-cored lines are readily available in this country.

CHAPTER EIGHTEEN

Terminal Tackle

One of the great pleasures of lure fishing in general, and of plug fishing in our case, is that the terminal tackle is relatively simple. When working a plug for perch or chub, or even trout, it is only necessary to have a link swivel on the end of the reel line, and an anti-kink vane some distance up the line from the link swivel. The link swivel is simply for rapid attachment of lures. The only change in this arrangement that is ever necessary is to add a wire trace, for example when pike are the quarry.

Great variation is possible in trace wires these days, so it would be best if we explained our preferences, whilst not intimating that other types are no good. Alasticum wire is a widely-used and quite cheap form of trace wire, coming in two types, single strand and cabled. The single strand is perfectly all right for plug fishing unless you are in the habit of making jerky casts which may, during the flight of one cast, introduce a kink and almost simultaneously snap the wire. We think single strand Alasticum is best avoided.

Cabled Alasticum was really excellent wire until about 1973, when for some reason it appeared in the shops in a more loosely cabled form. Not only was the wire slightly thicker for the same breaking strain, but it wasn't stained as well as previously and it tended to unravel rather easily. We still use it and keep a small supply, but it qute simply is not as good as it was. Similar wire by PDQ is just as good.

One of the good features of Alasticum was its dull colour. We now use Tidemaster Steelstrand which in the 20 lb breaking strain category is actually thinner than 15 lb Alasticum. The colour is sorrel, and the wire stainless steel in seven fine strands. It has the slight disadvantage of being rather stiffer than Alasticum but that this is not really serious can be judged from the fact that one can still twist it with the fingers when attaching a link swivel.

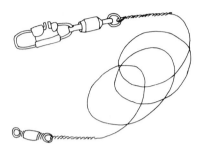

It would be nice to see Tidemaster in 15 lb, 10 lb and 6 lb breaking strains for other uses than heavy pike fishing, but we fear this is not to be. Quite a few nylon-coated traces are made these days. They certainly look nice, are usually a little bit stiff, and the nylon coating doesn't seem to last very long: some are also rather shiny. But almost all modern wires for traces are so much better than the thick, black hawsers of a few years ago, that one can probably pay rather too much attention to the details of them. The aim should always be as fine a wire as possible, preferably dull in colour, and preferably soft and supple enough to make attachment of link swivels an easy matter.

Swivels in our experience are pretty reliable. All you need is a range of sizes from the smallest you can get, about size 10, up to about size 4. If you intended using plugs for shark at sea, as some anglers do, then you might go up to size 2/0 or one of the ball-bearing swivels. Incidentally, Sharpe's ball-bearing swivel is of just the right size for use with 20 lb b.s. Tidemaster for pike traces.

With today's products one, or at the most two swivels should be sufficient, although there are some grotty efforts on the market and it does literally pay to be choosy. Consider the straightforward barrel swivel. It looks efficient, turns comfortably in your hand when first it is mounted, but after an outing or two it is an even bet that weed, grit and water will have forced themselves under the casing leaving it with about a fifty per cent efficiency. Moral? Check and lubricate all swivels after a day's fishing. When did you last check yours? Ah!

Next up the scale – and a long way at that financially – is the ball-bearing swivel. This is the Rolls Royce that purrs on forever, needing only an occasional service. Trouble is that it is very difficult to manufacture a small ball-bearing swivel, and those on the market are too big for some of our work.

We have plumped for the diamond swivel for our lighter spinning. The join is a rivet head type that can be seen, and should anything in the way of debris catch round it, can be cleared within seconds. Half a dozen loose swivels in a tackle box can be as elusive as an eel when you want to get hold of one. We clip ours together on a safety pin, which also serves as a good drying rack when we have run a little 3 in 1 oil over them. It's amazing how often you need a safety pin too! The strain of lifting our huge catches can play havoc with buttons.

Link swivels are more tricky. Avoid like the plague those which have a kind of elongated split-ring attached to one end: it is quite easy to attach your plug before casting, and almost as easy to unattach it *during* casting. What you need is some form of safety-pin link swivel of which there are numerous forms in most tackle shops. In some the wire of the safety-pin part is rather soft, but since you can hardly go pulling them about in the tackle shop, only experience will tell you which makes are reliable.

ANTI-KINKS AND LEADS

On the majority of days that you spin, line kink will be eliminated by the swivels mounted on the trace or line. But when there is heavy water – a fast current – then the speed at which the lure will turn can present some kinky problems. That is when an anti-kink device of some sort becomes a necessity.

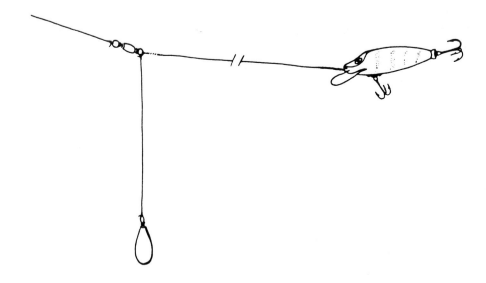

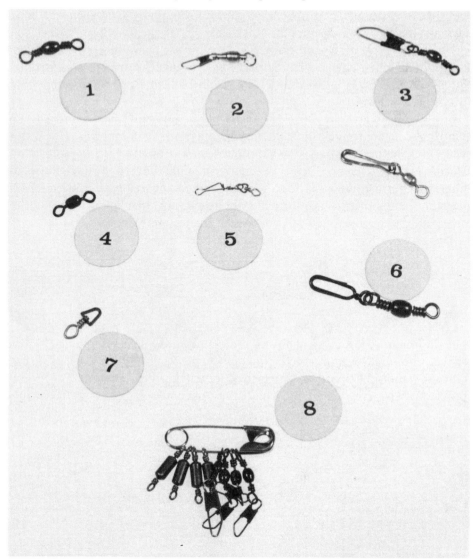

SWIVELS. *1. Barrel   2. American Link   3. Safety-pin   4. Berkeley   5. Diamond Link   6. Split-link swivels   7. Diamond   8. A safe way of carrying. Mixed ball-bearing and safety-pin swivels.*

Celluloid anti-kink vanes either clip on to the line with a series of slots, or have a length of looped wire running through them to which the line and trace are attached. The clip-on type will often allow a fine line to turn within the slots, but cope reasonably well with thicker monofilament. Those that are made with a line attachment are better, but again provide yet another joining link between the angler and his fish. We like to keep the number of links on the line to a minimum.

One of our favourite anti-kinks was a vaned torpedo-shaped device called a Kneverkink that slid up the line, and then fastened down on to one half of the swivel from where it could not move. Unfortunately it appears to be out of production now.

But Hardy's have filled the bill with their anti-kink vane that clips on their ball-bearing swivel. Very efficient in clear water, but weed can dislodge the vane from the swivel body. Note well, and check regularly. The alternative to celluloid or plastic anti-kink vanes is lead in some form or other. Properly applied it will make the swivels work, and as weight will probably be required to keep the lure well down, two purposes can be served with the one application.

The Jardine spiral lead is probably the most popular for spinning. Quite frankly we cannot get on with it. They tend to unravel, and the pulling of line through the bent spiral tends to stretch, kink and weaken it. A much better proposition is the Wye lead, its boat shape hanging in such a way that

Trace-making equipment – with two proprietary traces.

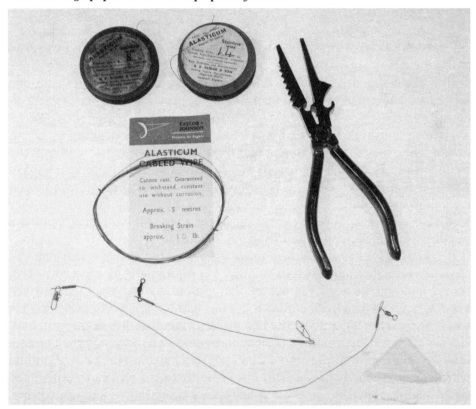

161

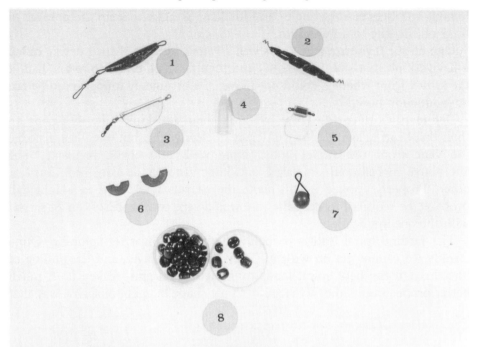

ANTI-KINKS AND LEADS. *1. Wye lead 2. Jardine spiral 3. Celluloid vane 4. Kneverlink 5. Hardy Anti-kink 6. Half-moon leads 7. Hillman lead 8. Swan shot.*

swivels are compelled to move. But they need attaching by either end, and our earlier comment on too many links applies equally here. Care, as always. . . .

Hillman anti-kink leads that clip on to one eye of a swivel are excellent, except when they catch on the bottom or in weed beds, something they tend to do with monotonous regularity. Which leaves us with large split shot or fold-over half moon leads, and these are our favourites. But we are cautious enough to test both types of lead when we buy them, making sure that they really are soft. It is so very easy to pinch the line with hard shot, causing a weakness that is concealed and irreparable damage.

It takes only a few minutes to make up a wire trace, that much must be obvious from the above. Quite simply, cut the length of wire you need, thread one end through the eye of the appropriate swivel or link swivel, bend back about one inch and lay it parallel and touching the trace wire just before the swivel. Then twist the two pieces firmly together so that you have at least half an inch of double thickness, twisted wire. If you are making up traces at home and have plenty of time, you can touch up the twisted portion with Araldite. This makes a rather posh finish to the job, but also has the added advantage of stopping the reel line getting caught up in the twisted wire.

That outlines the basic terminal tackle needed, but you will learn lots of tricks in addition. For example, our technique of fishing a buoyant plug *deep* in the Great Ouse is depicted. The line from swivel to lead is weaker than the trace or reel line so that if it gets snagged up all we lose is the lead. The plug, a floater by inclination, can be worked very slowly through deep water with a kind of sink-and-draw motion.

CHAPTER NINETEEN

Miscellaneous Tackle

The trouble with any branch of angling, or perhaps the joy of it, is that it needs a great deal of equipment which is largely peripheral to the main items such as rods and reels. Much of it is used only at infrequent intervals, but its use at those times can be quite critical in many respects. A good tip to remember, for close season blues, is to lay out *all* your tackle in the garage or on the floor of the lounge: not just main equipment but every small item. Then sit back, look at each item in turn and ask yourself a series of questions: 'Do I really need it?'; 'What is its use?'; 'Can I get or make a better one?'; 'Is there a better way of doing this job?'. Always remember that you have to *carry* these things. Usually you find several bits of gear that can be dispensed with, and always you find something that can be improved upon. In this account we want to give a personal view of the bits and pieces *we* carry and why: some will be carried in the vehicle, if not in the haversack or lure box.

SHARPENING STONE

What you need here is a small stone with a small grain size, say perhaps four to five inches long at the most, and not one of those huge, coarse carborundum stones that farmers use for sharpening scythes. Ours looks like an ancient slate (it probably is). The stone can be dropped in the pocket or left in the lure box, and it really doesn't matter much if it gets dirty: in use a little water will soon bring out the best in it. Others need oil, but most are reasonably effective when dry. After all, it is not really a precision engineering job that we are looking for, but simply a needle-like point on each and every hook.

The treble hooks on plugs get blunt remarkably quickly on snags as well as by knocking against the body of the plug, and since the trebles tend to be larger than those you would use on natural baits it is all the more difficult to keep a sharp point. But it is an extremely important matter. On several occaions we've seen anglers lose fish after fish simply because the hooks fell out during playing: and it never occurred to them to check the hook points. Other factors were involved, but as with motor-car mechanics, when you find one thing wrong there are usually other things as well! As with motor-cars, too, regular servicing minimises risks of failure.

THERMOMETERS

To put it bluntly, when the water temperature gets really low in winter lure fishing can be a waste of time. We know some waters that are exceptions to this rule, and if you prefer plug fishing, or indeed any artificial lure fishing, to other fishing, then you'd better find some winter waters in your region. On one water near St Ives we took, with some friends, more than fifty pike on plugs in three afternoon sessions. The water temperature was 38°F, but weather relatively mild for January.

As an absolute minimum therefore, a thermometer will tell the ardent autumn fisherman when things are going to get a little slow. Of course, taking the temperature is a little more important than that, since it can suggest for example when the prey might be on the shallows and hence well within the range of lures: or the converse.

We use an Autotherm, a four inch remarkably cheap alcohol thermometer. Alcohol thermometers may not be as accurate as mercury thermometers at the extremes of temperature, but since we are fishing in water which is neither near boiling nor 30° below, this is not important – and you can *read* alcohol thermometers because the manufacturers colour it red or blue. Usually we tape ours to the plastic backing and then keep it in a foam-lined spectacle case. This type can be bought in large department stores, in tourist souvenir shops, and in chemists. There are many more sophisticated versions costing upwards of £1, but they are quite unnecessary.

BAROMETERS

If you don't believe in these, then here is one item that can be dispensed with. We do believe, and we use a small (four to five inch diameter) aneroid barometer which is always kept in the glove compartment. We became convinced many years ago that in pike fishing, for example, a period of prolonged low pressure put the pike on the bottom, and scientific research on trout has tended to confirm this. For the lure angler, therefore, we need *high* pressure, or, better still, a rapidly rising barometer.

We are not suggesting that barometers and thermometers will tell you everything you need to know for a day's lure fishing, since there are the additional problems of wind and rain, sun and cloud, and water colour to think about, but they are useful in defining some of the basic facts of the environment, a combination of which determine whether the fish will move to food or not.

ARTERY FORCEPS

Most wandering anglers can be seen these days with a pair of artery forceps clipped to their lapels. Whether or not one likes this kind of exhibitionism is irrelevant to the fact that artery forceps are *indispensible* to the roving lure fisherman. They are better than long-nosed pliers simply because they have just as good a grip but are thinner, and hence are more manoeuvrable in the fish's jaws. Anyway, one cannot clip a pair of pliers to one's lapel! For us, personally, gags are not necessary and the only unhooking equipment required are forceps. With larger lures and larger hooks there *is* a case for good pliers as most forceps do not have much leverage strength.

In bait fishing for pike our usual practice is to grip the pike's lower jaw in a gloved or cloth-covered hand in such a way that the thumb is *outside* the pike's mouth. The fish is then turned on its back or held up and the lower jaw pulled a little so that the mouth opens, and the forceps (in the right hand) are used to remove the hooks. Whan plug fishing a little more care is needed since the plug itself may be well inside the mouth, and when you stick your index thumb inside it is as well to know just where all those treble hooks are situated. A pike's tooth will go into your fingers and then out again; a treble hook *stays* in because of the barb! People have been known to get themselves hooked up on a treble in this very way, and then have the pike start leaping about the bankside! They might just as well feed their fingers into the kitchen mincer.

Obviously, therefore, if you are at all nervous and if the fish will not open its mouth when gripped at the back of its head, then a gag could be used. In the case of trout and salmon, of course, the danger is much less, but since you intend killing it to eat anyway you might just as well kill it first and remove the hooks afterwards. Smaller species like perch, or toothless creatures like chub, can be gripped at the back of the head and pose no real problem to anyone. Again, artery forceps are the tools to use.

SILICA GEL

A small packet of silica gel in the lure box, hook box, rucksack etc. will help to stave off the angler's worse enemy, namely, damp. One of the ugliest sights in angling is a boxful of lures opened after a season of inattention, and one of the biggest temptations in angling is to fish on with a rusty hook just because the point is sharp! The point usually *is* sharp, but the shank, or behind the barb, is very weak. As well as silica gel one can liberally sprinkle 3 in 1 oil on some items, but it is rather messy.

PRIESTS ETC.

We are convinced that trout and salmon anglers should have one of these, but elsewhere the occasional blow with a rod-rest is all that is needed. We only kill for the table the occasional pike, perch or zander in addition to game fish. We are not experts at killing things and perhaps the reader had better look elsewhere for advice on this subject. The only time Barrie tried to kill a pike with a knife he very nearly pinned himself to the ground as the knife slid off the pike's skull. Boy-scouts always carry knives it seems, and since many anglers are a little bit that way inclined, we suppose they do too, but it is one more item of dubious necessity. With reluctance we agree that knives do have their uses – in cooking, for example, carving rod-rests (not in plugging), carving emergency wooden gaffs etc. If you really *must* get one, then get a good one, like those Normark Vibro used to make called fillet knives, in a leather safety case.

BOXES

Some say you can tell a lure fisherman who is out on the banks by the rattle of the lures in his portmanteau. Others say you can tell a bad plug fisherman by the rattle – he is so unsure of himself that he takes everything. To which you can immediately counter that if you take everything you are sure...

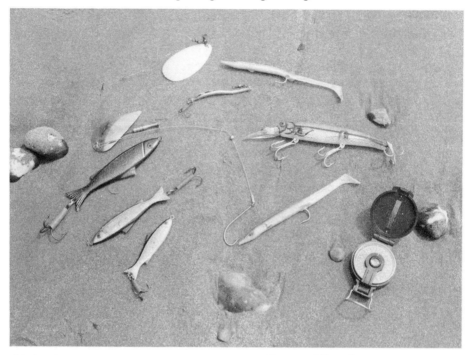

Aiming for depth on land or sea – jigs, perks, deep divers and flounder spoons

The point at issue of course is carrying lures in the most convenient way without giving the impression of being a scrap-iron merchant on an annual outing. So perhaps it is best to start with the supreme optimist who takes three of four lures only for the day.

Plastic boxes divided into partitions that can fit flat into large pockets take some beating, and the noise factor can be cut down if the bottom of each partition is lined with foam rubber, glued into position. A separate flat box into which traces, spare hooks and swivels, a sharpening stone etc. can be placed, and that is sufficient for the small-plug man. Small, because there is not a box on the market that can take three or four really big lures.

Big plugs can be rolled in a strip of canvas – in fact, Hardy's, in the dim and distant past, manufactured a canvas roll-pack complete with sections that was ideal for this sort of carrying. If you have a little flair with needle and thread it would be possible to make one at home. With a small pocket into which each plug can be placed, the roll can be tied off with tape and slipped into the jacket.

Other than that it usually means carting a big box. There are treble-protectors on the market, designed to fit over the points of a treble hook, and in theory this should mean that they can be carried loose in the pocket.

They are a fiddle each time you are out, though – and things can go bent on you. Young Adrian Lawson, an angler who works, eats and sleeps fishing, thought this was the complete answer – until he lost a first-rate pike fishing on the North Met. Pit at Cheshunt. When he reeled in he discovered that he had forgotten to remove one treble guard, hence the fish, not properly hooked, escaped. We think that it was Richard Walker who once referred to the buggeration factor!

So the only successful way to carry a small assortment of plugs is to adapt your own boxes, and there are umpteen varieties of Tupperware that can be divided up. Mind you, one feels a bit of a Charlie going through a pile of boxes in your local store measuring each one for size against your favourite plug – but shop assistants tend to accept angling eccentrics. Talking of eccentrics, if you are one of the types who permanently drops small boxes etc. into the water, plug one or two of the partitions with plastic padding material. It works – at the expense, admittedly, of a little plug space.

The penultimate stage in plug-carrying is the full-blown tackle box, properly rigged with space in the base for reels, and expanding shelves which are ready partitioned for the various plugs. There are many varieties on the market, all of them made from plastic – which is a pity, for this looks like becoming an expensive material, and today's high prices are likely to become higher.

We have found that all of the models on the market are useful, but that it certainly pays to have thoughts about the inside diameters and one or two other points before making the final decision. Remember that because the

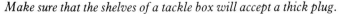

Make sure that the shelves of a tackle box will accept a thick plug.

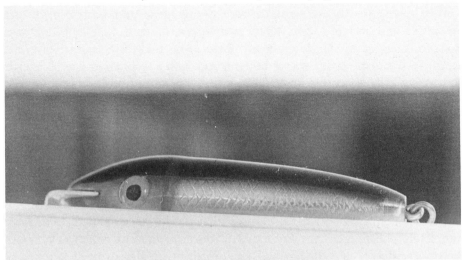

Both lid and base of this box fit firmly on the ground, and balance. But note also that the two top shelves are not closing because of a thick plug.

outside measurement appear to be what you are looking for, it doesn't follow that your plug collection will fit the inside partitions. There is only one way of making sure – and that is to try an assortment of plugs, plus a reel or two that you use, before parting with your hard-earned bawbies at the tackle shop.

Most partitions in the boxes will be found ideal from the point of size by length and width – but depth is another matter. For instance, try a Gudebrod Sniper and find how many shelves will fold flush over it. They are exceptionally thick across the shoulders, and with a treble mid-way along the body leave little space for manoeuvring into low fitting position.

Other small things can become very important; catches, for instance. Odds-on chances are that at some time or other you will overfill the box, so that extra strain will be thrust on the lock mechanism, and also the hinges. Make sure that the welding of lock and hinge to the body is strong, or better still, that it is an integral part of the construction. The more expensive models, especially in the Abu range, have a safety catch, so that the lock cannot fly open at an inappropriate moment to spread the contents acrss the bank.

Another point well worth checking is that the lid once opened, folds back completely and touches the ground. If it doesn't, the box will tip over once the upper shelves are concertinad backwards, with disastrous results. The photograph shows exactly what we mean, and it also shows an over-thick plug that will not fit flush into its partition. The ultimate lure holder is, of course, the roll-up version designed by BR and discussed briefly earlier on.

There are some excellent substitutes for a big tackle box on the market, most made from plastic, but at a much cheaper price than the custom built article. At a car accessory shop Ken discovered one that was designed to hold small electrical tools and parts, and Barrie took to a toolbox from Woolworths that filled the bill pretty well. They need occasional adaptation in the form of extra partitions, but the handyman could certainly get by with one. The same advice is offered though; that you could go to the shop armed with one or two 'awkward' plugs, and a reel, for a trial fitting before completing the purchase.

Neither of us have seen a box with a carrying strap and feel that there is a possibility here for the manufacturers to make a killing in the large-box range. Remembering how cold hands tend to get when walking on the banks, and how stiff fingers tend to become when cramped in one position round a small handle, a strap could be a boon. It would also tend to shift a large amount of weight from that small handle – a weak part of construction in all boxes we have seen.

How and what you pack is a matter of personal choice. We both are united in carrying a couple of packs of silica gel to absorb excessive dampness and prevent rusting of hooks etc., but do remember that the gel-mix needs drying out itself on occasions.

The biggest break-through in tackle boxes that we have seen is the new one from the Abu stable. They realised that baits laid flat occupy two or three times the amount of space occupied by baits suspended vertically. A quick glance at the photograph shows what we mean – and just how neatly baits slot by their end trebles into the plastic frame that fits into the outer case.

The only box they have at the moment is designed for spinners, but Ken has used small plugs in it with success, and has twisted Tony Perrin's arm as hard as he can to produce a deeper edition that can cope with the biggest plugs. Despite its small size and large capacity, the designers have had enough thought to provide a body-moulded hasp, so that the case can be padlocked.

Compared to the coarse and plug fisherman the spinning enthusiast's problem of carrying his lures around is relatively easy. No tremendous bulk, no chunky thickness or diving vanes with odd angles; on the contrary, the majority of spinning lures are fairly flat, and although perhaps rather heavy, only present a problem where hooks and swivels can tangle. Of course, few anglers are solely one kind of fisherman or the other.

We select boxes that are slim and small so they fit easily into a pocket. There are umpteen proprietary makes on the market that are admirable, but we prefer those that have a transparent lid – not so much that we can see

Vertical plug storage – the box from Abu.

Buzzer, one of the very best spinners on the market.

what we want, but because the effect of opening a box held upside down produces a fall-out too horrific for words. Most purchased boxes are ready divided, and the majority of lures can be fitted in one way or another. But, of course, this way of packaging does lead to a certain amount of tangle.

The only way of curing this time-waster is to glue strips of balsa wood or cork into small tin boxes, and firmly hook each treble into them. By further adding foam to the bottom of the box it is also possible to kill an enormous amount of metallic jangle that sounds great at the beginning of the day, but soul-destroying at its end. One of the best materials for this is Etherfoam, obtainable in bulk from Dons of Edmonton.

Barrie has tried making his own boxes following advice from Dave Holden (see also his article in the magazine *Coarse Fisherman* for Dec. 1976). All you

Pickled baits and an old Nottingham star back spinning reel. Both authors learnt to spin with one of these reels.

need is Slater's plasticard in various thicknesses and colours, a glue such as Weldite, a Stanley knife, and a ruler. You can make strong boxes of almost any shape or size with very little practice.

One thing is certain, that after a few years' spinning you will, like the fly fisherman, collect an awful amount of surplus baits of various sorts, sizes and condition. Hardy favourites wax and wane, and a new spinner becomes top of the pops; but, of course, one never thinks of ditching that which is out-dated. The only sensible way of keeping a check on things and preventing good material from rusting and rotting is to use a base camp, a large lure box into which the excesses and reserves can be kept. Despite the amount of room it occupies in his den, it remains a thing of beauty, and a source of pleasurable winter rummaging.

CHAPTER TWENTY

Clothing

There is only one thing worse than being wet when you are fishing – and that is being cold. If you think of all the work that goes into making a day's sport – the preparation, planning, expense of extra tackle, and then consider the sheer misery of being totally unprepared for the weather, you quickly realise that putting on a coat and rushing out of the house can be a criminal waste of time.

There is another side of the coin that is also frequently overlooked. When you are cold then both physically and mentally your power of concentration and reactions are impaired, a fact that our American cousins are well aware of, as any reader of *Field and Stream* during the winter months' issues quickly gathers.

It is not suggested that one should prepare for the Arctic, but few will dispute that better lure fishing is *sometimes* enjoyed during the cold months, so a little thought on the question of clothing is well spent. These pages so far have concentrated on minimising weight, and this is equally important in this sphere. Several thin layers of clothing that trap air between each item are better than one thick heavy coat. Mobility, allowing blood to circulate, is equally important.

Perhaps that is why we feel those one-piece suits, ideal though they may be for the specimen-hunter who camps on the bank, are unsuited for plug fishing. The gap of 'separates', i.e. jacket and trousers, allows much greater movement. A string vest, one or two woollen sweaters, and a Barbour-type coat will be found proof for the majority of English winters. Thigh waders over thick trousers, or Wellingtons with waterproof trousers (preferably a little on the baggy side) take care of the lower regions. Incidentally, the trouser legs fit *over* the Wellingtons, and not into them. We can cite at least one angler who always wondered why he got wet feet when he fished in the rain.

Annual outing of the Old Plugonians Club. Martin Gay, Barrie Rickards, Ken Whitehead and Ray Webb preparing to lose some tackle.

But it is the 'etceteras' that are really important. As an instance we glibly mention waders. Thigh waders must be at least one or two sizes too big to allow for either woollen oversocks or Husky-type bootees – plus enough room for the toes to wriggle around and keep the circulation on the move. Equally important is the necessity to hang waders up by the feet so that air can circulate through them and dry perspiration etc. before the next outing. Of course, the same applies to Wellingtons, except that when it comes to drying the latter they are better filled with bran (used later for roach fishing) or screwed-up dry newspaper.

At the other extremity we are both agreed that when headgear has to be worn then there is nothing to beat a hood for keeping out wind and rain. Those tweed fore-and-aft deerstalkers, and poncey pork-pie titfers are ideal for bar-room boasting and emergency boat-sickness, but useless for keeping rain out of the back of your neck. Mention of the neck reveals a weak chink in the angler's garb, one which Ken learned to cure in the navy by the simple expedient of rolling a large soft hand-towel and using it as a scarf. It keeps all the draughts out as well, and when wet, only requires refolding to present a dry portion to the skin.

Hands are perhaps the most difficult of the extremities to warm, and many gloves are obviously useless. Millarmitts are ideal, warm and possessed of long wrist pieces that tuck well up into the coat sleeves. Two pairs are better than one, so that a change can be made when it is really raining hard, and half the morning has been spent clearing weed from the trebles of the plug. Slightly more expensive are the shooting mitts made of leather by the same firm, but they are completely finger-free, only the hand and backs of the fingers being covered. They possess the extra virtue of being more hook-repellant than their cheaper woollen counterparts. Hand-warmers are worth carrying and when fingers go too blue too feel, then five minutes with one in each hand works wonders. They tuck into the inside pockets when not in hands, still giving warmth to the body.

Fishing in the orthodox style provides a means for an angler to sit, either on box or stool. When lure fishing one is forever roaming, and a seat of any sort is an encumbrance. But sit one must, and this is when it is possible to collect the supreme accolade of the wet backside, worn for the remainder of the day in extreme discomfort. One sure and simple way to avoid it is by folding and tucking a large plastic bag into an inside pocket. It can be produced to sit on in seconds, and serves a dual purpose as a fish carrier if one turns up for the pot.

The fly-fisherman's waistcoat – equally useful for the spinning man.

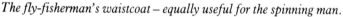

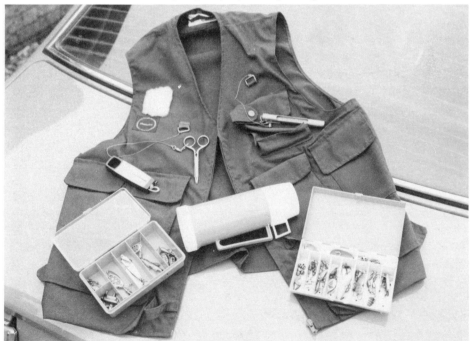

Warmth and concentration do not only centre on clothing. Food and drink are equally important. Each to his own when it comes to the likes, but we tend to avoid hot curries, Oxo or Bovril in a Thermos, all of which tend to leave one with a severe thirst. Scotch, rum and other spirits are warming for a time, but rapidly produce a chilling effect as the 'glow' wears off. A half-pint of tea or coffee in a Thermos, with sugar and dried milk carried separately, occupies little space and genuinely warms, especially if the contents are generously sweetened.

We mentioned the American scene earlier, and the severe weather they may encounter during winter. It is very easy to scoff, and say that England provides nothing like that – but each individual feels the cold in different ways. Hypothermia – cooling of the body – is silent, insidious, and can be lethal. It is so easy to play the 'he-man', and carry on even if you feel chilled to the very marrow. Nature gave us an in-built warning of this situation, the simple act of shivering. When it starts, run round, eat, drink, and in most cases it will stop because the body has warmed. But if despite everything that you do, the shivers continue, then is the time to head for home, or at least shelter and warmth. There is nothing great about collapsing from the cold miles from anywhere, and inconveniencing others who have to look for you. Think and plan for the cold, and immediately your fishing will improve.

PART FOUR

CHAPTER TWENTY-ONE

Plugs and Pike

It is not possible to learn *everything* about the pike and its activities by just going plug fishing all the time: but it is possible to learn more of them at this branch of the sport than at any other. Of the many thousands of anglers live- and deadbaiting for pike, including ourselves we would add, few have seen a pike take the bait. But in plug fishing and, indeed, in spinning, even a poor angler can observe the take of a pike quite frequently – always assuming that the angler is not so poor that he gets no takes! You get a terrific idea, for example, of the pike's vision in *clear* water. When Barrie used to fish Saltmarshe Lake in the East Riding with a small, yellow, plastic floater the pike seemed to see it clearly from at least ten yards away and they came at it like arrows. It was no good waiting for the bow-wave of the charging pike to reach the lure: the pike was always some feet ahead of the bow-wave, rather like the way in which the boil of water is some distance away from the rock which causes it in a trout stream. You can imagine the tension before the strike. There you are, craftily working a four inch shallow-diving floater over the tops of semi-submerged soft weed beds, when you see a bow-wave start off at ten to fifteen yards away as the pike homes in over the top of the same weed beds. If it's a small pike it will be only a foot or so ahead of the ripple, but if it is a big one it will be at least five feet in advance of the wave. Everything happens so fast that you get just about enough time to take a firm grip on the rod with one hand, and the reel handle with the other. Too often the pike slows down just before the impact you hope for, and follows the plug to the bank. It is at this point that you get a good view as it slides along. It may be a tiddler or a giant – and will it take just as you lift out the lure?

When a pike follows the plug right to the bankside it often *does* take just as it thinks the prey is escaping. If it sees you, however, it either stops and sidles away slowly, looking agitated, or else it departs with tremendous acceleration and you are left with your plug swirling in the boil of water the pike leaves behind. Thirty yards away you see the bow wave subside, and then you lift the plug from the water for the next cast knowing that in all probability you frightened *one* pike for an hour or two. It is impossible not to be impressed by the take-off of a pike from a standing start, and it is this power that overhauls the prey, unlike the wearing down tactics used by perch and zander as they worry away at the tail of their prey.

Of course, this kind of excitement is best enjoyed in shallow, clear, weedy waters. In deeper waters the pike often appears from nowhere, gives you a terrific shock as it strikes, and has much of the advantage of any surprise attack, at least in the early stages of the battle: they often tear the reel handle out of your hand because you had lost concentration and held it lightly. At this point, with the rod flapping loose as it were, you often fail to set the hooks and lose the fish anyway.

The actual takes vary tremendously. Occasionally they *do* give the pluck-pluck type of take typical of perch, but more commonly they engulf the rear end of the plug and give the rod a tidy thump which is difficult to miss. Sometimes there seems to be a real ferocity in the attack, particularly it seems to us, if it has had to chase the plug across the weeds, or hit it before the plug leaves the pike's hole in the weeds. We've never been certain, because things happen so quickly, whether the pike comes at the lure with its mouth agape (a phrase beloved of many writers) or whether the gaping mouth and flaring gill-rakers are the pike's quicksilver responses to its realisation that something is wrong. We're inclined to think that the latter is the case, and that on the strike it only opens its mouth at the last split second, and then only the bare minimum necessary to grab the plug. If the attack is fast and violent, with little time to think on the part of the pike, it probably hooks itself, realises its mistake and *then* opens its mouth wide and shakes its head. The angler's reaction is invariably a little slower and he probably *sees* the pike for the first time at the mouth-opening stage of the strike. Looked at like this the angler's strike is probably superfluous, except that it helps to knock the pike off an even keel at a very critical stage of the battle.

Another kind of take often ignored by the inexperienced is the slack-line bite. This happens when a pike follows a lure and hits it from behind but doesn't stop as it reaches the lure. The line goes slack as the pike continues its run. Any angler who has used a Veltic or Mepps spinner will know the feeling because these spinners 'go slack' if they pick up a little weed, and the best response is to reel faster until you catch up again. It's the same with a slack-line take on plug, except that we can't resist striking hard the moment things go slack! If you treat slack-line bites in this way, then the strike has to be sweeping enough to take up the slack *and* drive home the hooks, and remember you do not know how slack is slack....

The kind of situation when the pike follows the plug right to the bank is the most difficult one for the pike angler to live with. What should he do? Reel faster; slow down; stop? If the pike has not seen you and the plug is not too close to the rod tip then all you can do is stop reeling and hope. With some plugs the pike will take them as they stop and float to the surface. If the plug is a sinker they may follow it down and take it. We find, on the other hand, that merely slowing down a retrieve rarely seems to result in a positive take.

There are other ways of tackling this particular situation. Let's look at the whole problem of bringing the plug close to the bank. One difficulty is that the pike may see you; get round this by using every inch of bankside cover. On the Old Bedford River in the Fens there is little cover and the banks are very quakey, sending vibrations along ahead of the angler, so that it is necessary either to stand well back from the water with the merest inch of the rod tip sticking over the water, or to kneel behind what cover there is. Another trick is to use a longish rod, say ten feet or so, and bring in the plug to a position ten feet down the bank from where you are standing, rather than sticking the rod straight out over the water in front of you. One obvious disadvantage with short rods is that you *have* to bring in the lure to your feet.

Well-hooked, but the misshapen mouth suggests earlier hook damage.

There are many other things to be learnt from plug fishing in shallow waters than watching and getting used to the take. You learn the kind of lairs that small and big pike prefer, and you get an inkling of the presence of groups of pike in one place – hotspots – though the real recognition of these phenomena comes more easily through dead- and livebait fishing. On the other hand, a first-class plug fisherman can detect hotspots a little more quickly than a bait fisherman since the latter's techniques are necessarily a little slower. Barrie well remembers Basil Chilvers working his plugs along a Fenland drain and pinpointing a short stretch that he suggested we move into with baits. Since it was the depth of winter at the time, we expected – and found – that baits were rather better than plugs.

TIME OF YEAR

Time of year is an important consideration for the plug fisherman. Generally speaking the summer months are best for plug fishing for pike. In Eire, where there is no close season for coarse fish, plugs, like natural baits, seem to succeed best in May, give or take a little. In Britain the months of June and early July are good, late July and August usually poorer, as indeed they are for all aspects of piking; and then sport picks up again in September. How long into the winter one can keep on plug fishing with a real hope of often beating natural baits probably depends on the year in question: a good year will provide lively fishing until well into November. But when the water gets cold, say around 47°F or less, then sport falls off rapidly.

Naturally we are generalising above, and there are enough exceptions to keep the ardent plug fisherman going right through the winter. There is also a number of waters in every region which respond well to plug even in the depths of winter, and not neccessarily to small pike only. Find those waters and you have an added string to your bow if you are a general pike fisherman as well as a plug enthusiast.

Of course, temperature problems are not confined to the winter. In summer, during the occasional bouts of hot weather which we get, to carry plug box, net or gaff, and clothes through brambly undergrowth, from swim to swim, is a killer. Summer plugging is best enjoyed in the early morning or late in the evening, but it may well be that the best time for pike is just before lunch.

PLUGS VERSUS SPINNERS

We'll begin here with a generalisation. We have known a fair few occasions when a spinner has been taken by a dour pike in preference to a plug, but have many times observed the opposite. Barrie first came across a clear instance of this many years ago whilst fishing a tiny pond near Snaith in the West Riding of Yorkshire. A perch he was reeling in was attacked by a good pike, but after a few minutes the pike fell off, as they are wont to do! He gave it a few minutes to come unscared, then cast a variety of spinners at it: it showed interest, obviously hadn't seen him, but really didn't want to know. The first cast with a small jointed wooden floater produced a great take and a fine pike of over ten pounds.

Similarly, in Ireland, he had a fish of nine pounds follow a worm to the boat, refuse spinner after spinner, and then take a plug first cast. That fish solved the problem of lack of a large landing net by leaping into the boat. It might almost have said, 'Unhook me quickly and put me back.' Which he promptly did.

On another occasion, also on an Irish lough, a friend spotted a huge pike sunning itself on the shallows. He cast various spinners across its bows and, even though it hadn't been scared off, it showed no real interest. But the moment a plug tried to wiggle past, the pike took it in a flash. That fish went over twenty pounds. The many similar cases far outnumber the few occasions when a spinner or spoon has seemed to be better. On these rare occasions we have noticed that the pike will fall to a tiny twinkling spinner or spoon, such as a one inch minnow or a mackerel spinner, when they have been disturbed, or scared, or otherwise worked up by the use of big plugs. We'd certainly never be without a selection of spinners and spoons, as a back up to plugs which we prefer most of the time.

In view of some recent developments we expand some of these thoughts elsewhere. Whilst the above generalisation are true they do not apply to *all* spinners.

THE COMPLETE (TRAVELLING) PLUG FISHERMAN

It is obvious that anything but a *very* casual approach to plug fishing is going to be fairly arduous, and that the idea of rambling slowly from swim to swim is something of a daydream. What about the rod? If it is four to five feet long it will be no burden. The trouble is that delightful though these little

One method of carrying plugs too big to fit the box.

rods are for casting and firing a plug accurately into a hole in the weed, we find a long rod (ten feet) much better most of the time – and we fish in some pretty tight places, too, not just fenland drains, and reservoirs! It is easy to cast, even in heavy undergrowth, with a long rod. All you have to do is poke the rod through the trees and swing the plug out pendulum fashion. Perhaps the only problem is the fisherman's strike: a hefty strike will almost certainly take a branch or two along as well! And hitting a branch in mid-strike is one of the best ways of losing fish by failing to set the hooks properly. We've done it on several occasions. The important thing, of course, is to work out where you are going to strike, just as you should work out where you are going to land the fish.

APPROACH TO A SWIM

It is very common to see anglers march boldly up to the swim, stand bolt upright, lash out the plug as far as they can and then retrieve at considerable speed. A few more random casts are made, and then the angler marches stolidly on to the next swim. Such anglers may catch pike on plugs but

they'd catch a lot more if they didn't frighten the pike away first. Without question, the best way to tackle a new swim is to walk up quietly and stop well short of it: try a short cast into the few yards of water immediately in front of where the bottom fisherman normally sits. It is a fact that pike are often attracted to these swims simply because the roach angler has been attracting roach, and one of the deadliest ways of plug fishing is to work your way along a match length a few minutes after the matchmen have packed up and gone.

Try a few more casts like this, preferably using a relatively small plug which has less chance of scaring the pike, and then move cautiously up to the edge of the swim, making full use of any cover, before searching the whole area of the swim more thoroughly. It's a good idea to begin with short casts, particularly along the edges to your left and right. If you suspect a pike has plucked at or followed the lure, and nothing happens on the next cast, give that particular part of the swim a rest for a few minutes whilst you search the rest: then come back to it with a few more casts. By then there will be a good chance that the pike has made up its mind and has no intention of being frustrated again.

Gradually increase the lengths of your casts until you are satisfied you have given the area a good coverage. Then you'll have to think about trying

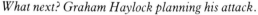

What next? Graham Haylock planning his attack.

A fine brace of sea trout.

a different plug: a darker-coloured one perhaps if the sun has come out. You can imagine that all this procedure takes time, particularly if you try several plugs. Now you move on to the next swim, and do the whole thing again trying not to become too automatic.

Personally we usually stick to one plug for a considerable stretch of water, and really give it a good trial. We do not work systematically through a swim: we try to cast to where we think the pike is most likely to be. In some swims we may make a few dozen casts, yet in others not make more than a couple. We reckon about an hour is long enough to fish at one stretch, for otherwise you lose concentration, and probably fish too, by fishing badly or missing the strike as the pike rips the reel handles out of your hand. So you need to have a relaxed, but careful and quiet approach to each swim, and try to *think* where the pike might be lying.

SIZE OF PLUGS

One thing that the modern trend to plug fishing and its publicity has done is to make anglers use plugs that are often too large. We're as guilty as the next man at this, for there is great attraction in the vast quantities of big American plugs now available. But plugs in the one inch to three inch category shouldn't be ignored, and as already explained, their very non-scaring qualities makes them a good bet to *begin* work on a swim.

There is another side to this question, however, and that is that pike often seem to *prefer* a small plug. We suspect that on many occasions a giant, shiny plug is not only fish-scaring because of the size of its splash, but fish-scaring because it is too new-looking and its counterfeit properties too apparent to the pike that sidles after it. So we would urge you to make a habit of using the smaller sizes of plugs like the River Runt Spook range or similar types. Of course, one major attraction of big plugs is that they cast a long way, but this is largely true of plugs in general when compared to spinners or spoons.

Big plugs seem to us to succeed best in big, shallow weedy waters. Imagine that your cast goes fifty yards, then it doesn't matter too much if you frighten pike for a radius of twenty yards around the splash, because you have another thirty yards of retrieve left. The pike will be in pockets in the weed and will only vaguely hear the splash somewhere on the lake, and the thing they see is a fish working briefly above their heads: so they up and follow it. In deeper waters a big splash is probably appreciated by the pike over a much greater distance, particularly if the surface is calm.

COLOURS OF PLUGS

The beginner, confronted with thousands of plugs of almost infinitely varied hues, might be forgiven for thinking that anyone prepared to talk about plug colour was a little light in the head. But there *are* certain basic colours and combinations of colours that have proved highly successful over the years. But before taking a somewhat rambling course through the world of plug colour let's briefly tackle one aspect of light behaviour in water that is ignored by most anglers with almost deliberate care. It is this: white light is broken down when passing through water, for a variety of reasons, and the result is that a deep-fished plug does not necessarily appear the same colour to the pike as it does to us at the surface. We ought to say immediately that it is possible that pike do not see colour in quite the same way as we do anyway, although it is inconceivable that they live only in a world of shades of grey. Light then is broken down into its constituent colours, and the light which penetrates deepest is the blue end of the spectrum. Therefore, at depth, a blue plug ought to show up more clearly than a plug of any other colour, which would in fact appear as a dark colour. Whether fluorescent blue would show up even more clearly we do not know.

We're not aware that in general blue plugs have proved more successful at depth, although in East Yorkshire Barrie did rather better with five inch jointed blue plugs fished deep than with any other plugs in his tackle box. So there is a possibility that in the future some kind of pattern will emerge relating plug colour to depth of water.

That said, we can go on to what we think is the most important factor about colour to be fully confirmed during the last decade, and that is on bright sunlit days a dull plug usually succeeds best, and the opposite on dull days. This has been known for a long time, but thanks to the efforts of the modern breed of ardent plugmen what was little more than a strong feeling before has been shown to be a matter of great importance.

It has been said, in explanation of this fact, that the bright light enables a pike to get too good a view of the lure before it hits it, and it seems a reasonable enough idea at first sight. However, we would expect that under bright light a dull plug would be more easily inspected simply because the flash from the flanks of a bright plug would tend to *obscure* details and dazzle the pike. Perhaps it's dazzle they don't like! Our own flume tank experiments support this interpretation.

You can see the problem that this question of colour raises: it's no good having three different sizes of one plug, but it begins to sound as though you need several different colours as well, and hence you'll need three tackle boxes! It isn't as bad as that, of course, but we'd never dream of going plug fishing without our full colour range of home-made wooden Hi-Los, for example. We have a basically white one with a red head for dawn and dusk fishing; a green one and a yellow one, both rather dull, that we use when the light is moderately strong (say average light of a winter's day), and a black one with flecks of silver and a silver belly for use during the middle of the day. On one day a couple of winters ago we took pike all day long, gradually changing from light-coloured Hi-Los to dark and back to light in the course of the day.

However, it is impossible to have a comprehensive selection of different types of plug with you, and at the same time have a full colour range of each type, so you can compromise by having, say, a white and red Hi-Lo, a darker Rapala, and a very dull River Runt Spook. In other words you have enough colour variation in each basic plug type – floaters, shallow divers, sinkers etc. – to cover most needs.

What about the actual colours themselves? Well, plugs which are basically either red or green we have not found very effective. There are exceptions, such as our dull green Hi-Lo and red and white Crazy Crawler, but the best colours seem to us to incorporate yellow in them somewhere. We had terrific success for years with a four inch yellow plastic plug that looked for all the world like a small pike nipping through the water. We have no doubt at all that a red throat and conspicuous eyes enhance the effectiveness of most plugs, whilst stripes of various colours, including green, upon the back-ground colour are very important. Gudebrod's perch-striped Sniper is an extremely effective lure once the bright light of mid-day is upon you: as opposed to the rather gaudy yellow one which succeeds best when the weather is dull.

Naturally there is immense scope for invention and the artistically inclined. You can make brown plugs with nice red spots on like trout: ours do not seem to be any more effective than other colours, and if pike accept them as trout then they must do so with a barely-concealed grin. Great fun can be had by taking pike on plugs of many different hues – jet black ones at night, white ones in the middle of the day – and it all adds interest to a very fascinating kind of fishing.

PLUGS FOR DIFFERENT CIRCUMSTANCES

It will be apparent from much of the content of this book that there are plugs for almost any circumstances: they'll do almost anything except fly, from bumping along the bottom to crawling along the surface, popping on a calm surface, standing on their heads, or fighting their way through big waves. If you have a look at our section on the classification of plugs you will find one to suit most circumstances, but there will come a general realisation that most plugs are floaters which dive to various depths: sinkers are less common and true poppers or crawlers perhaps less common still. But some imagination can be used here. For example, if you do not happen to have a surface crawler in your box at the time, you can use a buoyant floater and retrieve it *slowly* so that it doesn't dive! Similarly, lacking sinkers, you can weight a floating diver in the manner shown earlier, and often portrayed in American magazines, and work it through deep water knowing that if you get snagged up you will lose, in all probability, only the lead. We used this system with a little success on the deeper stretches of the Great Ouse.

Perhaps it is worth enlarging on this a little. Suppose you cast directly across the river, allow the plug to sink and then work it directly to your feet, repeating this about three feet further downstream, you cannot help at least disturbing if not attracting, at least several pike in every hundred yards. Most big pike sit down there on the bottom and they have to show interest or get out of the way. Looked at like that our results were not as good as they should have been.

One of the developments in the field of spoons during recent years in this country has been the use of weed guards on the treble hooks. Now with plugs you would not normally think of putting weed guards on several treble hooks, largely because weed is normally picked up by the diving vane first. But if you intend casting into sunken trees with sizeable branches then there is no reason at all why you should not have a plug or two complete with weed-guarded treble hooks. They'll not help the plug through soft weed, but they'll help through logs: the diving vane need not be protected.

Therefore, one of the few places it is difficult to fish a plug is in weed beds which would constantly foul the treble hooks. Here the plug man *has* to revert to weed-guarded spoons, which are reasonably effective. Pike are often found deep *in* the weed beds (though not in soft, clogging weed) and not just around the margins where it is easy, and necessary, to fish plugs. Otherwise, using our classification guide, it should be possible to fish a pikey plug on the surface, shallow or deep, small or large, and fast or slow.

SPEED AND DEPTH OF RETRIEVE

About the biggest mistake made by beginners spinning for pike is to fish too fast and too shallow. This is understandable, for to fish slow and deep can be expensive in terms of lost spinners. It would be a help, therefore, if

Come and get me! Action from a Crazy Crawler that lives up to its name.

beginners used plugs, because if not fished deep they can certainly be fished slowly, thereby increasing the chances of a take by fifty per cent. Bearing in mind that in many circumstances pike may, in our opinion, prefer plugs to spoons or spinners, it is obviously very much better for a beginner to use plugs. Before very long he will realise that he can fish them in deep water, and when he finally appreciates through his own experience that pike lie deep most of the time the worry about losing lures will be a thought in the past.

With plugs you can easily search a water from top to bottom, but in general it seems to us that plugs are more effective fished as deep as possible in deep water. In shallow lakes, say three to five feet, this is much less important and they can be effective at all depths.

In conclusion, therefore, try to fish plugs at their best working speeds, usually slow, but have a number that work well at high speeds and try them in the shallow swims.

TREBLE HOOKS

Treble hooks on plugs for pike have two functions, one to hook the pike, and the other to be an effective keel to make the plugs work well. On larger plugs these trebles are enormous and therefore make hook penetration much more difficult. But a more important problem, which prompts these remarks, is that very small pike will *often* take big plugs, and the trebles can be quite damaging to small mouths; far more so than any gaffs on the market. We would urge anglers to unhook small pike with great care, because they certainly cannot avoid taking them by using big plugs. We might add that this is the only worrying aspect of plug fishing for pike which is otherwise one of the pleasantest forms of fishing.

Since treble hooks on plugs are usually large they are quite strong and this, coupled with the fact that they *are* treble, means that it is unusual to have a hook straighten out on you. This is not the case with the occasional *double* hooks you see on plugs. We have never seen a good double hook on a plug.

Hook points on plug trebles are mostly poor: quite blunt with a ridiculously rank barb. The barb can be filed down, and the points kept sharp with a stone, as we described earlier in the book. However, we are strongly opposed to barbless hooks on plugs or, indeed, on any spinners: fish quite simply fall off far too often – like most of the time. So these local councils who, thinking they are supporting the *in* thing, ban barbed hooks, are doing a great disservice to one of the finest aspects of angling.

CHAPTER TWENTY-TWO

Spinners and Pike

This is the sport of which boyhood dreams are made, and one of the few branches of the sport which caters for that perennial problem of all youngsters, namely their inability to sit still for more than five minutes at a time. Spinning is essentially a mobile sport and like all mobile pike-fishing methods it teaches you a great deal about the species. Barrie spent hundreds of hours as a youngster spinning for pike in the shallow railway pits and clay workings around Eastrington in East Yorkshire, and has seen as many as five hungry jacks chasing one mackerel spinner. To a youngster in those days spinning meant just that, because plugs were expensive and spinners were easier to make anyway. Mackerel spinners were used by Barrie because they were cheap, could be cast a long way on 8 lb b.s. line, and they really catch pike. The best he ever saw, taken by an acquaintance out at the same game, was twenty-five pound, although several double-figure fish fell prey to the same lure over a period of two or three years. Sometimes, where a 'hole' went down to 3–5 feet a small Colorado was used, with the red wool tag removed: somehow, on these tiny intimate waters, a red wool tail (equivalent to the bucktail of many North American lures) seemed just too conspicuous. A better substitute was a piece of Rhode Island Red chicken feather tied to the treble hook in the form of a roach's tail: this certainly encouraged that bonus fish, the perch, to take hold – and pike too, when they were tending to follow the lure and snip at the end without firmly taking.

As an aside, we could mention that this 'coming short' problem has been solved in another way by some of today's anglers, in the creation of the Commando spoons. In this case a flying treble follows the main spoon treble; a technique also used by salmon anglers. No doubt the flying treble is often taken by the pike, but more often it is foul hooked by it when striking the spoon blade itself. The technique is highly effective, but has been roundly condemned by many anglers, including some of the leading writers. We never use this method, a matter of personal choice, but find it difficult ultimately to condemn it as unsporting. Clearly it is a matter for the individual to decide. If a tassle is added to the Commando spoon the pike certainly home in on it, so this technique satisfies us morally.

But returning to those shallow Eastrington railway ponds and the lessons learned. Probably the first thing was to appreciate that additions to the line in the form of traces, anti-kink vanes and weights was something to be borne with fortitude when necessary. Traces are absolutely vital for pike spinning. Barrie once had twenty-seven pike in succession without a trace, average weight about two pound each, then hooked three doubles in a row on Carlton Towers, and lost them all! The bigger the mouth, the easier it is to engulf a spinner. On one occasion a seven inch spoon completely disappeared into the back of the throat of a seventeen pounder that he had in Ireland. So if anybody tells you that traces are not necessary, make a booking for him in the local institution. He won't be lonely, for such places must be heavily populated by frustrated anglers.

Barrie has a very clear memory of fishing a dull Veltic on a shiny, plastic-coated trace, and from thirty yards away could see the trace, but not the lure, as it made its way to his vantage point part-way up a railway embankment. So use a thin, dark trace, say 10–15 lb b.s. for most spinning; about a foot or eighteen inches long, with a safety-pin link swivel at the business end, and a small bronze swivel at the other for attachment to the reel line. Personally, we feel that the reel line should *not* be tied direct to a loop in the trace wire, since the wire is so much finer than that of a swivel eye and *must* have a greater tendency to cut, cheese-wire fashion, the softer nylon line.

If weight cannot be added to the body of the spinner we add it, when necessary, to the line just above the trace rather than to the trace itself. It is much more convenient when changing lures or methods to remove the lead weight or weights from the line and then discard the bottom six inches of line and tie a new knot. Anti-kink vanes can be fixed in the same position, or a combination of the two in some instances. We think you have the attitude about right if you need your arm twisting to add anything other than a trace to your terminal tackle.

The main technique on those tiny waters, and one which has certainly worked all over Britain since then, was to spin over, under and around weed beds and snags, and along the bankside under overhanging trees. Line was usually 7 or 8 lb b.s. monofil, and despite the inferior monofil of the 1950s only certain spinners introduced 'spontaneous coiling' in the line. Colorados, minnows, and mackerel spinners, the three favourites, had little adverse effect and it was possible to wander from swim to swim flicking the tackle lightly under bushes and through small gaps in the floating or lightly-rooted mace beds. Little home-made minnows with reversible fins could always

195

take out the kinks, or the line could be laid out in a field and trailed behind the angler for a few minutes.

Rods, in those carefree days, were a joke. Not that good rods weren't available, but under the age of twenty-one it wasn't possible to take out a mortgage. So we used sawn-off roach rods, parts of steel tank aerial and so on. Indeed, the rod is not really so important, nice though it is to have a wand of beautiful action. When Barrie went back there on a flying visit, much later, he took only the reel, some sellotape, and a safety pin: the rod was cut from a hedge, the pin and reel bound to the 'rod' and three pike from 1½lb to 4lb were caught in three hours. Distance wasn't the object, in fact it would put you into the middle of a cornfield, but the real skill was from the split second the spinner hit the water to the split second of lifting it from the water.

You can of course, stick a ten foot rod through the foliage and 'dap', much after the fashion of chub fishing. When Barrie was a youngster jigs were not readily available, but he took a number of pike by jigging a spinner in just such circumstances, even amongst thick *Potamogeton* beds. The trouble was that although the spinner *attracted* the pike easily enough to within inches of the bait, they came short much more commonly than with conventionally pulled spinners. It was found that a fly or a large lure with tied on jay feathers, or a small fly-spoon succeeded much better. Some of today's jigs would be better still. Nevertheless this technique did produce enough fish and certainly meant you could fish in places which other anglers walked past.

This kind of piking, producing small pike with the occasional double, is to be recommended for many of the reasons given, but perhaps above all for the way in which it forces you to cast in any and all directions, and with any and all obstructions, whether above the water or below it. It also teaches you to *plan* the landing of a fish in advance: every swim you approach needs looking at from two standpoints, firstly, where to lay the net down to draw the fish over; secondly, where to strike so that half a hawthorn bush isn't included in the pantomime. Talking of snags, one pike took a spinner, one treble point of which was buried in a thin springy underwater branch, the strike being so savage that it pulled the spinner free and hooked the pike, a two pound fish, simultaneously. The variety of interest, observation, and spectacle in such fishing is quite unending.

On the big waters piking takes on a new dimension, with a proportionate increase of the chance of some boring spinning. Don't misunderstand us here, for most of our spinning has been done on big waters; rivers, drains, lakes, loughs and lochs. And there is always the chance of a really giant pike to fire the imagination and keep the spinners and spoons working busily away! But faced with a lot of water, where on earth and how on earth does

Small spinner produced these pike within an hour when Ken fished a Lea valley pit.

one make start? Remember that the fishing itself has to be enjoyable, not just the catching of fish. It is true that a systematic approach sometimes pays dividends. Two instances come to mind. The first concerned some friends, spinner/spoon men only, who used systematically to fish the lower Great Ouse and the Relief Channel: each swim was given one or two casts with a biggish Toby which was fired to the far bank and then retrieved close to the bottom. They reckoned that a couple of casts showed the spoon to any pike that was interested and then they moved on, leap-frogging each other, looking for big, actively feeding pike. A second concerned fishing on the Market Weighton canal where Barrie used to make a cast to the far bank, at right-angles to the flow, retrieve, and then take one step and cast again. The idea was that the small Copper and Silver (with red inside) would be certain to pass by a sizeable pike at least every few casts and it could not avoid seeing the spoon. This worked very well and he caught plenty of pike averaging 3–4 lb His companion at the time was Phil Reeves, who worked ahead of Barrie, casting as his fancy took him. It was noticeable that Barrie took more pike.

Even on that water, however, the better fish, over ten pounds, fell to Veltic spinners worked through junction pools, at points where ditches and dykes entered the canal, and in some of the shelving holes between sandbars and weed beds. The same techniques worked well on the Yorkshire Derwent, which is a pretty sizeable river in places: find a feature such as the sunken barges at Sutton, and you have located pike more quickly.

Returning to the subject of large lochs and loughs, the standard technique is trolling (colloquial) or trailing (supposedly correct terminology), but whether this or any other method is used the idea is to break down the loch, mentally, into a series of smaller waters. Not only is this psychologically better, but it has a basis in pike ecology, for the species is not evenly distributed throughout a water. Find yourself a bay, perhaps a hundred yards or more across, a stream entering in the corner, shallows with soft weeds and fringing emergent reeds, a drop off to twenty-five feet plus at the mouth of the bay, and you have found a potential pike holding area, perhaps even a hotspot. You can fish such a bay quietly by anchoring and spinning round the boat, the technique which Ray Webb, Fred Wagstaffe and others found so successful in Eire. A variety of spinners can be tried, and then the boat can be up-anchored and a different part of the bay tried. These are the circumstances where we would normally use sizeable spoons; Tobys, Pikers, and homemade monstrosities of various lengths and colours. Generally speaking, such large waters are crystal clear and the tone of the spoon is important.

A simple and effective way of colouring sprats – after drying and sealing!

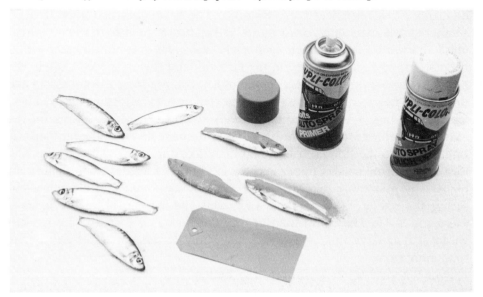

Spinning from the standing position.

Trolling is often condemned as boring, but probably becomes so only to people not fishing properly. The same rules about finding the pike apply: *never* troll on mile after mile in an unthinking fashion. Try the bays, the contours, changes of depth, changes of lures and so on. In fact, trolling is a skilled business whether one has the rods more or less inboard, pointing over the gunwhales, or has them on outriggers. The line for trolling big lochs for big pike probably needs to be in the 18–25 lb b.s. bracket, not because that is needed to land the fish, but because in the event of a take (with the anti-reverse lever *on*, of course) the pike hooks itself and the boat's forward movement must be stopped pronto otherwise a snapped line will result. If the anti-reverse lever is off, or the clutch set light, the pike will not necessarily hook itself, and by the time the rod is picked up, in say 3–5 seconds, the fish has thrown the lure.

Both trolling and spinning from a stationary boat are techniques that can be continued with natural bait fishing at lunchtimes! Simply hook a few sprats on the trebles and chuck it out to lay on the bottom. Barrie had an eight pound fish on the R. Hull like this, and on two occasions has had a pike pick up a static spinner on the bottom, the first a sizeable fish on the R. Hull which picked up Veltic but eventually got off, and the second a four pound fish on L. Ree which picked up a Colorado and didn't get off.

Lunchtime on a big loch is also a useful time for breaking with these traditional methods and trying something a little different. What we often do is look for an extensive area of rocky, reedy shallows or flooded fields, and drift quietly into them looking for basking pike which are then approached from either the boat or the bank depending upon which is most convenient. This is an essentially good way to relax after lunch, and after a full morning on the open water, but does not necessarily mean small pike only: on one occasion a friend took one of twenty-seven pound. It is also a good way of getting to know a loch before facing up to venturing forth on the open water. Barrie can remember on many occasions catching several pike at lunchtime, spinning the shallows, and collecting nothing at all during the rest of the day!

On Loch Lomond on one occasion, the pike had obviously moved into some flooded fields, and strikes could be seen amongst emergent lesser bulrush clumps and the long grass. On closer investigation we found that the pike were feeding on toads which had gathered for spawning. Most of the time these toads were sitting on the bottom, in the grass, and safely out of sight. But the moment one came up for air a v-shaped wake was seen coming at it like a torpedo, often from ten or more yards away: the pike were clearly watching and waiting. Under these circumstances one would have thought that a plug would succeed with the pike, but they failed, including a floating rubber frog, yet spinners succeeded in taking three! It is, of course, quite easy to fish in emergent grass since most of the stems are firm yet flexible so that the treble hooks slide through them quite easily. It is a situation that calls for a return to the earlier methods of this chapter, namely small shallow water spinners, although if the surface of the water is really rough a big Piker spoon worked very shallow, even from wave to wave, can be highly effective. Even quite small pike will chase a big spoon in a swim of this nature.

The kind of pike spinning we have been talking about is clearly very variable, and you must learn to cast and fish the lures in a manner of ways, ranging from the trolled downrigger to the flicked one inch minnow on 7 lb b.s. line. But there is a casting stance that we like to adopt, given that the situation is not too cramped. We face the water, standing. The cast is usually double-handed over the right shoulder, the rod coming through at an angle of 60° to the ground. All these factors vary with the circumstances, of course, but less variable is the retrieve position. Here it is necessary to point the rod nearly at the lure, at an angle of perhaps 25° as seen in plan view. If you point directly at the lure there is a slight risk of snapping on the take. If the rod is at right-angles to the retrieve line of the spinner, as it sometimes has to be, then it may be difficult to get in a full-blooded strike to drive home the hooks.

Probably the worst thing than can happen is a pike following the spinner right to the bank edge. With a floating plug or wobbled deadbait you can stop the retrieve, allowing the plug to float and the deadbait to sink, but with a spinner or spoon you have to keep on reeling. Some advise speeding-up the retrieve, but we try to continue it, while making it clear to the pike by raising the spinner's route to the surface that very shortly the lure will reach the bank. If the pike still refuses, and you are able to creep away without frightening it off, try another cast from about ten yards along the-bank, casting back to where the pike is lying. You can also change to a small spinner at the same time. When spinning fish baits, as on Archer flights or home-made versions, the strike of the pike is treated in the same way as when using a spinner or spoon, but when wobbling deadbaits, even small ones like sprats, it is as well to ease off in the event of a take and treat it much as you would a dead or livebait run. This takes a great deal of will-power for us, but luckily the take on a wobbled deadbait is often gentle. The savage takes to sprats *can* be struck immediately, but we usually miss most of them if we do this, probably as a result of the soft sprat balling up and masking the hooks.

The jaw which shows why the ironmongery is needed.

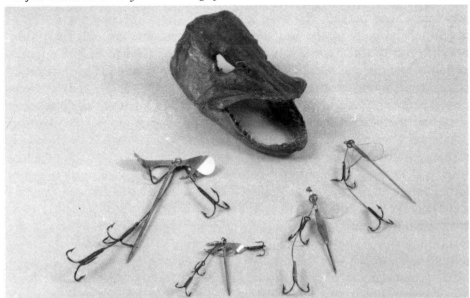

201

So far we have outlined the spinners and spoons and the natural bait approach, but there is a combination of the two which may well be one of the methods of the future. We refer to the baited spoon technique. This has been used extensively in sea fishing and North American 'sportfishing', found to be effective in perch fishing and, in our chapter on that subject, we refer to our feeling that this species homes in on a scent trail through the water. The diagram is of a rig considered by some to be very effective for pike, and it must be admitted that here is a potential method of pike fishing that might work well on waters where the pike are sick of the sight of spinners and wobbled deadbaits. In ancient days the baited spinner or spoon was certainly used much more than today, and just as night fishing for pike needed a few pioneers in the later 1960s, this technique really needs trying. It would surely be wrong to say that a wobbled deadbait can achieve anything a baited spoon can, because the flashing spoon acts as an attractor, and the bait itself can be quite small to encourage the pike which come short. As far as the natural bait is concerned strips of mackerel or trout, or chunks of freshly killed roach would have an undoubted attraction.

When it comes to considering baits for wobbling techniques the choice is legion. Sprats last about half an hour if frozen to start with, but mounting up a new sprat is such a quick and easy business – we often merely put the sliding treble of a snap tackle through the snout and tie it firmly in position – and sprats are so small and light, that it hardly matters if you have to change baits every fifteen minutes. Whole herrings and mackerel soon get pretty scraggy but may be no less effective for that, except that they don't cast too well. But a good solid roach in the 5–8 oz. bracket is the most convenient, and perhaps the most killing bait. Jim Gibbinson's idea (1974) of slitting the belly of the bait to remove the insides, not only allows the wobbled bait to sink very slowly indeed, but actually seems to give a longer period before the bait breaks up. The only time we've had trouble with such baits disintegrating is when they really do a belly flop at the end of a long cast. There really can be no doubt that the smell of a freshly killed roach is attractive to pike. A bait that is firm at the beginning of the day can sometimes be used all day unless the pike chew it to pieces, and in that case no one would complain.

In our chapter on spinning natural baits we refer to our favourite technique of preserving them, failing a deep-freeze that is. At one time we were not too worried about formalin-soaked baits, but more recently have come round to using sugar solution at a stage immediately following the formalin soak. While it would be much better to con your supplier into putting a few roach into his deep freeze, it is worth remembering that the freezer compartment of an ordinary household fridge will keep baits fresh for several weeks at least. In the winter months a bag full of deadbaits will

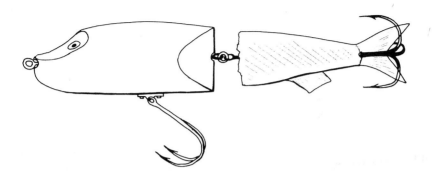

stay solidly frozen all day, but in summer it is better to attempt to calculate more or less the number needed for the day, because frozen baits soon thaw. Preserved baits are probably better in the warmer months, but at this time of the year it is much easier to get freshly killed baits.

Wobbled deadbait fishing, or deadbait spinning as it is often called (slightly erroneously), can be carried out extremely slowly. In fact there is a gradual transition as follows: static deadbait; twitched deadbait; wobbled deadbait; spun deadbait. The first of these usually has the head end of the deadbait hanging downwards, whereas all the more mobile methods have the bait head upwards along the trace. In order to be thoroughly flexible in approach on the day it is quite possible to fish static deadbaits head upwards too.

Wobbling deadbaits in really deep water is not easy, but from a boat it is possible to drift along bumping them and twitching them along the bottom, a technique found to work well on Irish loughs. This particular method is transitional to trolled deadbaits, where the usual role of the spoon is played by a slowly drawn deadbait mounted in exactly the same way as for wobbled deadbaiting from the bank. In really shallow water rough conditions seem to be best for chucking out deadbaits, but we are uncertain whether our observations are really objective on this issue. We shouldn't be at all surprised to hear of anglers succeeding well in calm waters. Jim Gibbinson has succeeded well with a smallish deadbait allowed to float on calm water and twitched gently at intervals. As a matter of fact we haven't yet had a fish like this but have seen several pike take a small dead roach just after we've thrown it back in! The deadbait can be retrieved from wave to wave, but not with the same speed as a big Jim Vincent style spoon. Takes are usually pretty savage to both lures, but on the deadbait it is fairly common to get a crafty grab in which the pike takes the bait and then simply sinks out of sight, often creating slack line.

It must be clear from the foregoing that the use of spinners, spoons, spun baits and wobbled baits for pike is a very variable art. This does not mean that it is necessary for you to carry a huge load. In fact the only (necessary) nuisance item is a large landing net. Spoons etc. can be carried in boxes inthe pockets of a good waistcoat or Bob Church jacket, and we prefer rucksacks on our backs (rather than shoulder bags), using these to carry our food and small items of gear – camera, waterproof trousers, drink and so on. Of course, Barrie's roll-up lure bag accomplishes *all* this very efficiently and neatly. One day you might be able to buy them.... Waders we always consider valuable, not only for wading, but for keeping the legs warm. In fact the only improvement we can suggest as far as both go is to well-vaseline your toes before putting on an old pair of socks to go into bootees and sea boot socks. Equipped in the way the angler should be both mobile and warm for winter pike spinning. And the waders can be fur-lined down to the knees simply by sticking on fur with Copydex.

CHAPTER TWENTY-THREE

Plugs and Perch

The perch, alas, has declined over the past years to the point that capture of one in any size and by any method will be guaranteed to bring a string of fellow anglers round to have a look. What was once an everyday occurrence, and in many cases the first real fish that a young angler caught, is now a relative rarity. True, things improved fairly dramatically during 1984 to 1986, and it is to be hoped that they continue to do so.

So it must follow that much of this chapter is drawn from our past experience, although Barrie has access to lakes that hold a good head of perch, albeit of no great size.

Although they are not separate species, perch have always been divided mentally by anglers into lake and river fish – with most serious angling being directed at the still water, as opposed to the more widely dispersed fish in the rivers. Undoubtedly the cream of perching has been in the big reservoirs and gravel pits, especially the various groups around London. Big shoals of fish would cram around the water inlets and valve towers, pretty uniform in weight and size, and if the angler hit a day when they were 'on', then sport could be fast and furious.

The areas occupied by perch lent themselves perfectly to plug fishing; large open stretches, weedless and deep. Using a large sinking plug – a double-weighted Hardy Jock Scott was one favourite – one cast as far as possible, allowed the plug to sink, and both twitched the rod tip and worked a slow retrieve at the same time. When a fish took it was always with a decided bang, and the majority of fish were hooked well inside the mouth on the tail treble.

The main problem lay in getting the plug down to the deep water where the biggest specimens would be feeding. Time after time it was seized by small (½ to ¾ lb) fish within the first ten to fifteen feet of sinking. Eventually we took to clipping a small lead on to the trace fifteen inches or so above the plug, and although in theory that should have ruined the action, to all intents and purposes it made not the slightest difference.

A tight corner. Barrie plugging for winter perch on a lake.

Of course, there were times when the perch were just not on feed, and could in fact be as finnicky as any roach. On those days, no matter how or with what one fished, there was a distinct nervousness when a fish did take, apparent by the gentle plucks and the swirls of fish turning away at the angler's feet, having followed the lure in to the bank. Often a gimmick could tip the scales in the fisherman's favour, and a lobworm hooked on to the tail treble and left to trail was one of the more rewarding ideas.

Turning over some old copies of *Field and Stream* the other day it was interesting to note that pork strips are one of the things used in America, and now we wonder whether these, mounted in the same way as our lobworms were, would perhaps pay better dividends: bacon strips certainly work well with chub and pike.

Pond and lake perch have very definite areas that they prefer to live in, apparently regardless of the time of year, or the temperature of the water. But they can be as temperamental as Paddy McGinty's goat when it comes to a taking depth. Surface thrashers can be tremendously successful in pike styles and colours, Barrie already having described some of his 'tearing' experiences with the Crazy Crawler.

During the winter we have had most success around the reed beds – in fact there are times when perch can be heard moving the stems, rooting for food. This is when a good loud splash from a floating-diving plug can pull fish, and the conditions for which a popping plug was designed. Mr Thirteen, Tiger, Trouble Maker, Sinner Spinner – all, in every combination of size and colour, are worth a try.

Occasionally it has been worth the trouble of groundbaiting where good perch are known to exist – especially where they are rather thin over the water, and fruitless hours would be spent in 'chuck and chance' fishing. We have used this method successfully on one particular Lea Valley pit, where the perch run big, but are few in number; we have also had success with it on the Thames, where perch are 'at home' in the deep water of sweeping beds. The principle is simple; just groundbait with a fine cereal mix, and fish for roach or bream in the normal way. When the small fry start cartwheeling and skimming on the surface, take to the plug outfit (after removing all bottom fishing gear from the swim) and work the water systematically.

The reverse can be worked; in fact Gerry Savage, who has access to some superb perch fishing in Kent, uses the style with great success. Here the angler suspends a livebait to work out in the water, and then works the water over with a large plug around the suspended bait. result? In many cases nothing scores on the plug, but down goes the livebait float. It would appear that the plug incites the feeding urge in the perch which then goes for the livebait, to the satisfaction of the angler.

Gravel pits can be a never-ending source of surprise in perch fishing. During the working when excavation takes place, large amounts of spoil – clay and earth – are tipped back at irregular intervals, leaving a series of ridges and valleys across the bed. Occasionally a deeper hole remains – and one, perhaps two big perch take up residence in that small spot. The difficulty of course lies in getting a plug into just that one position where it can be presented properly to the fish, bearing in mind that there are usually no landmarks to establish an exact location.

We know of one position like this, where a Gudebrod Bump 'n Grind will do the trick, providing it hits an underwater obstruction during the retrieve, at a distance of about thirty feet from the bank. In nine cases out of ten you can work the lure back across the bottom without success – then, on the tenth time it hits the rock, log, or whatever it is that projects on the underwater ridge, and after scraping over it, it will sink into deep water and be immediately taken. A foot to the right or left, and the hole is missed. One fish is usually all that the angler catches, until the next time out, when another fish will have taken up residence.

All man-made fissures on river or canals are favourite perch haunts – locks, lock cuttings, weirs, bridges, bank reinforcements (the famous 'camp sheathing' of the Victorian era), to name just a few places. But time and again the plug angler just doesn't give himself a chance to really get a fish. He merely

Colin Simpson of Ardingly Reservoir provided the frog, and Rod Poole the team of Crazy Crawler lures.

appears on the scene, has a few chucks with whatever happens to be his 'in' lure of the day, and wanders off convinced that nothing is to be caught.

These areas often hold exceptionally deep water, and we cannot repeat too often our earlier advice about finding a taking depth. Start on the surface, then change to a shallow diving plug, and work through the range to the bump and grind models. Remember to count the plug down – five seconds perhaps for the first cast, six for the second and so forth – until you are really scraping the bottom. Lose tackle? Yes, of course you may. But if you are really set on getting one of the big perch it is the only way of going about things.

Surprisingly few anglers who want to catch perch ever use anything approaching even a fair-sized plug. The myth of the small glittering perch lure has been going for years, and we feel sure that this is one of the reasons why few big perch ever seem to fall to the plug man. A nine inch perch can comfortably manage a three inch plug in its mouth and still give a fight, size for size, equal to any other fish that swims.

Think big for perch – study the plugs we have discussed for pike plugging, and work on those lines, within reason. Remember also that perch eat perch, and when it comes to colour, a perch finish is often one of the most successful.

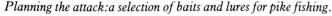

Planning the attack: a selection of baits and lures for pike fishing.

CHAPTER TWENTY-THREE

Spinners and Perch

We wrote the section Plugs and Perch with a lament at the temporary passing of that fine species. Now, not much later we find a rather different picture with perch creeping back into the news – and good fish too, weighing pounds in the plural and from a cross-section of waters as widely divergent as industrial stretches of the River Lea, gravel pits and private lakes and, best of all, reports indicating sizeable fish again appearing in some of the big reservoirs.

We suggest that there is probably a good head of perch in some waters today, but that they are not being chased by the specialist angler, if ever they really were before the mysterious disease and demise occurred a few years back. In fact, we would even suggest that, prior to the disease, perch were never desperately sought after and mostly were caught accidentally.

Fortunately for us, the authors of old angling books excelled in telling anglers where fish could be found, something writers of today rarely bother to do. What many writers failed to give were the reasons *why* you should look for perch in those locations: the simple fact that this is where small fry can congregate in reasonable safety, and where natural food in the form of insects will wash and accumulate to form a natural hunting ground for predatory fish like the perch. Moral? To find good perch, think like one that is looking for a meal, and you will usually score. Find one perch and it is odds-on that you will find a shoal, probably evenly graded in size and stupid enough in the smaller sizes to let you catch fish after fish from the same place, always providing that you do not become careless and prick or lose one. Even the lowest I.Q. has its break factor, and a prick from an angler's hook happens to be the one possessed by a perch.

We have been perch fishing for enough years now to have learned where not to look for them, and when not to fish. We avoid very fast water; that hump of flesh on the shoulders of a perch would disappear at a rapid rate with exercise. We leave mud bottoms on river or lake beds well alone, our experience telling us that perch may well be there 'hoovering' the bottom for food, but if they are, they are not likely to be very interested in a spinner of any sort. Flood water, or water that is coloured in any way can also take the edge off a day's fishing. Whether it is the suspended grit and mud content that puts them off feed, or just the fact that their eyesight is poor, is anyone's guess.

Weather plays an enormous part in perch feeding patterns. Excessive rain, as we have pointed out, can put them off feed, and cold, real biting cold, will also put them off but on a diminishing scale. The longer the cold lasts and the lower the temperature drops, so interest in food falls. Not only that, but cold also drives them into deeper water and down to the bottom until eventually they become nearly as torpid as tench. Natural baits score better at these times.

The most influential factor affecting feeding is the degree of brightness in the weather. On bright, sunny days perch will be close to the surface, working into the shallows and interested only in playing at feeding, although everything that comes before them will be well investigated. Warm, dull days when there is plenty of light behind a cloud base but no direct sunlight are just about the best for spinning and a good shoal will feed hard, barely questioning anything that is spun before them. By far the best day for a big fish has for us been one of those back end, late February, early March days

Seeking perch among moored boats.

when a gradual warm-up has given just a hint of spring. A little weak sunshine and we have both hit good perch when we have been pike spinning and using large baits that we would not at one time have considered for a perch.

There is a school of thought that brackets pike and perch together, maintaining that what is good for one must hold good for the other, be it rod, strength of line or size of lure. Nothing could be further from the truth. We have described the odd day when a perch will conform to the principles of pike feeding, but those occasions are few and far between. For all their schoolboy, first fish, big-mouthed, hungry image they are as delicate at feeding as a roach, at least where sizeable fish are concerned, and deserve as much consideration as that species in deciding on tackle and tactics.

Our chapter on tackle selection decreed that size of lure should govern the line, rod and reel. We work to a bait weight of approximately ten grams as the maximum we wish to use for perch fishing, and consider that this supports a line with no greater breaking strain than four pounds and a rod six to seven feet long with matching reel. Of course, this size of outfit tends to minimise the distance one can cast, but serious perch fishing is not a long and repeated series of massive casts into the very middle of a water where one happens to be fishing. Imagination is the thing that catches perch; imagining where small fry are likely to be, and that is rarely going to be miles away from the bankside.

Instead of worrying about distance we think of ways to reach obvious perch holds without disturbing them or being seen – a thought often omitted by the spinning angler. A cast of fifteen feet made with the angler standing in a concealed position is more likely to achieve success than one of fifty feet made with the angler standing above the skyline, and after ten minutes of bank-swamping and bush-whacking to get into position. Where it is not possible to get near to a good casting position by using the bank, one can often reach it by using the water, providing that it is safe. Vic Gibson sold us on that idea – he invested in a set of breast-chest waders and found that with a little care he could reach areas on some of his local gravel pits where no-one had ever spun before. Not only that, his position low down in the water gave him the obvious advantage of keeping out of sight of the fish.

Obviously, weather must govern the type of lure that you spin with. A warm, sunny day and fish in the shallows demand the smallest bait possible – and this for us is a tiny copper fly-spoon with perhaps one small shot to help in making the cast unless, of course, we are using the ultra-light rod and closed face reel. The tiny Shakespeare Dorado bar spinner is another excellent worker, and available in a variety of colours that allow ringing the changes until the right one is found. Whether colour on a revolving blade has any influence or not (and we are still in some doubt after our tank tests) the black and yellow model has been our most successful.

Fresh woods and pastures new. Vic Gibson making good use of breast-high waders.

No matter how attractive a lure may be, it can prove useless when it is worked inconsistently or thoughtlessly. For fishing an area where perch are known to lie, a direct cast right over them followed by a retrieve through the shoal will lead to disaster. Line falling across the surface in good visibility can literally be seen in a flash. Far better is a cast made to one side or other of the shoal and a steady retrieve with the hope of enticing a fish out to take it.

One can get away with casting beyond and retrieving over fish in rough water conditions such as those around a weirpool, and of course you can scale-up the lure size considerably. Several spoons are absolutely great for this type of work, notable the Paravan type of Norwegian spoon, beautifully finished and producing a firm, half-wobbled part-spin that really pulls them in. Other spoons in this category are the Shakespeare Jim Vincent and Catcher, and the Abu Flamingo. As far as is possible we plump for near-perch colours or, failing that, a part red and gold finish.

One lure has been especially useful to us when fishing weirpools and lock areas during the autumn months. At this time large shoals of small (and often not so small) fish are up against timbers and supports, feeding on silkweed, which is just beginning to die off and flake away. The little Mepps Adour worked around these places seems to beat the ordinary bar spinners at this time. It looks like a small fish, but even better, responds to a sink and draw retrieve that pulls perch when a straighforward wind leaves them cold. The woollen tassle on the tail is an optional extra – we have taken our fish both with and without it. The only disadvantage of wool around any hook is that it tends to encourage rusting.

Weirpool fishing can be a labour of love at times. The best time to spin is when the water level is low and there is plenty of slack water either side of the main run and around the closed gates. Directly there is a hard pull of water one's chances disappear. But the attraction of a weir with its 'fishy' atmosphere can often lead one to waste hours of unproductive fishing.

Stillwaters and large open stretches of river where there is a reasonable depth are the places where we spin with larger baits, such as the Toby and Nobby lures, the Abu Atom and Little Wiggley spoons and, where the water is really deep, a Shakespeare Geneva spoon. The last-named is heavier than most we use – but it is probably the most compact wobbler in its weight/size ratio. Gladdings Flectolight and Mepps Rainbo bar spinners in large sizes have proved excellent in stillwaters, and are probably the most 'gaudy' lures that we use for perch, despite the general doctrine that one should use a flashy, showy spinner at all times.

With large waters we use the countdown principle of spinning. Once the bait has hit the water we count off a few seconds and then retrieve. We then repeat the cast, adding one or two more seconds to our counting after the bait has reached the water, thereby increasing the depth to which it will sink

Winter perch-fishing at a weirpool.

before we wind in. By casting fan-wise from the rushes or reeds at the left side of the water through 180° to the bank on our right, and counting before we start the bait working, we will eventually find the depth at which perch are feeding, besides carrying out a systematic search over the likely areas.

215

Often we locate a shoal and then find that we gets lots of bumps at the lure, but no fish on the strike. Occasionally this is caused by fish hitting at a swivel or anti-kink device, in which case the cure is to remove it or use a smaller one where this is possible. Another reason for this behaviour is that perch will often hit at the lure broadside-on or from ahead, thereby missing the hooks. We have especially noticed this behaviour when using bar-spoons, and have a pretty fair idea that fish are actually going for the revolving blade itself and travelling at an oblique angle to do so. The only cure we know, when this happens consistently, is to increase slightly the rate of wind on the retrieve so that perch finish up chasing and hitting the lure from astern.

Yet another problem we have had is with foul-hooking, usually under the jaw. Again, we think that this is a question of too slow a retrieve, with fish accelerating beyond the hook to grab at the body of the spinner. Speeding up the retrieve helps, so does a change to a large single hook instead of the treble, or occasionally reducing the size of the lure itself so that it becomes a single mouthful. Mostly, these problems occur in running water, where any current helps the spinner to revolve faster than one is used to in stillwater. One feels this increase through the rod and tends to slow the retrieve to get the lure back to its imagined normal rate of spin.

Foul-hooked perch – the result of the perch striking high?

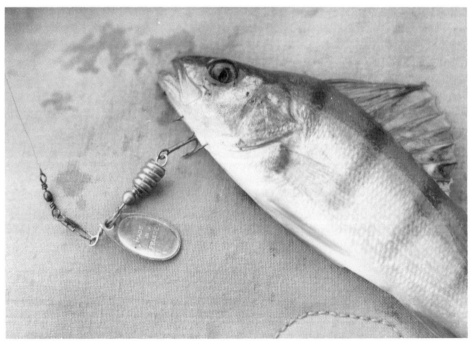

With one possible exception, striking is hardly necessary when perch spinning. Providing that hooks are regularly sharpened, a light pull back on the rod to tighten the line is sufficient to drive the point home. Anything harder is asking for damage to the soft tissue of the mouth and the hook to tear free.

Our exception is when we are wobbling a small deadbait on the sink-and-draw principle – something particularly deadly between weed beds when any attempt to spin an artificial lure would lead to disaster. Minnows or sprats threaded on the line with a single treble at the vent and a small weight in the mouth can be worked up and down through the smallest area clear of the weed.

Once the cast is made, the rod tip does the work, raising the bait and allowing it to wobble slowly down again. It is when the bait sinks that the take usually occurs – and it is not felt until the rod tip is raised again. In that short time a perch often realises the deception and is on the point of expelling it as resistance is felt. Only a short, sharp strike will save a lost fish under these circumstances.

Our latest experiment in perch fishing which so far has been extremely successful is with what we call the spinner cocktail. We make no claim to have originated the idea – it has been the vogue in America for a number of years. The American anglers attach strips of pork or bacon rind (it is sold ready preserved in packs) to the trebles at the tail of a lure and then spin with it in the normal way. We have not gone so far as using bacon rind (yet!) but have found that worms – red or small lobs – head hooked on one or two points of the treble, certainly do improve results. We have thoroughly combed an area where we know good fish to have been in residence without the cocktail and then mounted the worms and spun again only to connect with good fish.

Why? Well, we don't know. To all intents and purposes the trailing worm merely follows the path of the lure in front. But perhaps there is a scent of some sort that perch pick up and are attracted to. Come to think of it, weed caught around the trebles and trailed in a like fashion has never aroused attention, so that would seem the most logical conclusion. Anyway, next season we intend to start using strips of fresh-killed fish, rather in the fashion of the strip of mackerel attached to the sea spinner lures. Which highlights the whole beauty of perch fishing with a spinner – there is always some new approach, some new and untried idea with which to tempt this sporting fish.

Our last thoughts on perch concern night fishing. We had never stopped to give it serious thought until we picked up reflective types of lure, which sowed the seeds of the idea in our heads. We experimented, and certainly it is a successful method within certain limitations. First of all, we must define

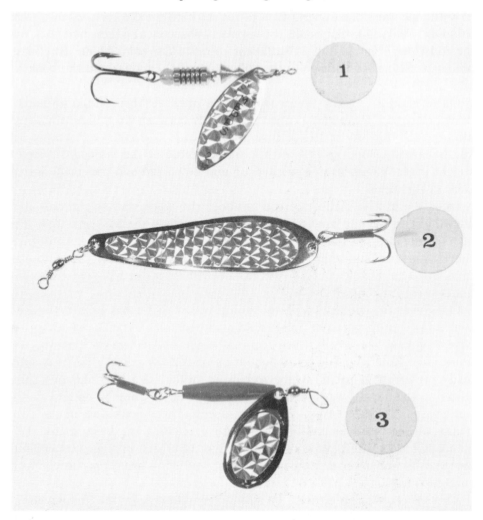

REFLECTIVE SPINNERS. *1. Mapps Aglia Rainbo   2. Intrepid Flasha   3. Intrepid Spinflasha (Red/Gold).*

night. We have had no success in the middle hours of darkness, say between midnight and 4 a.m. And definitely no success other than in the more open months of the year, June to early October, when there is the very long dusk period and an early false dawn.

This proves pretty conclusively that these has to be *some* light available to reflect off the lure. We have also found that areas where perch are conditioned to artificial light – lakes and river banks beside a road, or where a bridge with street lights crosses the river – are far better bets than the waters where natural light only is available.

Ken mentioned night spinning to Henri Limouzin, the celebrated French angling writer, during the course of a letter and it is interesting to note that his observations entirely agree with ours. Night fishing is banned in France, but their very early and late fishing for perch, which overlaps into the pre-dawn and dusk periods can be excellent, and he also confirms our success with the Rainbo and Flectolite type of lure.

CHAPTER TWENTY-FIVE

Plugs and Chub

Angling literature through the ages leaves the reader with a firm impression that the chub is a rather coarse character that spends his whole time looking for the slightest excuse to disappear; an easy-to-catch but difficult-to-approach fish that might turn up in a roach swim – providing he deigns to leave the shade of the willow trees on the opposite bank. Always it is the willow trees – and always they are on the opposite bank!

Charlie Landells was responsible for Ken's conversion to plug fishing for chub. One back end day he took him to the Upper Ouse in a shooting brake, the engine noise of which was nearly drowned by the slurping and slooshing of a few hundred large slugs in varying colours busy gorging themselves in a large drum of garden refuse. Using a near spinning-type rod Charlie mounted a slug on to a spliced hook, and proceeded to throw this into just about every place that no angler in his right mind would ever consider casting – and produced fish after fish.

Ken sat and watched, soon realising that the sexual habits of the slug, apropos home-breeding in the garage, did not appeal to him in the slightest, nor did the aura of slime that covered hands, rod handles, and sandwiches. From there it was an easy mental exertion to imagine a plug landing in the water instead of a slug, and yet another chub-plugger was born.

It would be no exaggeration to state that three-quarters of all coarse fishermen do not believe that a chub would look at a plug for one second, let alone would take it thinking it was natural food. Probably the reasoning against the acceptance of this idea is that chub take fright easily, and a plug splashing on to the water would provide that fright, so Q.E.D., the plug fisherman must come home chubless.

Quite the reverse is the actual case. Chub are probably the most inquisitive fish that swim, and a 'plop' of any sort, providing it is not that caused by a half-brick, can be guaranteed to bring them immediately to investigate. *But only if they have no reason to suppose that an angler was or could be responsible for that happening.*

Charlie Landells slugging a few chub out of the Upper Ouse.

If you are using a leger or float ring you are constantly performing mental calculations around the possible action of the bait once it is in that difficult corner where you feel the fish might be. With a plug one has only to fit the bait into the corner, and control can be dictated by the angler from the second it hits the water. No float or lead preceding the bait, hang-ups, or fruitless fishing with a bait that has come off during the cast.

Long distance casting is the exception rather than the rule in chubbing. Accuracy, however, is all-important, and only the man who knows and uses his tackle can hope to get where the best chub lie. Light, single-handed sensitive rods, rather on the short side and balanced with a sensible fixed spool reel take a lot of beating. In fact this is one of those occasions where the closed-face reel comes into its own.

Add a shoulder bag or fishing waistcoat into which a selection of lures can be packed with a few sandwiches – and the plugman is prepared. No long-distance heavyweight stuff – a light landing net and off you can go with as much or as little water to cover as you can manage.

Perhaps a word on distance would not be out of place at this point. Take a long section of good chubbing river, and times without number the angler starts to flail the water and charge along the banks at a rate of knots. It is infectious – a touch of the water in the next swim being greener than that in

Lazer lures, spoons with a beautiful fish print on one side and a silver outline of the same on the reverse.

A SELECTION OF FAVOURITE PLUGS FOR CHUB. *They all appear in sections for other fish as well, but these are our 'musts'. 1. Mr Thirteen   2. Mr Murder   3. Beno 4. Punkin Seed   5. Snoky   6. Prowler   7. Trouble Maker   8. Lazy Ike   9. Basspin   10. Sinner Spinner   11. Shad.*

the one you are fishing. But it is a forerunner of failure. To catch chub with a plug one must examine every possible hold, think like a chub, the chub that is possibly sitting there, and plan his downfall.

A preliminary reconnoitre is often useful on a strange water, an evening walk without tackle (if that is possible!) where the best parts can be earmarked for special attention. And of course, the more important detail – how to approach the possible fish without putting him down.

This is where the luxury of a boat can bring immense pleasure and reward, and where the electric motor comes into its own. Launch the boat upstream, drift down casting across the banks on either side, or explore a small backwater, a weirpool, under the arches of a bridge; wonderful sport, the thing that angling memories are made from.

Where else do good fish lie? We talked about this one day at great length, and came to the conclusion that the large chub is a frustrated tortoise. He loves an armoured plating around and if possible below him.

So trees that overhang, roots that grow out into water, and sunken branches that have silted solid with bank and bottom make the obvious holds. Reed beds – especially thick rafts of reed mace and bulrush where it is possible to wade through long sections – rather like Amazon stuff – is great fishing, providing cover for the angler who moves quietly and allowing him to reach a hundred little channels and pools where the current has cleaned a passage. Bridges, and the pools that usually lie above and below them, landing stages, boathouse creeks off the main river and lock cuttings (especially where there is a reasonable current – the Kennet and Avon canal is an instance) also come immediately to mind.

Whilst thinking of man-made chub haunts there are few better places in which to enjoy sport than a weirpool. Part of this is a fascination for fast running water that acts as a magnet for a large majority of fishermen; you never know what might turn up! Quite apart from this, chub use the whole area as a natural feeding ground and lose a lot of their natural caution in so doing. Happy memories exist for Ken who has had great fishing on the Britford water, combing the whole weirpool for salmon and finishing with king-sized chub.

Kingsweir is another good weir chub haunt, where they lie just below the sill. Once hit, they double back under the rush of water and under the sill itself, which stands on stilts. Exciting and frustrating moments. Erosion and chub are well suited, and undercuts in the bank can usually produce a fish. Jack Hilton can read a water as few other men can, and to watch him size up one of his Norfolk rivers and point out the undercut sections – that are not always on the concave side of a bend – is an education in itself.

Having described the seemingly impossible places to fish we shall obviously be hammered by the critics if we don't give some idea of how to get a bait to them. Going back to our chub and tortoise comparison, it seems reasonable to suppose that where the tortoise sticks his head and tail out of the shell so, metaphorically speaking, the chub must stick out one end for food, if for nothing else. Once that chink in the armour is found – exploit it.

It isn't necessary to cast directly into the chub all the time. Dapping, the time-honoured and oft-described action of poking a rod tip under or through the undergrowth along the bank, and then allowing the bait to drop on to the water, can be rewarding; it can also be frustrating and damaging to waders, trousers and dignity. Many plugs are designed to be 'twitched' and generally teased on the surface, and it is in these situations that they pay a dividend.

If the particular chub you want to reach is right at the back of heavily overhung trees, then don't try and cast to him. Select a floating plug, cast well upstream, allow plenty of slack line and leave the plug to drift down under the branches. Start the action when the plug reaches your fish – and you could be in business.

Underwater obstructions require a little imagination. It isn't always possible to see their full extent, so try probing. Using a shallow- or medium-running floating plug, and delicately 'feel' the plug back to you via the reel

'Popping'. Note the two surface patterns caused by plug action when the rod tip is twitched.

handle. The moment it hits an obstruction, stop reeling, drop the rod tip and in the majority of cases the plug will float up to the surface, free of the obstruction. The emphasis is on the word *feel*. Ham-handed reeling will only lose tackle. How does one tell the difference between the bump of an obstruction and the bump of a taking fish? Experience only, we fear – something that no amount of 'flannel' or 'bull' in writing will teach.

Lost plugs, especially at around a pound or two a time, is a worry that we feel puts many anglers off plug fishing. Our descriptions so far of how to handle tight corners has saved us a good few pounds – so has the angler's 'otter', a disc of plastic that can be slipped on to the line, fed down the water, and allowed by its shape to provide a side-strain above the lure. Ours has been well worth its keep. But they only work in running water, where current provides the lateral pull.

One of the most difficult places to fish without tackle loss is in and around weed beds of any sort. It is possible to tie weed guards to hooks, but they are nowhere near wholly efficient. If a big chub is lying in the weeds and waving two tail-segments at you, your only chance of making contact will be to look for a possible clearing nearby, land a plug right in it and fish as much of the open water as possible. When you reach the weeds, reel like mad and make an enormous strike so that the plug lifts from the water and (in theory at least) over the weeds. It is also not a bad idea to duck at the same time!

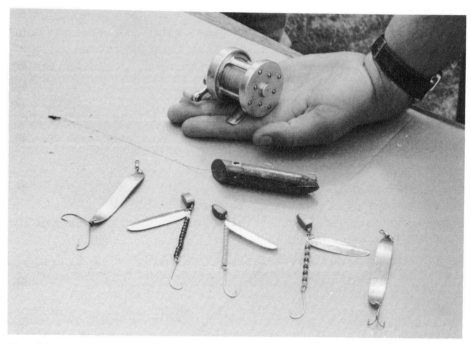

The ultimate in home-made tackle, barspoons, spoons, a Kynoch style plug which runs up the trace on the take, and a multiplier, all by Sussex expert Peter Truman.

Now to the nitty-gritty – plugs themselves. By and large it is the small plug that brings the best possible results. Not that a chub cannot manage a big one – they don't call him satchel-mouth for nothing – but because it is action that counts where attraction is concerned, and a small plug is more versatile in this than its larger brethren, especially in confined spaces. How to describe them without making a book read like a tackle-dealer's catalogue is difficult, but we decided to 'zone' plugs into their main action heading earlier, so we shall take them in that order.

SURFACE LURES

Two Shakespeare models are first-rate surface lures for chubbing. The Slim Jim is a wooden torpedo with propellors at either end and fishes on the 'try it and see' principle. You can guess what we mean by that – the sort of large hole that should hold a chub, and so you try the Slim Jim across the surface where it kicks up hell's delight. Usually the chub cannot resist having a look-see, and the rest should follow. This one definitely needs space though, otherwise the propellors can't really send out the message.

Mr Thirteen we have described elsewhere. The junior model measuring in at 2⅝ inches and in the Yellow Coach Dog finish looks good, and fishes superbly. Another model more difficult to obtain in this country, but worth the effort of getting hold of, is the Lucky popper. This is an absolute natural among the lily pads with its 'popping' action.

The Bomber Stick and Spinstick models are similar to the Slim Jim in action, the Stick being rather unique in its fishing position of nearly vertical, and leaning slightly forward out of the water. We are in no doubt that noise from a lure across the surface can be a tremendous attraction, but we find extreme difficulty in convincing many anglers of this. The Arbogast Jitterbug is a good example of the noise attracters. The large down-turned shield at the nose of the plugs sends twin jets of water spraying outward and at first sight would tend to put off even the most ardent fisherman. But times without number this lure has scored for us.

Sinner Spinner, showing the surface disturbance that revolving blades can produce.

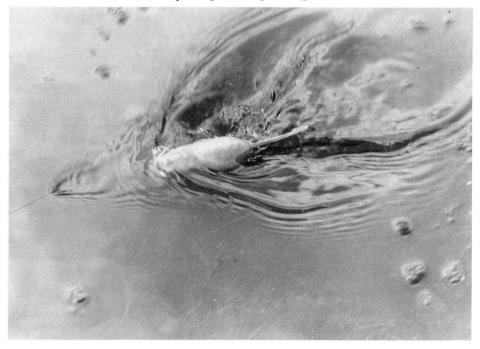

The Meadow Mouse in action.

Heddon floating and diving plugs are first-rate, starting of course with the Meadow Mouse that is just about the most natural artificial that we have ever seen. The Spooks, Wood Vamp, Vamp and River Runt have proved themselves not only for chub, but every other type of coarse and game fish. Shakespeare's Dapper Dan, the Abu Hi-Lo, Rapala originals, and the Midge Oreno from Gladding's stables are also useful additions to the tackle box.

DEEP-DIVING AND SINKING LURES

These are more out of the tackle box in the winter months than during the summer, when weed has died back and it is possible to bump and grind (to quote the American jargon) along the river bed. They are also great in a weirpool during the summer months – providing you have guts. At about £2 or so a time, it certainly takes guts in every sense of the word to pull on a well-snagged plug. But the fish are there, and deep work in the deep holes that infest every weirpool can bring wonderful results.

Abu's Killer and Snoky, Bomber Baits' 200 and Punkfish, Shakespeare's Klatter Kat and Big 'S', Heddon's Deep 6, Spooks and Sonars give some ideas of our other fancies and the Punkin Seed. The last *looks* fishy, which we feel always instils confidence in the fisherman and is so necessary to bring results.

So far we have said little or nothing on the question of colour. There are two ways of looking at this; one is from the fishes' point of view, where one supposes that whatever is offered should look as life-like as possible, be it fish, insect or what-have-you. In this case the green, brown and predominantly yellow plugs would seem to be a must. Viewed from the angler's point of view, it is whatever takes his eye, and may result in some of the bright blues, reds, purples and orange colours that hit you when so many tackle box lids are raised. Perhaps this may be the root of the maxim that runs 'Plugs catch fishermen, not fish'. We would be the first to agree, however, that some of those with more garish decorations *do* produce fish, often when the more obvious natural doesn't arouse the slightest interest.

WEATHER AND WATER-TEMPERATURE

Obviously, so much must depend on the day. We were both brought up on the old spinning maxim that dull colours should be used on bright days and in clear waters, bright colours being the order when the water is dark and the light poor. Light has an enormous influence on fish, and strange though it may seem, the reverse is true of plug fishing for chub. When it is dull and overcast then get out the deep golds and blacks, keeping the light colours for the bright sunny days when the water is clear. Ken vividly recalls talking to an American visitor in Pall Mall on the question of plug colour and light, and remembers his advice. 'Son', he said, 'when the water is not quite thick enough to plough, and not quite thin enough to drink, and when the camera needs an exposure of f5.6 with a fast film – that's the time to go fishing.' Unfortunately he didn't say anything about shutter speeds.

Floodwater is an exception that proves a rule, and when the banks are nearly under water then the biggest, most agile plug in the box, regardless of colour, should be worked through every inch of slack water possible, and kept on or near to the bottom. Actually, the fisherman is in double dilemma with these conditions. Using a floater he can catch on surface debris and suffer a break; with a deep dive or bump and grind he is pretty sure to catch on freshly exposed obstructions. But gamble one must.

Obviously, weather conditions are of great influence to any sport and an understanding of them can only increase one's chances of a fish – even be it only by making sure that you pick up the rod on a taking day. But chub can be the most difficult fish to understand where weather is concerned. Think about it. There it is, well down to freezing, ice all over the banks and rushes bent down by its weight. Lines of brass monkeys nipping down the towpath on their way to get lagged when suddenly there comes a shout from a crowd of fishermen. Something has been caught – and in nine cases out of ten that something is a chub. Now to the other extreme. Blinding heat that brings practically all wild life except courting couples to a standstill, the river near-warm enough to boil an egg – and again, it is the chub that allows his stomach to overrule his brain and so finishes up on the bank.

Earlier, we mentioned the barometer and the fact that we believe in its use. Obviously it cannot tell you when to fish or, better still, perhaps, when not. But two or three rules of thumb are well worth remembering about its prophecies. A rapid rise foretells unsettled weather, whilst a slow rise foretells the reverse. A slow, continued rise over a period of time indicates to any sensible angler that it is high time he told the office that grandma has just died, and to check that the plug box is really full and ready. Our best days have been those when the barometer has risen slowly in summer and the weather has been 'soft', i.e. the light has been plentiful but not harsh, and there has been a touch of moisture in the air – perhaps even light rain – that has caused the temperature of the water to rise a little.

Obviously the better (higher) the water temperature, then the better one's chances of sport, but there can be no hard and fast rule with this, e.g. our description of the chub, so often caught when nothing else moves. Again, Ken has often looked from his bedroom window on to the Lea, and seen that delightful and fascinating water-mist that comes when water temperature is higher than that of the air. In theory the perfect setting and conditions under which to catch fish; but time after time Ken has dropped everything and flailed the water without success.

Although the weather conditions can to some great extent influence sport, few anglers are going to let it influence them away from the water. It's just a question of trying that much harder when the cards seem stacked against success – and through all our talk of plug types, colour, size, the weather and the temperature, it is application that really matters.

Take each plug that you use and fish it as though it were the best in the world. Try to imagine what it will look like in the water from the fishes' point of view; run it back and forth at your feet until you are really sure of its action, then cast to the fish and get every ounce of teasing and attraction from it that is possible. Don't change it until you are sure that it has been presented to its best advantage – and then repeat the whole pattern with the next offering from the box.

Usually, a taking chub mouths the plug hard enough to be hooked without the need of a strike from the angler, especially when the lure is on the big side. It is when the smaller plugs are being used that a strike is

Flood time. Adrian Lawson looking for slack water after the river has left its banks.

necessary, just in case one of the small trebles hasn't found a hold inside that big mouth. But under no circumstances should this be the full-bloodied swing that is associated with pike fishing. Although there is a large amount of hard bone and gristle around the mouth area, there is also a considerable amount of soft tissue from which the hook can easily be pulled, some of it on the outside, and a chub takes with such a rush that often he is hooked on the outside of the mouth, especially when the plug is being retrieved quickly.

Where one chub has been caught another will be found often within half-an-hour of taking the original fish. It would appear that on many rivers there is a housing shortage, and another fish of similar size to the first will take up residence as a vacancy occurs in a good lie. With this in mind, the effort of keeping a diary – even on very abbreviated lines – is well worth the effort, so that the known places where fish have been found in the past can receive regular attention.

CHAPTER TWENTY-SIX

Spinners and Chub

We would be the last to suggest that it is possible to take a spinner and catch a chub on it every day of the week, anymore than the fly or trotted cereal bait would produce consistent results. But at certain times of the year and under favourable weather conditions a spun bait can be a very profitable way of fishing.

At what age chub turn cannibal is hard to tell. But it is interesting that neither of us has caught a fish smaller than ten inches long by spinning, which would probably be in their fourth year and at a time when they are just about sexually mature. We believe that this size and sexual maturity link are important where spinning is concerned – because there is no doubt that the cream of the sport is to be found during the early part of the season, during June and July when spawning is taking or has just taken place, and enormous amounts of freshly hatched fry are present and spawning minnows are on the shallows.

It is during this period that chub move into fast water around weirpools and between narrow banks of a river where the current really speeds up. If you stand quietly using a pair of Polaroid glasses they can often be seen hunting and driving small fry as they dash across the shallows, in much the same way as perch and pike do. It would seem that, having spawned, they then set about systematically eating their own and every other fishes' current and previous season's offspring.

During those warm months we spin with the lightest possible tackle – until we developed the ultra-light rod we would use a No. 6 fly rod and fixed spool reel – and an assortment of matching spinners to comb the faster water. Deep spinning is definitely out where summer chubbing is concerned and, in direct opposition to perch fishing, the brighter and more flashy the lure the better the results will be.

Naturally, small fly-spoons are good except in the very fast runs, where they seem to get lost in the welter of foam and broken water. Mackerel spinners have turned up some good fish; their size/weight ratio is ideal, and if one stops fishing the lure it will sink with a wobbling action that can often pull a fish into making a take.

Mepps Mouche bar spinners with a fly tied on to the rear treble are absolutely grand fished in the 0 to 2 sizes. We have a very soft spot for Mouche Jaune that has a Palmer type fly body tied with a red tail. Also in the fly spinner category is the Abu Reflex bait, and the little Abu Fly, with nose mounted spinning vane to help keep an even body keel on the retrieve. Shakespeare's Marble spinner and its crimped blade reflect well, and the thin wire hooks are especially easy to drive home on the strike.

Our method of fishing these spinners is to cast slightly upstream and across, keeping the rod tip up and allowing the current to carry the bait below us, holding back so that the current does as much of the work as is possible. Once the bait is completely downstream we retrieve small amounts of line, allowing the spinner to hang and revolve as long as is possible. Naturally, if one can get on a weir platform, or the sill of the lasher, or on a projecting piece of bank, then the cast can be made to last practically indefinitely.

Never worry if the spinner is only in the broken water for a short time. Most of the fry and a large amount of the action will take place relatively close to the bankside. Which leads us directly to problems, for just because there is one devil of a lot of noise and confusion where fast water is running, it does not necessarily follow that fish can neither see nor hear you. A chub might be a big-mouthed bomb head, but he is probably the most cautious fish swimming where disturbance is concerned. You can hook and lose him without disturbing the shoal he has come from. But once you visibly or physically frighten one and he stampedes, then the rest of those near to him will follow suit – period. Keep low, keep quiet, and avoid sudden movement.

With the post-spawning period over, madness seems to go out of a chub's fish-eating habits. This does not mean to say that they are not as cannibalistic as before: it is merely that they will drop back into quieter water, using the very considerable amount of cover that a bank has to offer in the summer months. Small fish will continue to cruise around and can be caught relatively freely, but the better fish, appreciating perhaps that clear and low water has made them particularly vulnerable to danger, take up a stance with plenty of cover from reed, weed, bushes, trees and sunken branches around and over them. At this time they are at their most difficult to catch with a spinner. With legering, a lobworm could be anchored at the entrance to their shelter. With a plug, a small surface lure, it could be plopped like a falling insect directly into their safe area. But a spinner can only commit suicide when chub are positioned like this, as it frequently gets snagged.

The only hope that the angler has is to spin something close by that hold, so attractively that a fish could not help but swim out and intercept it. Instinctively one would think that this would be the situation for the spun natural bait, but our results have proved this to be far from the case; in fact spun natural baits for chub are, in our experience at least, the most unsuccessful. Other people have had a different experience; Dave Steuart, for example, has had lots of chub on the spun natural minnow.

One lure with which we have had success when attempting this type of spinning is the Devon minnow. The wooden or plastic types, about an inch to two inches in length, are light enough to spin within the top two feet or so of the surface and can easily be controlled by using the rod tip if snagging seems inevitable where a cast is misjudged. Colour seems to be immaterial. Ken favours blue back and silver belly, a combination he accidentally stumbled across when trout spinning on a well-known river. The trout just ignored everything that he fished, but the chub, three of which were taken from the same pool, left a welter of tree roots and literally smashed at the Devon.

Three other lures we have used to attract fish into open water have been the Mepps Mino and the Abu Drop-Fish and Morrum. The Drop-Fish and Mino are both artificial minnows perfectly reproduced in soft plastic, with a bar spinner mounted at the head. Although they are quite long, their weight ratio is low and they search the upper layer of water providing that the rate of retrieve is kept high. Fortunately, speed seems to be an incentive to chub at this time of year, in fact pulling the spinner up to the surface where it makes one hell of a clatter is a trick worth trying.

The Morrum is a lure we reserve for very deep holes where fish can be lying down below the surface. Weight carried by this lure is in the artificial head which is made from lead, and the spinner blade is mounted behind it, making it also an excellent sink and draw bait. There are times when this scores, though in fairness we should state that most of our fish have been taken on the straight retrieve.

During the winter months chub tend to be taken more on the open river. Whilst they may use their summer areas as a retreat, fluctuations in water levels and temperatures can scatter them over a wide area that makes objective spinning very difficult. Most of our chub 'turn-up' at this time of year, often when we are perch spinning or spinning for pike with a small lure. From our fishing logs (we both keep one – they provide endless information and ideas over the season) we have noted that three lures have provided most of our cold weather sport.

The Abu Droppen makes the best deepwater spinner, an enormous weight ratio in the body helping the count-down method of spinning described in the perch section, besides ensuring that the lure works on an even keel. For working the middle and upper layers the Mepps Aglia has been successful

Mepps Mino – a small mouthful for a hungry chub.

– surprisingly in its largest (no. 5) size. This bar spinner and small Copper and Silvers have provided us with our only stillwater chub, taken on mild January days when pike were the objective. The fish took at the end of the retrieve, when the lures were being lifted from the water prior to re-casting, and it was thought they had followed them in over a considerable distance.

Our only spoon to meet with success in chub spinning has been the plain Copper and Silver type, unadorned, and fished slowly just over the bottom. It seems to do the trick after a prolonged period of frost and we have noticed that it is taken with only a little of a chub's usual smash-and-grab enthusiasm. Experimenting with our cocktail style in using small worms mounted on the rear treble has not been successful, which rather surprises us. But we have decided not to leave this idea, and there are fresh thoughts along these lines planned for next season.

There is one final suggestion we would commend to anyone who is thinking seriously of spinning for chub; consider the use of a boat. Boats and chub spinning are not usually associated, yet without a boat one is always looking regretfully at a small stretch of water that just cannot be covered because of an obstruction either on your side, or on the opposite bank. There are times when you can use only a few angles in retrieving a lure – usually those obliquely across the area that you want to cover – and how often has the angler wished that he could cross over to the opposite bank to cover a fish unapproachable from his position on the bank! The independence that a boat can bring when chub fishing, the ability to drop quietly downstream covering either bank or both from the same position, the chances that are given to spin at any one of several angles to reach a fish, make the financial and physical efforts required to get a boat on the water more than worthwhile.

CHAPTER TWENTY-SEVEN

Spinning for Zander

Zander have been around on the continent for a long while, and their North American counterparts, the walleyes, likewise; but in Britain, although of restricted distribution since 1878 they have been widespread in East Anglia for only a few years. Hence they are not *settled*, and the techniques used in their capture nowadays will probably have to be modified in years to come. Zander were introduced into the Great Ouse Relief Channel in 1963 and they have spread incredibly throughout much of the system including the rivers Wissey, Lark, Little Ouse, and Cam and the drains such as the Old Bedford, Sixteen Foot and Delph, as well as numerous other waters. Many of these waters are now good zander fisheries, and it all happened in less than ten years from an original stock of ninety-seven fish.

In this recent period of spreading, livebaits and deadbaits have accounted for far more fish than have plug baits or spinners. It may be that as the zander spread into a new water and concentrate so strongly on mopping up the new larder of available small fish they become preoccupied with the natural fish to such an extent that they ignore things which do not quite conform to the pattern of dead and live fish. Nevertheless, plugs do succeed well at times; and the contrast between European and North American zander and walleye is worth pursuing further. In the longer-established populations where the zander or walleye do not form such an irregular percentage of the total fish population, and where there is more of a fine balance between prey and predator, the latter may be more on the lookout for anything worth eating. In any event, many more Dutch zander are taken on plugs than in this country, and plugging is an essential part of the North American walleye hunters' repertoire.

Quite a number of magazines and catalogues list particular plugs as being exceptionally good with zander or walleye. Creek Chub specifically mention the Cahokie, Crazy-z-fish and Viper; Bomber Baits list the Midget Bomberette; Heddon's rate the River Runt Spook, Punkin Seed, Sonar and Punkin

Spin as walleye plugs. On the other hand, one does detect a certain reticence on the part of the publishers of these catalogues: pike, perch, game fish, crappie and bass are mentioned much more commonly than zanders or walleyes. We did a survey of those admirable Abu annuals called *Tight Lines*. It was surprising that very few zander were listed amongst their exceptional fish, notable exceptions being, in 1968, a fourteen and a half pounder on a Hi-Lo and in 1972, a 13 lb 3 oz fish on an Abu Killer. In 1970 Abu rated their Killer as a 'must' for zander. But in their catalogues in general few plugs are listed as 'musts', and the 1974 version of *Tight Lines* lists only a spinner (Atom) with a specific link-up to zander.

It is of interest that Abu's Killer is not unlike Normark's Rapala and Creek Chub's Viper, also rated highly as zander plugs. These resemble long, slim, silvery fish, and similar plugs have succeeded on occasions in Britain. We would tentatively suggest that in our experience, and on present evidence, live- and deadbaits are more successful than plugs on most occasions. The great attraction of plug fishing for zander is that when these occasions arise great sport can be had and probably more fish hooked and landed than when fish baits are used. It may be that the zander, being a rather sluggish fish without the turn of speed of the pike, is simply not prepared to chase a moderately fast-moving plug. Or it may well be that zander spend more time scavenging on the bottom than do pike and perch. We know one lake, admittedly not crowded with zander, where despite intensive use of spinners and plugs, not a single zander has been caught on anything other than fish baits or lobworms.

The last water was a crystal-clear gravel pit, and it is a fact that a considerable number of plug-caught zander in this country were taken under muddy or slightly coloured conditions on the Great Ouse Relief Channel. The fish were located as a shoal or hunting pack and the plugs were worked slowly through them. The fish caught were mostly in the two to three pound range and almost all of them were caught by casting parallel to the bank where the zander were chasing fry.

Most of these zander fell to single plugs of the River Runt Spook type or small Rapalas, or to relatively small jointed plugs. Just as many fell to spoons as to plugs. There is one major difference between the Great Ouse Relief Channel on the one hand and many other fenland drains and the Dutch drains on the other, and that is that the GORC is very wide (about one hundred yards) and relatively deep (about twelve feet). On the narrower and shallower Dutch drains plugs have succeeded well with zander for years and we fully expect that in the Fens they will really come into their own in future years.

For the present we would suggest using plugs like the Viper, Whopper Stopper's Hellcat, Norman's Shiner-minnow, Normark's Rapalas, and Abu's

At last big zander like this are being caught on lures in this country.

Killer and Hi-Lo, preferably in the smaller sizes and preferably in silver. The best times for plug fishing in clear water conditions seem to be at dawn for the first hour and at dusk, just as in bait fishing. There is no doubt that the zander come on the feed at this time.

Night plugging has also been successful on some still waters. Naturally you have to know the water well both with respect to where you put the cast and also where you put your feet! A fish taking in the dark when you least expect it does your heart no good at all. At one time Barrie did a great deal of night plugging and spinning for trout and would confirm that too many surprises in the dead of a dark night are no good for anyone's well-being. Three such takes, particularly if you are dreaming at the time, are enough to send you off home for a short rest. Trout and perch both give a little warning pluck, however, before the main pull, but with pike and zander this is not usually the case: they hit the lure and that's that. If you are taken by surprise it is an easy matter to miss.

Results on plugs during coloured water conditions on the Relief Channel have been better than under clear water conditions. We remember one youngster taking four nice zander in as many casts by working a small silvery plug along the edge of the water. Several other anglers have taken nice fish *between* the reed beds and the bank when the river has been in flood: in these conditions the water is not merely coloured but *dirty*, carrying rafts of rubbish and quantities of submerged debris. But the zander get close to the bank, behind the reeds, and despite the oxtail soup appearance of the water good fish can be taken on bright plugs.

Another way to take zander on this water is to use a deep-diving or sinking plug and work it close to the bottom, particularly over the last few yards of the retrieve. Quite a few zander sit at the break of slope down at about eleven to twelve feet and will follow a plug that creeps up the slope. If the plug snatches at the bottom, kicking up little puffs of mud, then so much the better. They'll also tackle a plummet or paternoster lead retrieved in this way, as Barrie knows from his own experiences!

Even in coloured water conditions it seems that dawn and dusk are the best times, although ones's chances during the day are far better if the water is not clear. One technique is to keep a careful watch on the water surface about ten yards out from the bank and cast to any strikes. Zander often strike at fish near the surface when there is a good chop on the water, but of course the strike may easily pass unnoticed. Best of all is to spot a pack and detect the direction in which they are moving. By adopting a quiet approach they can be followed for some distance.

We think that, in the future, plug fishing in the Fen drains in general will become easier: quite a lot of the shallower drains will respond to more varied types of plug and to more varied techniques. But we cannot see zander chasing plugs with the ferocity of a hunting pike. Having watched zander take a plug it must be said that they follow it almost leisurely before taking a firm hold. Like perch, they really take a good look at it first. Occasionally they may take a pluck-pluck at it but then usually come short in the end. Clearly, from what we have said, plug fishing for zander has a long way to go in this country and we suspect that this may be to some extent true for the continental fisheries.

In 1985 we discovered an especially good zander catching spoon, the Lazer Lure made by Renosky Lures of the USA. These have a fish painted on one side (a shad, trout, perch etc.) and have a smooth silver finish on the other. They are wobbly spoons, cast well, and can be fished at any depth from three inches deep downwards. It would seem that the prime feature of attraction is the simulated fish, Barrie's zander coming on a water full of bleak where the Lazer Lure closely resembled bleak. This selective behaviour possibly ties in with the zander's fish eating habits for it is known to ignore sea fish deadbaits whilst readily taking freshwater deadbaits of species upon which it normally feeds. Once again these zander fell under very coloured water conditions and it is becoming increasingly obvious that these conditions are ideal for lure fishing for zander. Normally very coloured, dirty water puts off the lure fishing enthusiast, but now we have a common species that revels in just those conditions.

CHAPTER TWENTY-EIGHT

Spinning for other fish, including Coarse Fish

In these islands where lure fishing for pike and perch has always been popular, interest in recent years has received a fillip with the importing of North American techniques, and yet it is need of much greater exploitation as far as other species are concerned. Lure fishing for salmon is a well-trodden path, and not really within our compass, so we shall say no more about it except to note that relating taking colour and the lure size to the exact water spate conditions on different waters is almost an exact science to many salmon anglers. We have taken many hill-stream trout on small plugs, but on most trout waters today plug fishing is at least frowned upon, if not banned altogether. Not so in Ireland, where many of the big loughs are open to plug fishing. And the Irish trout provide a case of the required 'exploitation' that we have mentioned: on one large and famous lough the locals had for years used small spinners in the lea of the islands to take smallish trout in shallow water, and yet Wagstaffe and colleagues caught several trout over ten pounds in weight by braving the open lough and following the contours with an echo-sounder. They used plugs and other lures to find the taking depths, really stuck to their task, and eventually came up with a superb technique, the possibility of which had existed for years and yet had not been exploited.

Big sea-trout certainly take plugs well on some fenland waters, as do the fewer big brownies in with them, but the locations are well-guarded secrets. What interests us is that the lures should be fished deep even when the sea-trout are leaping in numbers. At dusk and dawn a few will fall to a fast, shallow-fished silver plug or spinner, but mostly a deep and moderately fast retrieve is needed – faster than you would retrieve for pike and perch for example.

Very occasionally we read of other coarse fish being caught on lures – bream, tench, carp, eels, and even roach. Most species are predatory to the extent that they will sometimes eat fish, particularly in spring and early summer when fry abound in the weedy shallows. Probably exploitation will be difficult. Bream will certainly take large lures, both spoons and plugs, but usually in spring and in our experience, usually in Ireland! Even the bream of the Norfolk Broads do not seem to fall regularly to spinners during the Easter break in the close season, but Barrie has had six in a day on Veltic on one Fenland drain.

What seems a real possibility is the construction of very small plugs, less than one and a half inches in length, and fishing them on fine lines through shoals of roach, tench etc. in the early part of the season. Of course, very small plugs are already on the market, but it would be much easier and cheaper to make your own, particularly bearing in mind the probable loss of them to marauding pike. The smaller the plug is, the nearer it will approach some 'flies' in construction – the polystickle for example. We now know that these various trout flies or lures are highly successful with coarse fish, whether they are fished on standard fly tackle or on float-fished outfits, and there is little doubt that tiny plugs would succeed. The important thing may be to fish them through big shoals of surface-priming fish, since this is where we have best succeeded in Ireland.

Barrie's best bream on spinner (Mepps) went 6½lb, and on one occasion he had several seven pound plus bream fall off a six inch Jim Vincent spoon. This was in Ireland, but in Fenland he took three bream averaging 4½lb from a small drain in winter, two of which were fairly hooked with the tail treble of a Veltic in their mouths. His son Jeremy had a 6¾lb fully scaled common carp on a two and a half inch Veltic, this one being an autumn fish. Most anglers who do a lot of spinning will have caught the occasional carp species: barbel and tench, if not bream or smaller species. On the Continent large roach and hybrids are taken on small bar-spoons, and bream too. The question is, can the method be adapted in some way to make it more regularly productive? Various anglers have suggested that the use of very small spinners of the bar-spoon type might be productive, but it is not something which has yet caught on.

If we look at the problem from another viewpoint we may get a clue or two. Fly fishing has long been known to catch plenty of carp species: rudd, dace and chub in particular, but the advent of reservoir trouting and the use of fast stripped lures and large flies, has opened up yet other possibilities. Probably most anglers will have heard of the bream catches from Grafham water, made by trout anglers, and these were not small bream either. Now some of these large 'flies' are rather plug-like, and others have enough flash in them to resemble tiny spinners, so it may well be that tiny bar-spoons, with single hooks, could prove very attractive to the larger specimens of the carp family. However, it would be difficult to fish such spinners on fly tackle, and ludicrous to fish them on the spinning tackle normally used by anglers after pike, or even perch. What is needed is the ultra-light approach, using lines in the 2–4 lb b.s. bracket, no traces, and tiny spinners. We have had some extremely light but steely rods made in recent years. They are a delight to use, and with this equipment we have hopes of a much greater variety of species. It might be added that the kind of fixed spool reel you need for this fishing is one of the tiny but well made types – a small Shakespeare for example, or a Mitchell 408. The places to try are the known shoaling areas at the beginning of the season, or likely holes in a variable river. So far we've had a lot of perch and chub.

CHAPTER TWENTY-NINE

Spinning for salmon

by

D. L. Steuart

The first thing to understand when trying to catch salmon is that they don't eat in freshwater; they cannot, their stomachs won't allow it – so you're on a loser to start with! Having grasped this fact one can appreciate that it is factors other than *necessity* to eat that causes a salmon to take hold of spinner, plug, fly, worm, prawn or whatever, whether it be a predatory reflex action, aggressiveness, territorial assertion, or downright stupidity. Our non-migratory species, will, when in feeding mood, eat a variety of foods, and depending upon quantity, the tiniest food forms to the largest they can swallow, and although conditions effect their feeding patterns to a certain extent, they have got to eat sometime and so are vulnerable to the angler. The 'prodigals', however, fat with excesses from 'overseas', and with stomach atrophied, have to be induced to take a bait* by the application of a well-known general procedure, based on the experiences of the past and present experts of the written word, and aligned to one's own lore.

This generally accepted basic set of rules is closely allied to water temperatures, for the obvious reason that all fishes' metabolism is tied to this, and in this respect a salmon is no different to any other fish. When the water is cold, and the salmon's metabolic rate is low, it has neither the inclination nor the energy to move far for a bait, and so the salmon angler endeavours to present his bait as close as possible to the fish, at eye level. As the water warms and a salmon becomes capable of greater energy, the angler fishes higher in the water and generally a little faster.

*In this chapter the word 'bait' means spinner of whatever type is being used.

The well known temperature of 48°F which most salmon fly-fishermen use as a guide to decide whether to fish near the surface with a floating line, or deeper with sunk line, can also be used as a guide by the spinning man to change his style or manner of presenting his bait. Some salmon fishers tend to use one method for the whole season, and doubtless lose some possible chances of a fish because of it.

There are reasons other than temperature, of course, for fishing with a certain size or type of spinner in a certain way, and I will try and elaborate on these by explaining why I use a particular method and bait as we explore the field of 'Spinning for Salmon'.

You cannot catch fish if you're not fishing where they are, so it is as well to familiarise oneself with the current speeds and river-bed contours where salmon like to rest, while awaiting conditions to urge them to move upstream. They generally like to lie in fast water, or appear to, in similarconditions to those one would associate with barbel swims. I say, 'appear to'. I have perceived that although a salmon is at first glance lying in fast, strong, water, it is usually positioned where a division of current or turbulence creates backflow, an easier flow in which the fish can maintain position with little effort. This can be seen when particles of detritus are travelling with the flow, and the behaviour of such matter is observed as it enters the salmon's 'lie'. However, as a generalisation, we look for salmon where the water flows fast.

The obvious lies therefore are the outside of bends, where the river flows strong and deep; in our southern rivers, often where piles have been hammered to contain the river by arresting bank erosion. Deep-cut banks caused by fast currents; narrow stretches creating a speeding-up of flow; gradients; all create possible lies. Fish like to lie just upstream of a gradient where there is a pull over their backs as the flow accelerates, influenced by the increased velocity down the incline. Sometimes it is the tail of a pool – sometimes not, but a 'run-in' to a pool.

Dictated by the angle of the gradient, fish may or may not lie in the water flowing over them. It may be too fast, too turbulent, and without obstruction to create short-rest lies, as some rocky waterfalls give to ascending fish.

The pool below a gradient will hold fish in various places, dependent upon its character. There could be fish lying alongside the main flow into the pool: if it is deep, they might lie in a back-current underneath the white water where it enters the pool, and not always near the bottom, alienating to flow. If the flow enters to one side of the pool they may lie at the current's edge or alongside the bank edge – smooth rock faces, piling, or straight-cut banking of any sort they favour, and will lie at all depths between the river bed and surface alongside these, again the depth at which they lie subjected by a flow to their liking.

Cover is important. Salmon will sometimes prefer lying in shallow water where there is cover, rather than in deep water where conditions would cause them to be easily visible, i.e. slow flows and gin-clear water. High banks will give cover, as will trees, bridges, and any overhang. Remove the cover as some misinformed anglers and fishery administrators are inclined to do, and you remove the fish.

Groynes generally create the conditions that fish like, but it is unlikely such features would not be recognisable even to the novice.

One very important consideration, as much when spinning for salmon as any other fish – *keep out of sight of the fish*!

It's about time we did some fishing.

PATERNOSTER-SPINNING

Early season fishing for 'springers' can be a hard, cold, fruitless job, but if successful, the prize is so great that all the effort and discomfort becomes well worth while. In my view, there is no other fish so beautiful and symmetrically perfect as a white-bellied, silver-flanked, steel-blue-backed, spring salmon. I live in the south, near London, and the nearest salmon fishing available to me is the river Test, the Hampshire Avon, and the Dorset Stour. All these rivers are fairly fast-flowing and gravel-bottomed, and when fishing for the few springers that still enter these rivers, from the opening day of February 1st for a couple of months or so, for reasons that I will explain later, I favour spinning paternoster fashion. This is a fairly simple way of fishing a bait very close to the river bed, a bait that travels very slowly through the spring lies.

Basically, terminal tackle is simple. The chosen line, 15–20 lb breaking strain, is tied to a ball-ring swivel; a nylon trace approximately three foot long of the same strength as the line is attached to the other end of the swivel, and to the trace is tied a link swivel to attach the bait of your choice. From the top-eye of the ball-bearing swivel a six to ten inch length of nylon hangs, of much lighter b.s. in case it gets snagged (I favour 6 lb b.s.), and to this nylon I tie a link for the easy changing of pear leads.

During the course of a day's fishing the pear lead size may be altered several times to counteract different pressures on the line of current speed and depth, which would cause a bait to travel too fast across the river, too high in the water, or in the case of too heavy a lead, not to travel across by the current's pressure on the line at all, but remained anchored. Lead size is all-important; don't be afraid of it. In some lies in heavy water you sometimes need two ounces or more.

246

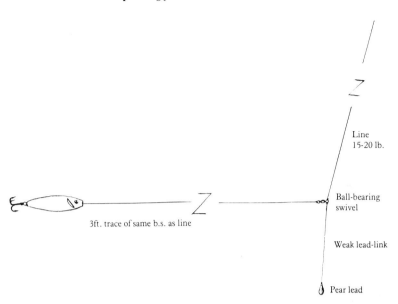

The method of fishing is to cast across the river in a downstream direction at an angle of about 45°. Line is allowed to flow from the spool to shoot the lead to the 'bottom', the bail is closed (fixed spool reel) or the gears engaged (multiplier), and with rod held high, the tackle travels in an arc from its cast position to the near bank as the current pushes on the across-stream line, lead, and bait. The farther downstream one casts and the higher the rod is held, the slower the tackle will travel across, but avoid casting too far down – a very long line will make hook penetration more difficult.

If lead size is right one can feel it dragging bottom as it comes over, and if it occasionally catches, a slight lift of the rod will free it to continue its journey. When the tackle reaches the angler's bank, it is rewound, the angler takes a few steps downstream, and recasts.

By this method the river is searched methodically yard after yard in the hope of putting the bait very close to the fish, right on the bottom, for as mentioned early on in this chapter, when the water is cold, as it is in early season, a salmon has neither the inclination nor the energy to chase a bait far or fast.

Salmon will enter a river readily enough in water at almost freezing point, 33°F anyway, especially on a spring tide, and will move slowly upriver until confronted by any obstruction such as a weir, waterfall, or any gradient that is steep enough to cause white water. In the cold water they haven't the energy to surmount difficult water, so if one is lucky enough to be able to fish the lower beats in early spring – especially the first major obstacles –

before the water temperature rises to approximately 10°F above freezing, there should be a few new fish waiting to be caught by correct bait presentation. After the water reaches the low 'forties', fish will start negotiating falls and move upstream at a faster pace.

So we hope we are fishing water where early salmon have reached; we are using the paternoster method as we know we must get down to the fish and fish slowly, and as fish may be very scarce we know we must search the 'ground' thoroughly, but what of baits? There are several considerations here and if we start with the salmon we realise that in its cold state it needs a jolt, a high impact to cause a reaction, and so we start with size – we use a large bait. We must then consider the water in which the salmon is lying. Is it clear or dirty, deep or shallow? We assume it is going to be fairly heavy, fast water, in February/March, the time of rains and melting snows; and we also take notice of that in our bait assessment.

Assuming rains have made the river a bit coloured, as well as needing a large bait, for the salmon to really get the message we need a bright colour. The Avon favourite is yellow; in devons, the yellow-belly, and in heavy, coloured conditions, I would use a three and a half inch bait. There is nothing to beat a light wooden or plastic devon, for paternoster work. Any heavy metal job fished by the method would soon catch bottom and snag; the wooden devon, however, in any situation where the current eases, instead of fishing deeper will float up and keep clear, and plastic patterns, Dibro for example, need such little flow to keep them working that they rarely ever snag either. Without wooden or plasic devons we couldn't fish a *short*-link paternoster with the bait only a few inches from the river bed, following the contours. As depth increases, the lead takes down the bait; as it shallows, the lead bounces up the slope with bait following instead of catching up.

In very dirty water the big three and a half inch yellow-belly is necessary even in shallow rivers to give enough impact, whereas in shallow water three foot or less, with just a touch of colour, I would either change down to a two and a half inch yellow-belly, or change the colour and retain the large size – brown/gold, black/gold – considering a three and a half inch yellow-belly to be just too much on shallows, that might put a fish off. In deeper water with only a little colour, it would be as well to use the large size and bright colour while temperatures are low, as even slight turbidity causes a deterioration in visibility the deeper it gets, remembering it is 'impact' we are after.

In gin-clear water – and we've found this at the beginning of the season once or twice in recent years – I would still take my first consideration as read and start with a large bait, but a brown/gold, or black/gold, wooden devon, or a natural sprat, golden sprat, or what I call my kipper-devon. Natural sprats are soft, but mounted on a spinning flight (a celluloid-vaned flight is light enough to be used paternoster fashion) they catch salmon, *and*

Three nice fish on plastic devon.

they smell nice. Golden sprat catches a lot of fish but I've never liked the smell much, although Ken and Barrie's method of de-formalising might help in this direction. I've tried smoked sprat – they look OK and smell OK, but break up. If you are lazy, stick with the sober-coloured devons, but for a change-bait that lasts I have recently been using my 'kipper-devon'. This is simply a celluloid-vaned flight with a devon-shaped length of cork glued to the mounting-pin. The cork is made slim to allow a wrapping of skin, taken from the flank of a lovely golden kipper. It is kept in place by a winding of elastic cotton. The skin, shading from blue-black to golden, can be wrapped in such a way as to give the bait a dark back and a golden belly. It's a devon that smells nice, and when a fish takes hold, perhaps tastes nice. The cork body gives it buoyancy to fish paternoster style.

As the water warms – getting into the low forties – it is usually clearer, and with the fish a little livelier we cut down bait size to two and a half inch, lengthen the lead-link a few inches to fish the bait a *little* above the salmon, and decrease lead size slightly so that the bait fishes across a mite faster. Bait colour is sober. But despite the salmon's slightly increased liveliness, if the

249

river is still very coloured we return to the early method of big bait – perhaps three inch instead of three and a half inch inch – yellow-belly,shorter lead-link, and fish very slowly. This is not so much for high impact, but to give the fish a chance to see the bait.

Later in the spring, when water temperatures are in the upper forties, we may dispense with the paternoster altogether and fish a different method, but will always return to it after heavy rains, when conditions dictate that we again have to put the bait right into the salmon's mouth.

A further point about fishing the paternoster when temperatures have reached the low forties and rising, and the water is clear; we can start increasing the number of steps between casts. The fish will see a bait farther away, and when in taking mood be prepared to move farther to intercept it or chase it, and so we can work through the river much faster. We can also confine ourselves to fishing the obvious lies that are appearing as the river levels drop – they're not always so easily read when the river is high, and then a fish could turn up anywhere! Going through faster, plus the lengthening of daylight, will mean that we have time to work through a pool twice. The second time through will sometimes produce a fish. Probably, first time through woke it up, and second time through decided its interest.

I favour the paternoster and the light devons as *the* method for early season for so many reasons. It fishes slowly; it takes the bait right down to the fish; if the lead gets snagged the weak lead-link will break and the bait is retained; the bait rarely gets snagged; in the fast water of early season the devon does not create drag and increase speed as it comes across; it commences fishing as soon as it enters the water; being buoyant, the devon will spin even if the lead is allowed to act as an anchor to hold the bait in one position for a known difficult fish; it will fish right under the far bank by allowing the lead to shoot to the bottom upon entry, before the current acts on the line and brings it across; and it's the easiest of ways to correctly present a bait early season. When fish are scarce it can also be the most boring and tiring – what I call 'the hard flog of spring salmon fishing.'

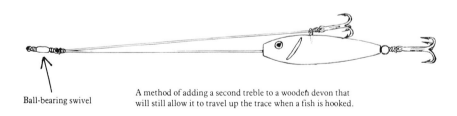

Ball-bearing swivel

A method of adding a second treble to a wooden devon that will still allow it to travel up the trace when a fish is hooked.

ORTHODOX SPINNING

Unfortunately (or fortunately; depends how you look at it), it is not possible to use the paternoster in all rivers. In turbulent rocky rivers, small and large, much associated with salmon fishing, it is not practical to fish with a hanging lead, unless you own a lead mine, for it will continually be getting snagged. One then fishes in far more orthodox fashion with up-trace lead, Wye lead, or Jardine lead, and fishes as deep as possible consistent with keeping the tackle from getting snagged. I still favour the wooden or plastic devons and apply all the aforegoing lore as to bait size, colour etc., but some anglers who know their rivers very well will use a heavy metal devon, with or without up-trace lead as conditions demand, knowing just how deep they can allow it to go, and just where to raise it out of trouble. The knowledge probably cost them dear at first.

With the wooden devon, if the lead is felt to touch bottom or rock, a slight lift to clear it should also lift the devon out of trouble.

The method of fishing is still across and down, trying to cover as much holding water as possible. I have the feeling that were it possible, the paternoster would outfish the orthodox in early season, although many hundreds of fish fall to the latter method. Compared to the rivers where we can fish paternoster-style, the others hold so many fish that sooner or later any method of bait presentation is bound to pass near a fool fish willing to take.

Long spoons and bar-spoons can be used to fish salmon early season in shallow streams by making a fairly long cast downstream, to fish them across as slow as possible. The trouble arises when trying to get them to go deep, especially bar-spoons. They create such a pull when fished downstream, that unless very heavily leaded they fish close to the surface. Such spoons are best left until the water warms up, when they can be fished in a different manner.

With river temperatures in the upper forties we can start on more interesting ways of spinning providing the water is a good colour – clear or just slightly coloured. With a slight colour we might still fish paternoster-style, but make our casts at a lesser angle downstream so that it will fish round faster. In clear water we can dispense with the link-lead and fish more orthodox with up-trace leads to devons, toby spoons, bar-spoons, wobbling spoons, plugs – anything that the angler thinks might interest a fish. Sizes of devons will have dropped to two or two and a half inch, and other baits will range about that size, with wobbling spoons and plugs perhaps just slightly larger. Bar-spoons with their greater vibration impact can be a little smaller, although I personally will still use, say, a Mepp No. 5 Aglia in the Avon or Stour where the fish run large. On the River Test though, I will drop to a size 4 during the same period, for the salmon are a few pounds lighter, so there we have yet another consideration factor in choice of bait size.

We might fish a few square casts so that the bait travels across as we *wind* back, controlling the fishing depth by rod angle and winding speed, with the bait coming across slightly downstream, and making an inviting turn as we wind when the bait has come three-quarters of the way across to the angler's bank.

Once temperatures have reached the fifties I will fish some of the day with Mepps or similar bar-spoons in preference to other baits, and do a deal of casting *slightly* upstream, winding back so that the bait comes across square to the current with the blade giving a broader image to the upstream-facing fish. One must fish small rivers very carefully when adopting this method for you are fishing for fish that are opposite you in the river, and careless movement on the bank or in the water, although it may not always frighten fish away, will make them nervous and unlikely to take a bait.

UPSTREAM SPINNING

Providing the water is clear, the low fifties are also the river temperatures when I have the occasional throw directly upstream in fast water, winding back fairly rapidly. Although some anglers are under the impression that a fish has to move fast to take a bait coming downstream at speed, it is a fallacy, and requires less effort from the fish than the taking of a bait just dangled in the fast water. The fish seeing the bait coming down, may move its position slightly and simply intercept it with little effort, and even if it chases the bait downstream, no extra energy is required. If we assume the fast water is travelling at 4 mph and it needs a speed of 1 mph to work the bar-spoon, to make it revolve we must wind at a speed in excess of 5 mph. But a fish travelling with the current has only to swim at a little over 1 mph to overtake the bait as the current takes it downstream. To take a bait dangled in the current it must swim a little more than the current speed.

Come the summer and low water conditions, very much more of my spinning is then directly upstream. There are, in my opinion, lots of advantages to be had by fishing in this manner, which increase as the summer advances. One of them, and a very important one where salmon are concerned, is that I seem to have a more successful number of landings to takes. I have always had a few salmon come adrift during the course of a season, and every salmon angler I know has similar experiences, so if casting up and winding down increases the chance of a hook taking a fair hold, it's very important.

'Tis' a grand fellow ye are!'

If a salmon intercepts the bait as it comes down, the hook should lodge in a corner of its mouth; if it follows down and turns back as it takes, which salmon often do, the hold should also be in the scissors. This is a very secure hook-hold, although the 'kiting' effect of such a hold on a large, long-jawed, cock fish, can be a little disconcerting.

When a fish is hooked, the downstream angler is already in a better position for playing it from below, than is the angler who hooks a fish from upstream. The salmon will often take off upriver, and this gives the down-stream angler the advantage of having the fish fighting the current as well as himself. If weeds have grown, there is less fear of entanglement in playing a fish from below; if weeds are abundant, it is often advisable to cast up and spin down the runs between them when it is not possible to fish downstream.

If cut weed is coming down, providing it isn't too damn much, it is also feasible to get a few casts in by throwing upstream and winding down with the stuff.

Another advantage is that as the current bears upon the line, one can cast a longish line upstream to the far bank, and spin down that bank a long way before the bait leaves it and starts coming across. And because the bait will come down in a fairly straight line it is a very quick way of covering a lot of water, for the bait must have been seen and been in close proximity to all the fish, by casting up alongside the lies.

The depth at which the bait fishes can also be fairly easily controlled.

In the low fifties I will have used Mepp size 4, or 3 if very clear, with devons of a half to two inches, and as I concentrate more on upstream work toward and during summer, I will have dropped to a Mepp 2. Should I feel like a change I use metal devons for their ease in casting without up-trace lead. In very low water even a tiny one inch devon or no. 1 or 0 Mepp will take fish. These small baits can be cast to a fish several times without worrying it unduly.

Over the last couple of years when upstream spinning, if fishing a small bar-spoon where I have needed lead to aid casting, or to fish it deeper, I have placed the lead right down near the spinner to act as a head for the bait – like a Voblex. I have fished this way since having a hell of a pull when winding down fast, but not connecting. As I finished the retrieve I saw a salmon swimming down directly behind the up-trace lead and it occurred to me that on occasions when I have had a pull and not hooked the fish, it could well be a fish that hit the up-trace lead. When casting up and retrieving a bait and using an up-trace lead, the first thing the fish sees is the

A brace to the Mepp 3.

lead, and if it's really in a taking mood, it may well hit the lead before the following spinner. The trouble is, it rarely gives one a second chance!

It will be noticed that as the temperature of the river has risen through the year, so we have used smaller baits, fished higher in the water, and faster. As fish become livelier through the year, so they will refuse larger baits, or even be frightened by them. I don't pretend to understand this but have observed fish that have refused a bait, been rested, then taken a smaller one. Although I have caught salmon by continually casting to them with small baits, quite often continually showing them a large bait will cause them to move house.

There are many observations one can make about salmon taking spinning baits. For example, fresh run fish will sometimes take a larger bait of fish that have been in the river for a while, and yet, toward the autumn, stale fish may well start hitting large baits again. In the latter case it could be an aggressiveness that becomes positive as the spawning season nears commencement, as I have watched cock salmon chasing trout and salmon parr off the redds during cutting.

SMALL RIVERS

Fishing some of the smaller, natural, rocky rivers, often with heavily bushed and treed banks, does tend to cut down on one's ability to cover all the water where a fish might rest, but then such waters are usually fairly easy to read and the salmon lies rather obvious. It may be that one has only one or two stances from which to fish a stretch of water, and to cover it as well as possible will require upstream, downstream, and square casting, all from one position. This may mean adding or removing lead to cast to a new position and fish at the right depth and speed – not so critical later in the year in the small river, but important early in the season. This, I think, is why so many of the locals prefer worming – an art if fished well, and more certain of fishing right.

Some of the casting must be very acurate in streams, as when placing a bait into a small gap amid or beneath foliage on the far bank, flicking it across from amidst foliage on one's side, or trying a long one upstream between branches that try and pluck at the offering with gnarled fingertips – sometimes successfully.

Such casting is much easier when all the weight is in one place – at the end of the line – so either use baits with sufficient weight 'built-in', or place the lead close to it, as I have suggested for upstream fishing. Some anglers like heavy metal devons for this sort of work, and catch a lot of fish on them too!

Temperature changes affect the fish of small streams more readily than in the larger river, as such changes can happen more quickly. A large river is less likely to be affected by a small change in air temperature, but the lesser volume of a stream may well be affected enough to stop fish taking, or start them showing an interest!

HOOKING

I once saw three salmon holding station over eight feet of water. They were only some three feet below the surface, sitting comfortably on top of a backflow, although the current over their backs was fast and strong. I flicked a devon upstream of them, watched it come flickering downstream past them and saw the smallest of the three, a fish about seven pounds, swing out and follow the devon. As it swung round into the slack water the salmon closed its mouth over it. I did nothing except continue winding, expecting to feel the rod go down. In the same second as it took the bait the salmon opened its mouth and the devon came out *spinning*. I didn't feel a thing! The fish turned back to lie with the other two and showed no further interest. Although I intermittently tried various baits during the course of the day, all three fish took no notice, although in the evening the seven pounder did take a prawn. Pity about the other two. One was 20lb. and the other about 14lb.

I have seen salmon swim up to the bait and knock it with their nose with mouth shut. I mention this and the previous instance to show that there can be problems with hooking salmon. Occasionally one gets a very sharp knock as a bait comes across, and I often wonder if it is a warning to the intruder to keep away, and whether a salmon does it with the mouth closed. It always excites me anyway, as another cast to the same spot often results in a proper take.

The main difficulty lies in the strength of a salmon's jaw, for as in nearly all animals, the jaw muscle are the strongest. When a salmon takes hold of a bait and the angler strikes, I don't think he moves it within the fish's mouth at all and so doesn't drive in the hooks. Instead, the salmon feels the pull, opens its mouth and ejects the lot. When fishing down and across early in the season, and the salmon hasn't moved far for the bait and is probably still facing upstream while holding the bait, a good hook-hold is least likely. Later in the season when one is fishing square, faster, or upstream, when a salmon moves farther to a bait and then *turns* back to its lie, a good hook-hold is much more on the cards.

A hook-hold here might not penetrate the maxillary and fall out.

Some experts say that you should never strike, but let the weight of the fish set the hook, as it *will* turn away if it doesn't feel a pull. Some anglers I know, use very stiff rods and strike hard. I've tried both methods, but still fish fall off. Probably a delayed hard pull is best, but a quicker strike in summer when grilse are running – fish which are lively and eject a bait quickly.

Another problem is the long bait – devon, Toby, etc. specially early in the season, or in dirty water when one is using large sizes. I'm positive that salmon often take hold crosswise, and with only a treble at the tail the hook isn't within the mouth of the fish. I have got over this problem a little by adding a centre-treble to some of my devons and spoons, but in a manner that still allows the devon to slide up the line out of the salmon's mouth when the fish is hooked, and for the spoon to swing free. A devon or spoon that remains in a hooked salmon's jaw may be waggled about in its effort to get rid of it, and so lever out the hooks.

If one is prepared to go the trouble of replacing baits that continual casting will destroy, one way of overcoming the hooking difficulties to some extent is to use natural baits whenever possible. Natural sprat and a hard strike rarely result in a missed fish, as the soft bait doesn't stop the hooks moving when the strike is made. Golden sprat will last longer, as the formalin preservative toughens the flesh, but hooks can still be struck through it.

257

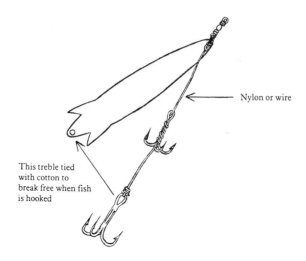

Nylon or wire

This treble tied
with cotton to
break free when fish
is hooked

Superior hooking is possible with twin trebles
for fish that take crosswise.

When a small bait is wanted, a natural minnow makes a good spinning bait although I haven't yet had success with it, but I haven't used it much for salmon. I've caught a lot of trout with it though. Some old-time anglers have taken pretty hefty bags of salmon with natural minnow, so I guess it's only the modern angler's terrific choice of baits that has caused it to fall out of favour. I was going to fish it hard in 1976, but with the drought conditions there weren't any fish to throw at!

There are times when a fresh, lively salmon will hammer into a bait with terrific enthusiasm, hooking itself solidly. They have smashed into floats when I have been retrieving them along the surface on days when I've been coarse fishing. Such suicidal fish are rare unfortunately, but knowing they will sometimes have a go at a surface bait wound upstream, did give me the idea of trotting a spinner to a difficult lie and retrieving slowly back. I have caught one or two fish like this. One was caught where the high but sloping bank made the angler very obviously visible when he cast to fish, so a spinner was trotted, retrieved, a good fish took and was landed. Another angler, seeing the float from a distance, thought the fish was caught on worm. I didn't enlighten him.

But back to this hooking business. Remember that when spinning, the length of line is ever-changing, and should you strike, you must strike damned hard on a long line, but a lot less hard on a short one; the latter specially when fishing lighter tackle in low water conditions. And don't fish with the rod pointing down the line, or a really hard take can then cause tackle failure.

Things to be wary of when a salmon is hooked is head-shaking for one. It thumps the rod like hell, can loosen the hook hold, and frightens me to death if it's a big fish. I always ease pressure when this happens, the fish usually stops and then goes off on a long run. Another time the hook-hold may give, is when a fish explodes from the water, but as this is usually the termination of a run the angler is not holding it hard anyway, so there's little can be done – unless one believes in the power of prayer.

PLAYING A SALMON

Whether or not Barrie and Ken wish me to write about playing the fish I don't know, but it's not much good solidly hooking the thing if you don't get it on the bank.

A salmon is often a big fish. It is also a strong fish, a fast fish, an acrobatic fish, and a fish that often likes to move around relieving the angler of a lot of line in the process. And this last is one thing that novice anglers don't really appreciate; that it is always best to keep a fish on as short a line as possible. If a fish takes off downstream – get off after it. If it takes off up-stream – get off after it. The more line you lose from the reel, the longer it will take to get the fish back into a controllable position.

Now I don't mean by that last remark that if a big fish takes off you should hang on hard – that's the last thing you should do even with heavy tackle, for either the hook will tear out or break, or the line will break, or something disastrous will happen. What you should do is chase it upstream or down, letting as little line off the reel as you can, and retrieving as you near the animal. With a fish that's run downstream, pass it by and get below it, for you should try and play a big fish from downstream of it.

The foregoing is fine for clear banks, but what of obstructed banks? Sometimes the obstructions can be traversed, trees can be passed by taking the rod around; the river may be shallow enough to wade round and, if you have a companion, marvels can be accomplished. All this is necessary when a fish runs down, but not so if a fish goes up, as (unless it goes around a bend) the angler can usually get the fish back from below, since the fish is fighting both current and angler. If the bank is clear, however, as I said in the beginning, get off after it!

What if a big fish has gone a long way down and the obstructions are impassable? You can try pumping it up if you are restricted in either direction, but if the bank upstream is open, walk the fish up. When the fish has finished its downward rush and turned to face the current, wind tight, clamp your hand upon the reel drum and walk upriver. The fish will usually

Dave Steuart tails a salmon caught spinning with his 'toy reel'.

come up with you without fuss so long as you keep the pressure steady. Walk it up as far as you think necessary, or as far as you can go, then walk down retrieving line until you are opposite the fish or have to repeat the procedure. The fish may go down again and you may have to go 'walkies' a lot before eventually winning the day.

The first thing I do if I hook a salmon of any size upstream of a bridge, sluice, obstructed bank, or anywhere that I cannot follow down, is walk it up well away from trouble if it is at all feasible. I feel a lot happier and in a much more masterful position once I've done that.

If a fish has gone down and you cannot get it back, there are still a few courses open. You can let all the line from the reel and send a companion down to try and cast across it. If he is successful, cut your line, go down and re-tie. If you are on your own and possess a spare reel or spool of line, you can let off the line, tie it to a tree, go down with the rod and reel fitted with the spare line, cast and pick up the original line, try and gain some slack, then cut and tie to the new stuff. You can look for a largish tree branch (not waterlogged), tie your line to it, chuck it well out, and hope to pick it up below with the fish still attached – or you can go swimming. Rather you than me.

Salmon play pretty fair as a rule. They don't dive into weeds and snags, unless they are stale fish that have learnt the area. One place I fished last season, where because of the low water the new fish became potted, they used to disappear during the day beneath an old turbine house in dead slack water. When they came out in the evening, a fish hooked would belt straight back underneath.

Anglers will always argue amiably. When using a fixed spool reel, Barrie recommends back-pedalling to a running fish, but I disagree. It may be adequate to play some fish this way, but I personally don't like it for fast-moving fish like game fish, or when fishing with very fine lines. The reels are not balanced to revolve fast through the gears and one gets a 'rock' action when a fish is bolting. I admit that to play a fish from the clutch it is essential to have a reel with an ultra-smooth clutch, with no high spots, but there are such models and regular servicing to keep them so is entirely up to the angler.

After a big fish has been landed that has taken a lot of line, remove the terminal tackle and let the loose line flow freely downstream from the spool. This will remove the kinks put in the line by the drum revolving as the fish ran. It is a good idea to do this on any reel occasionally, for the line well down a spool will get crimped by the line pressure above.

TACKLE

As we have just talked of fixed spool reels I will mention reels before rods.

There are only two types worth bothering with when salmon spinning, and they are the fixed spool reel and the multiplier. I occasionally spin with a centre pin, but that is just the whim of a fool: the other two types are far more efficient for the job. If you are only interested in purchasing one model, buy a large fixed spool reel, but if you are going to fish the season through you will require two models; as a comparison, a Mitchell 300 and a Mitchell 306 or their equivalents.

For big fish, an open river, and heavy lines, the multiplier is nicer to use and is my choice, and *is* easy to cast with despite the talk of overruns. But it is easier to cast with a fixed spool reel in awkward places, in rocky, tree-lined rivers. Where following is not possible, heavy tackle is necessary even if the fish are not over-large. In these sorts of rivers, as mentioned previously, it is essential to be able to place a bait into little holes between branches, under foliage and so on. A reel needs to carry at least one hundred yards of 15–20 lb breaking strain for these conditions, and I would prefer it to carry one hundred and fifty to two hundred yards.

Removing a treble that was very well home.

For the open river with runs of big fish, a reel that will hold the same sort of lengths and breaking strains is ideal.

For summer, and upstream work, when a river is less strong, when the fish are smaller, where I am casting light baits, and where I have no fear of losses, a Mitchell 300 or equivalent, loaded with 8–12lb b.s. is ample. I often fish very much lighter than that, only half the recommended b.s., but 10lb b.s. is what I would recommend for summer salmon – only lighter stuff if I knew the angler's capabilities.

With big fish like salmon I work out first what line strength is sensible to give me a fair chance of success and, along with other factors, a rod (and reel) is dictated by that. For heavy lines on the big river, a double-handed ten foot job would be fine, but too awkward on a little river where single-handed, strong, eight or nine footer, capable of handling the same line strength, would be a better proposition. For summer work a medium action eight to nine footer, coupled to the ten pound line, gives an angler a deal of fun. Salmon are often full of fight in the warmer water and create hell – and heaven – for the angler!

I don't apologise for not giving the reader of this chapter much information on the multitude of spinning baits available, and their uses. I consider it more important that he or she know something about the fish, and its behaviour to the size of bait and the manner in which it is fished at different times of the year. As yet there is no infallible spinning bait, and if I *had* one, I wouldn't tell you!

CHAPTER THIRTY

Spinning for Trout

by

Fred J. Taylor

STILL WATERS

The late, great, Oliver Kite is reputed to have referred to still water trout fishing as 'spinning with a fly rod'. If he did (which I doubt) he was almost certainly referring to that branch of still water trouting which involves the casting and retrieving of flies dressed to look like minnows or the fry of other species. Oliver Kite was also credited with those immortal words, 'Chuck it out, pull it back and when you can't you've got one!' If he did, in fact, make such a remark (and I'm sure he did!) he was obviously referring to the use of the above-mentioned lure-type flies.

I would hesitate to disagree with Oliver Kite, and on matters entymological I would not do so at all, but there *is* more to lure fishing for trout than he would have had us believe. True, if you do no more than chuck-it-out-and-pull-it-back, you'll catch trout often enough to regard it as a reasonably effective method. But, although the casting of lure flies with a fly rod and traditional fly tackle requires a degree of skill, it does not take too long to reach a state of reasonable efficiency. Having cast the lure, however, the speed and manner of its retrieve probably require a little more than the sheer mechanical expertise needed for casting. Which is why, generally speaking, the fly-only ruling applied to most still water trout fisheries borders on the ridiculous.

If we accept the fact that 'flies' tied to represent small fish are strictly lures, and if lures, as suggested elsewhere in this book, are objects that flutter, spin, wobble or move in a manner attractive to bigger fish, why should we not be allowed to present those flies with a spinning rod and a casting reel?

Most of the trout fishing available to the average angler today is conducted on a daily permit, put-and-take basis. Waters are stocked, bag limits imposed, records kept and generally speaking it all works very well.

But why, I wonder, do public bodies controlling vast acreages of trout water which they claim to be 'open to the public', almost invariably enforce the fly-only rule? They have stocked their waters with trout, and now advertise the fact that they have, this year, introduced X number of browns and Y number of rainbows averaging so many pounds or parts of a pound apiece. They seek to attract the customers, to collect the revenue, to give sport to those who like to catch trout, to run and maintain good fisheries, and yet, despite their claims to be 'open to the public', they cater only for a small minority of the anglers in this country.

What of the angler who has no fly rod, no desire to purchase one and neither the wish nor time to learn the basics of fly casting? There is no way he can fish these so-called public waters because for some obscure reason his spinning tackle is strictly taboo.

It so happens that I *do* have a great deal of fly tackle, and despite the fact that I am not an expert fly fisher, I manage to catch my fair share of trout each season. What's more, I enjoy it, and to my way of thinking that's what fishing is all about, whatever the species. But not everyone *enjoys* fly fishing, and there are many situations where more pleasure could be achieved from the use of other tackle were it allowed. For the life of me I cannot figure out why spinning should *not* be allowed on *all* these public waters.

I've been told a hundred reasons of course. Fly fishers have argued emotionally but quite illogically about 'sporting methods' and 'unsporting methods', and I've listened to passionate outbursts from time to time about so-called 'unsporting tackle'. But I wonder. How can a method or a piece of tackle be sporting or unsporting? Only at the hands of someone who is not himself a sportsman can a method or a piece of tackle be put to an unsporting use. (Even a leister is not unsporting if it's propped up against a tree!)

Is it any more sportsmanlike to stand up to your thighs in water punching out a ten yard, high-density shooting head with a lure fly on the end than to flick out that same lure fly on – say – a two ounce spinning rod with a swan shot pinched on the line to aid casting? There are many situations where the latter presentation is likely to be more effective, less likely to spoil the pleasure of others, and much more enjoyable to practise. And whichever way the trout happens to be killed, it's worth remembering that it's still a dead trout!

I've heard it said that if spinning was allowed, anglers who practised it would get their limits too quickly. So what? If that is their pleasure, and provided they do not fish on or return hooked fish so that they may continue to exploit a situation, what's wrong with that? It's unlikely to happen very often, and it wouldn't make any difference anyway on a properly controlled fishery. If someone wants to get a limit and be off the water quickly, that's his business. If he can seek to do it with a fly rod, why not with a spinning rod?

I've also heard it argued that, in any case, a good man with a fly rod will outcast and outfish a spinning enthusiast nine times out of ten. I think that is probably very true, and all the more reason, in my book, for relaxing these method restrictions. The whole business is quite illogical.

'If we allow spinning we shall upset the fly fishers,' one fishery manager told me.

But why? And what about the other anglers who are already upset about a situation which virtually bars them from fishing these public waters? Is it not possible to set aside certain areas for both methods? A short stretch of bank for light spinning, the remainder for fly fishing? And strictly to enforce the ruling that these areas are reserved for the methods nominated? That is important.

If I'm trying to cast and fish a nymph, I do not want someone beside me hurling out a spoon; but by the same token, if I'm delicately casting my tiny $\frac{1}{32}$-ounce lures on my little spinning wand, I don't want someone beside me ripping the water open with a number 10 shooting head!

In its wisdom the Thames Water Authority has already experimented with 'all-method' waters. It is hoped, after a suitable period, to be able to compare the effectiveness of different angling methods, and *then* to decide upon policy, rules and regulations. A sensible attitude.

It has been suggested to me by those in control of certain fisheries that spinning areas would *not* be taken full advantage of and that this would result in less space for the fly fishers, but so far it has not been put to the test. If, after a given period, it was found that the spinning sections were not being exploited, there could be no argument; but I do not believe this would be the case. I do think, however, that a great many anglers using the spinning sectors would eventually take up fly fishing!

I think we might see a situation develop where a spinner, having all but taken his limit in the morning, might well spend the rest of the day with a fly rod. Alternatively, the fly fisher, having flogged away nearly all day for no reward, might feel justified in having the odd hour on the spinning sector in the hope of catching the brace of fish he's rashly promised his neighbour!

I'm quite certain in my mind that the overall result of such administration would be an increase in the number of fly fishers and an increase in revenue for the public undertakings generally.

A few snobs might stay away in protest, but snobs are unlikely to be true sportsmen and they would not be missed! They never tried spinning for trout, but they're prepared to condemn it out of hand. I *have* caught trout by *all* methods and many experiences have proved interesting. Henry's Lake in northern Idaho for instance holds large numbers of remarkably big trout. The fishing there is free. Facilities such as boat hire, cabin rental, etc., have to be paid for, and a state licence is required before the water can be fished. The money from the state licence is used for conservation generally, and it would seem that this fabulous water is very much self-supporting in the way of fish stocks. The rainbows and cutthroats hybridise and grow big; stocks take care of themselves.

Henry's Lake is referred to often by Americans as the 'fish factory', and yet there is absolutely no restriction on method. You may float fish with worms, bait cast with plugs or spoons, leger with cheese, troll or trail with minnows and, if you like, you can buy salmon eggs for bait from the local store!

It's quite the most exciting fishery I've ever visited. Spinning is widely practised but it happens to be a fact that over ninety per cent of the fish caught there are taken on fly! They are caught that way because for the most part it is the deadliest way of catching fish from that water. The spinners have been quick to learn this, but other methods are still permitted. I imagine it will always be so. There are times when the spinners have a ball but any suggestion of 'slaughtering fish' is taken care of by the bag limit imposed.

There have been times when great slaughter has been brought about by fly fishers over here, but there has never been any suggestion of banning the fly! The petty rules and restrictions applied on reservoirs and public waters, where the object is supposedly to attract customers, give pleasure and derive income, have done much to maintain the great wall between coarse and game fishers that has existed throughout this century.

In fairness, however, it must also be said that the development of these public waters has done much to break down the barrier. By now it should have been flattened!

Is it not a pity that we cannot all fish as we would like? To enjoy experimenting with methods and presentations? To be able to put your thoughts and ideas into action without fear? To be discouraged from 'bending' the rules without actually breaking them?

The list of forbidden methods increases, and pretty soon we shall be unable to experiment at all. If that happens there will be no more pleasure left in the sport of fishing for me and hundreds like me. That's the part of it all that worries me.

Don't misunderstand me. I *do not* wish *always* to spin for trout, but I would like to feel I could do so when I felt so inclined. I would like that freedom because I happen to know that there are situations where it is warranted, and where it could no harm whatsoever.

Thankfully, a few places remain where spinning is not a dirty word and, of course, if we forget those put-and-take waters, which provide an exciting but nevertheless somewhat artificial kind of fishing, and look further afield to the lochs of Scotland, and the loughs of Ireland, there's a wealth of stillwater spinning to be enjoyed. Strictly speaking, of course, lochs and loughs are not still waters but for the purposes of distinguishing between them and rivers I will refer to them as such. And, although the fish in these wild waters are produced naturally and without the help of stew ponds and trout pellets, there are certain similarities in their behaviour. In very hot weather, for example, the big browns tend to lie deep, and although I do not pretend to know why, there seems to be a certain magic about the forty foot depth layer. Fred Buller, using char rigs and trailing fly-type lures at depths of up to seventy feet caught a number of big brown trout at the forty foot level.

Similar results have been achieved in other waters, both here and abroad, and it seems utterly ridiculous to me that I should be forced to fish for these deep-lying brown trout in our put-and-take reservoirs with traditional fly tackle. There is no possible way of getting a fly down to that depth and fishing it in a manner likely to attract trout. It could be done with spinning tackle from a boat, and I see no reason why deep trolling with big spoons, plugs or spinners should not be allowed. These lures could be used with appropriate leads and where necessary, to reach extreme depths, modern down-riggers equipment could be used. Deep trolling with down-riggers is not a particularly exciting way of fishing until the actual moment of contact. Then it becomes something else!

It works extremely well on the Irish loughs and I've no doubt it could be made to work very effectively in our deep English reservoirs. The diagram shows roughly how it works. The plug, spoon, spinner or feathered lure is taken down in a quick release clip attached to a heavy paravane-shaped lead weighing several pounds. This lead is attached to a wire line and is lowered by means of markings (or a sophisticated depth-counter) to the appropriate depth. The lure works happily in its wake but, being attached to an otherwise completely unfurnished rod and line, it breaks away from the release clip when a trout hits. The lead remains at the right depth, the fish is played to the surface on the light, limber spinning rod and the lure is sent down again on a new release clip with a free-sliding ring attachment. All very uncomplicated *once* the rigs have been set.

Speed of the boat is important and must be allied to the lure's action and the mood of the trout. Only experience can tell you when the boat is moving too quickly or too slowly. It takes time and patience, but it *is* rewarding, and there's more than a fair degree of skill involved. You have to be more of a boat handler than a rodsman, but it all 'comes good' with practice. It is, I venture to say, the *only* way of coming to terms with big deep-lying trout in any vast still water.

The dam ends of many English reservoirs are so placed as to make fly casting impossible. The high wall behind allows no room for an extended

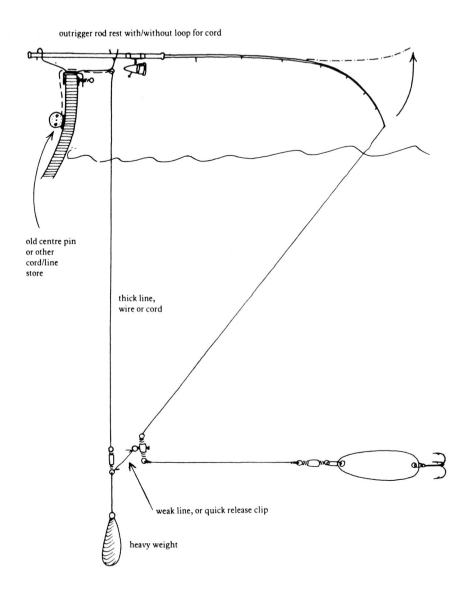

outrigger rod rest with/without loop for cord

old centre pin
or other
cord/line
store

thick line,
wire or cord

weak line, or quick release clip

heavy weight

back cast, the deep water immediately to the front cannot be exploited to the full with fly tackle. It is, however, an ideal spinning situation, and where it *is* allowed there is no better method for exploring the depths.

The techniques of spinning, rates of retrieve, how plugs and other lures work, have already been explained in other chapters. There is no need for me to elaborate. I do not believe it's necessary to use huge lures (despite the fact that rainbows will take them) and I have long since come to the conclusion that a violent action on the part of the lure is often quite unnecessary.

I have my own fancies, fads and favourites. I've used them in the wild waters of the Outer Hebrides, the Rocky Mountains, the Canadian Wilderness, the Oregon desert, Ireland and in four of the American Great Lakes as well as our own English waters. I have caught, from these many places, brookies, browns, lakers, rainbows, cutthroats and hybrids – *all* on traditional spinning tackle used one way or another. I do not make this statement to prove what a clever angler I am because, truthfully, I'm not so smart. But I do want to make it clear that spinning *is* an effective and sporting way of catching many kinds of trout in many different situations.

For the record I prefer (and it is purely a personal preference) to use lure-type flies of one kind or another rather than bar-spoons, plugs, Devon minnows, etc. But because I have restricted myself voluntarily to lure-type flies made of hair, fur, tinsel, feather, etc., I've had to learn to dress them or arm them with sufficient *weight* to allow me to cast them with a spinning rod.

There are many ways it can be done and possibly the simplest is to have already made-up, a number of swanshots painted with black and white markings to resemble eyes. One of these can be pinched on to the line at the very point of attachment to the hook; it makes an ordinary streamer of bucktail fly look even more like a small fish, *and* it allows it to be cast on a light spinning outfit. Extra weight may be needed for longer range casting, and in my experience it is better to attach this in the form of extra swan

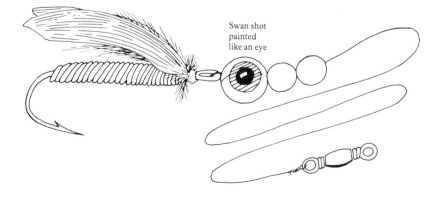

Swan shot
painted
like an eye

shots pinched on immediately above and more or less touching the first. Uptrace leads will certainly add distance to the cast, but they give a strange feeling of being 'out of touch' during the retrieve. Somehow you're never quite sure just what the lure is doing when you've a chunk of lead between you and it. But with the lead bulked at the extreme end of the tackle (you may pinch shots on to the shank of the hook if there's room) there's a feeling of contact which is both agreeable and effective.

It doesn't take much imagination to dream up ways and means of making simple fly-type lures with weight built into them for casting purposes. There's no great skill involved (even I can make them) but they're fun to play around with; *and* they catch fish.

All kinds of coloured embellishments may be added to any of the weighted hooks shown and I will not suggest any special dressings because they simply are not necessary. *Any* streamer fly dressing tied to one of these weighted hooks will catch fish on its day. Your problem is finding the right one for the day in question, but black, white, yellow and orange, or a combination of any two, are the colours I have found to be most effective.

Whichever way you choose to weight your hooks, use an Araldite-type glue generously in the process and let it set hard before adding the final dressings. Don't fuss about the dressing. It's easy to tie on a few more feathers or a wisp or two of hair when they've become worn. And remember too that very often these lure flies are most effective when they're well worn. They're often just 'coming good' when it's time to discard or re-dress them.

The diagram shows a fly vice being used to make up these lures, but you can work miracles with an ordinary pair of tweezers and a cotton reel. Think about it. Slide the cotton reel up the tweezers and the jaws will close tightly enough to hold almost any size of hook.

All this has little to do with the actual casting and retrieving of lures with a spinning rod. It has little to do with the playing and landing of trout, but you have my word for it that the lures I'm describing here *will* work excellently with a lightweight spinning outfit and that they *will* catch fish.

It's difficult to sit at a desk and tell someone *how* to fish, but I believe it *is* possible to pass on general information on *what to use*. These little snippets of information have been accumulated over many years of what I call open-minded angling. I do not believe they are common knowledge and I welcome the opportunity to pass them on, knowing that they have served me well in the past.

This is no place for a deep study of depth and temperature, but any observations in this particular field should be duly noted and allied to the speed, action, depth and colour of the lures being used. I cannot say: 'Do this when conditions are thus'. If I did it wouldn't work. All I can say is, 'Take note, experiment, and learn to put two and two together.'

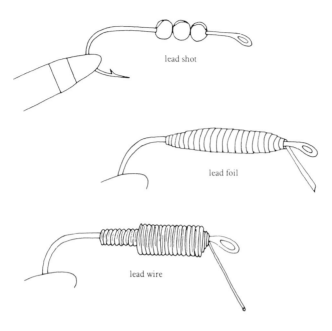

lead shot

lead foil

lead wire

There are, of course, many other factors to consider when fishing deep, still waters for trout, but again, observation is probably more important than technique. Finding fish, even without the restriction of the fly-only rule, is not always easy.

Catching one fish does not necessarily mean others are present, but it's at least a possibility. If you have caught a trout from – say – a drifting boat by casting a $\frac{1}{16}$-ounce lure, do you *know* at what depth the lure was working? After the fish has finally come to the net do you *know* now exactly where you hooked it? You'll have drifted some way since it happened; can you now go back to the same spot again? If you are trolling (or trailing) a spinning lure behind a boat (allowed on some waters and certainly encouraged in many Irish loughs and Scottish lochs) are you certain you know the depth at which the lure is working? If you change it – will the second lure fish at the same depth, or deeper? Small points, but all-important regarding the whereabouts of fish.

The figure shows a simple marker for pin-pointing a 'taking spot'. Immediately a trout is hooked, toss it over the side of the boat. Its oblong shape ensures that the weight will keep stripping off the line, turning the block over and over until the bottom is reached. Then it will stop and no more line will be pulled off. The 'buoy' will rest immediately above the lead and mark the spot with deadly accuracy.

271

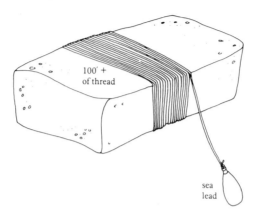

Big Irish and Scottish waters will be easier to understand if a transistorised sonar unit is put to use. Depth is then accurately recorded, but a simple way to ascertain the actual depth at which a lure is fishing is to row deliberately over a known shallow area and judge from what happens there. You may be surprised to find that your lure is fishing not eighteen feet as you'd thought, but less than half that depth!

There's much more, of course. I could go on discussing still water trout from now to eternity, but I'd probably be repeating some of the basics of spinning already dealt with in other chapters. I hope, however, that I've given you something to think about if and when the opportunity to spin for trout in still waters comes your way.

RIVERS AND STREAMS

The traditional way of spinning for trout in rivers is to tie on a small bar-spoon with a violent, vibrating action, cast it upstream and retrieve it slightly faster than the current speed. These tiny bar-spoons, mostly of French, Swedish or Norwegian origin, work extremely well even when travelling with the current and they catch fish. Because they are armed with treble hooks, however, they tend to be hard on small trout; and in the event that it is necessary or deemed advisable to return an unwanted or undersized specimen, these three points of penetration often make the task impossible.

It depends, of course, on what you want from your fishing. If, as I have done many times in wild and desolate areas, you are fishing for breakfast to be cooked over a camp fire, every fish, irrespective of size, will count – until sufficient have been caught. Then the fishing stops and the feeding begins! Half a dozen gudgeon-sized brownies taste just as good as one half-pounder when they're on the plate with an equal number of bacon rashers!

If, however, you're out to catch a brace or two of fish over a certain size and have no desire to hang on to the smaller ones, spinning with traditional treble-hooked spoons is not the answer.

Some of the fly-type lures already described and also those shown in the figure (1) and (2) will be equally effective and less harmful to any fish that is to be returned to the water alive.

Another way round the problem is to snip off two points of the bar-spoon treble and fish with only one. Odd fish will escape and almost certainly some of them will be of a takeable size, but at least they will be there for another time.

It is not always necessary to cast upstream to trout, however, and there are times when the action produced by retrieving *against* the current – i.e. by casting downstream and retrieving upstream, will prove to be a better proposition.

Remember one thing, however. Trout, like all other fish, spend much of their time headed into the current – which means that the downstream casting requires more caution on your part. You are more likely to be spotted when you are stationed upstream of a fish, but good use of cover and common sense will usually take care of that problem.

There are many tiny, overgrown streams where the trout are small and plentiful but which remain neglected by anglers either because their potential is not recognised or because the nearby salmon or sea trout are considered more worthwhile. Whatever turns you on! Me? I like to fish those waters. I like to get into the stream, work my way slowly up casting below the overhanging branches, flicking the tiny spoon or weighted fly into

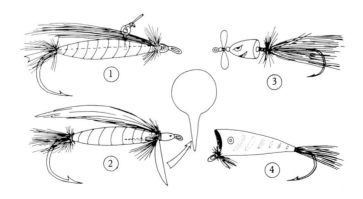

the likely looking spots. I like to force my way through the undergrowth and try some downstream casts through the areas I have not disturbed by wading, and while I will use fly and worm with equal pleasure if I think it is advisable, I often find the former quite impossible and the latter sometimes too easy. Worm-caught fish are also, in my experience, usually dead fish. There's no stopping a hungry little brownie from commiting suicide! In these waters a half-pounder is a veritable monster, and I'm never really sure about what to do with such fish. Should I return them because they are so few and far between? Or should I retain them because they've reached their peak anyway? I can't advise anyone with regard to this problem – because I don't know the answer myself. I doubt, however, if it makes much difference either way.

Many of the big salmon rivers of Scotland are fairly stiff with trout, but it's a safe bet that those in the pools have seen every conceivable type of lure before! The gentle glides, the wide shallows and some of the big deep eddies hold trout in abundance however, and they will often respond to sensible spinning with ultra-light gear.

Again, the basics of spinning with ultra-light tackle have already been explained and there is little more to add.

The peaty burns of Scotland, the Welsh hill streams, the tiny becks of Cumberland all abound with small trout, and whether or not you regard the effort involved in catching them as a worthwhile occupation depends entirely on your own temperament. I do. And again, I like to spin for these fish with weighted fly-type lures. The fish are easier to catch with baits like small worms and maggots; but why struggle with what amounts to coarse fishing tackle when a tiny wand weighing a mere couple of ounces and a hatful of weighted flies will serve almost as well? Traditional fly fishing will catch these fish too, but again there are very few places where it can be practised.

I hesitate to mention Thames trout because they are a breed of fish in a class of their own; but they are not extinct yet and every once in a while, a weir pool in the upper reaches produces a big brownie to a spinner. I have taken the odd fish from the Kennet on spun minnows and while these might possibly be regarded as Thames trout, I do not consider myself knowledge-able enough to delve deeply into the subject. I believe, however, that some of the weir pools are worth exploiting occasionally during the coarse fish close season if only to learn just how difficult a problem is presented!

Referring back briefly to the illustrated fly-spinners, (1) is made from a long-shanked hook with a wire loop soldered on about one third of the way along it. The whole is weighted with lead wire and almost any kind of feather or hair will do for dressing. The important point about this lure is that the line is attached to the wire loop and *not* the eye of the hook. This loop must be bent backwards or forwards until the lure is seen to be wobbling rapidly in the current. You need to see this effect before you can appreciate its deadliness. Retrieve *upstream* for best effect.

Fig. (2) shows a similar streamer fly with a wobbling disc (cut from an aluminium beer can) attached forward. Again, some bending and juggling is needed to get the required effect.

Fig. (3) shows a simple popping bug. Not normally associated with trout fishing at all, it has, on occasions, proved extremely effective for rainbows in deep smooth runs during the so-called dog days of July. It is hardly a spinning-rod lure, but it can be cast downstream, allowed to float down even farther, and then retrieved with a series of 'pops'. Sometimes the effect is very dramatic.

The same lure used at night sometimes produces similar results, but Fig. (4) shows an even better lure for that particular shady operation!

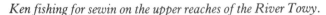

Ken fishing for sewin on the upper reaches of the River Towy.

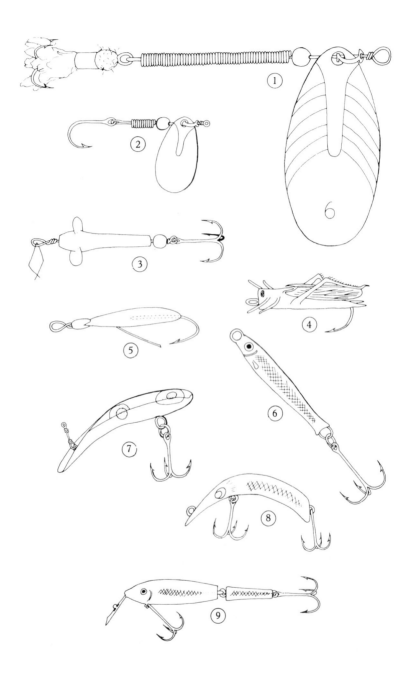

Lures that have proved very effective for trout, x 1.

Spinning for Trout

Sea Trout

by Ken Whitehead

For many, spinning for sea-trout is a part-time occupation to be practised when the water is out of condition for the fly, and not quite perfect for the worm. That attitude is a great mistake, for spinning for migratory trout is a deadly method – but only when the water is coloured (the degree of colour that brings success differing in various parts of the country) and only, as we have repeatedly indicated in this book, when the angler tackles the job with conviction. Chuck and chance just is not good enough

The tinge of colour that comes with falling water is something that can only be recognised with practice, but when there is sufficient for the spin pattern of a lure to be recognised by the fish is the time to use spinning tackle, the size of rod line and lure depending on the amount and pressure of water that is running off. Many anglers fish with tackle that is far too heavy and that, for those delicate fish, is to court disaster. The mouth of a sea trout – especially one that is fresh run – is tender to the extreme and more fish are lost through bully-boy tactics than ever are landed.

My attitude to the strength of tackle to be used centres around the weight of line. I try not to go above six pounds breaking strain and balance the rod and lure to that, though common sense dictates that when one is close to the estuary of a river then extra weight in both line and lure must be used.

Observations show that most who spin tend to use Mepps or Toby lures, their size depending on the flow of water. I have had my share of success with them, but find like many that the Toby is a better fish taker when fitted with an extra treble at the nose, looped with split ring through the swivel. For some reason fish often strike high at this bait as it flutters, and a fair percentage of missed takes are avoided with this inexpensive addition.

Most leaf spinners do well in the gold and silver range, the Toby lures in silver and blue, whilst that good old standby the quill minnow (or rather, the modern plastic imitation quill minnow) in brown and yellow or better still, the Irish minnow, with its added weight, are necessities in the lure box. One of the bigger lures that I have enjoyed success with is Shakespeare Catcher, and this often when fished without weight, with the spinner running just below the surface.

This business of taking depth, that part of the water in which fish are running is repeatedly overlooked by the majority. My experience is that the depth at which fish are moving below the surface will be governed by the amount of light that is around – something discussed in an earlier chapter. Dull days are far more productive on the whole than those of high sunshine and it is as well to use the 'count down' principle, where a number of

Being hard.

seconds are allowed to elapse before the retrieve is started, until some idea of a taking level is established.

The reverse is often the case at night when small plugs, fished up on the surface where they kick up a commotion will take fish even on the darkest night and without there being the need for colour on the water, or even to fish in areas of moving water which one normally covers when lure fishing.

Night fishing is a serious proposition that can provide results on some waters greatly out of proportion to those associated with coarse fishing. Especially so at the end of season when fish run hard and long, and seem keen to take any light coloured lure that is on the small size – probably reminiscent of small fry in the estuary. I have not had success with flecto-light type of lures which one would expect to bring results, and the same lack of interest seems to go for diving plugs.

Whilst the actual spinning for sea trout is a repetitive affair playing and landing fish is anything but. Each area into which a cast is made should be studied before spinning commences so that a fair idea can be built up of open water, snags, and gravel shallows over which fish rub the line to bring many a successful break.

Landing places where the net can be used, and more important where the angler can get out of the water with a clutter of rod, net and fish without breaking ones neck or drowning must be studied and remembered. Especially is this so at night and the old dodge of a white handkerchief tied to a bush or laid on the bank to show the way off the water can be a Godsend.

Above all, do keep the torch in its proper place – secured to the body – until it is essential for its use. Night vision is all important and easily lost.

CHAPTER THIRTY-ONE

All at Sea

A great deal of what has been written about in this book so far is as applicable to sea fishing as to spinning anywhere else, so we'll not duplicate any remarks. There is considerable scope for spinning at sea and certain areas are considerably under exploited. Take, for example, the usual spinning of which most sea anglers have some experience: feathers for mackerel, jigs and perks for cod, or baited spoons for flounders. This kind of spinning really requires little different from the sea anglers normal mode of fishing. He still has a weight on the end of the line – in the case of perk fishing this is the perk itself which may weigh up to a pound – and the feathers or silver papered hooks attached in various numbers and varying distances above the lead. There's nothing at all wrong with this, and it is a very productive way of spinning, although it must be said that real anglers soon tire of pulling in strings of mackerel all fighting against each other. And in perk fishing a lot of the skill is in getting to know the marks and the tidal role. Whilst this is also true of baited spoon flounder fishing there is in addition a great deal of skill in the way the lure is worked, requiring good boatsmanship and a precise judging of the up-trace weight. The baited spoon needs to bump gently along the bottom or just above the bottom and the taking speed found, for it varies from day to day and from one section of the shoreline to another. Thus there is a contrast between this mode of spinning and that of perking for cod and pollock or feathering for mackerel where once the taking depth or position is found the baits are simply jigged up and down.

Most sea anglers still bait fish most of the time though they'll take to the above forms of spinning readily enough if someone takes the plunge and starts to get results. And, of course, such spinning techniques may become traditional in certain parts of the coast, and at certain times of the year – as when a known run of mackerel is on.

But you *can* fish plugs and spinners much more frequently and by casting from the rocks or beach as well as from a boat. Estuaries also make good spinning grounds, not only for baited spoons and flounders but for bass too. Most sea fish are to some extent predatory and many different species will fall to the techniques described in this book. We've had quite a few pollack on plugs as well as spinners, and mackerel will, of course, take anything that moves at times. Plug fishing for bass has become quite an art in recent decades and we do not wish to attempt a synopsis here, but rather to point in the direction of the ocean the angler who comes to plug fishing through his freshwater interests. Quite recently some well-known pike fishermen tried plug fishing for shark from a small open boat. Perhaps a little foolhardy, but the shark were willing to take the plugs so the sport has definite possibilities.

You can even fish plugs much as you do perks or spinners, that is at depth, above a good-sized weight. We tried this years ago off Flamborough Head in Yorkshire and took codling on the plugs. Tangling the plug with the reel line was the main problem, but a little ingenuity for which sea anglers are well known would soon solve that problem: it is possible to fish the plug on a boom, just to mention one way around the problem.

Casting from the shore, especially a rocky shore, is an exciting way of spinning. Some of the heavier Tobys are superb for this and take a variety of species including sea trout as well as bass and mackerel. Not only do they throw considerable distances – up to seventy yards say – but they can be worked either deep or shallow. In many shores you have to raise the lure quickly in the last twenty or thirty yards or so or you'll snag up on the rocks or seaweed beds – or you can try fast retrieves just under the waves where the sea trout, bass, and mackerel lay on hot days. This kind of fishing is best done when the quarry have a reason for being there, such as when fry shoals mass in a quiet, sun-warmed bay. Under those circumstances the predatory fish will shoal them up in a corner using exactly the same tactics as pike and zander do in freshwater. Basically this tends to happen during the summer to early autumn, at different times presumably in different parts of our shoreline. In Yorkshire it is commonly August when the brit shoals hole up in the quiet bays.

For all our sea spinning we tend to use heavier gear than one would for catching the same weight fish in freshwater. It could be that this is unnecessary, that we are being unduly cautious. But we always up-rate the line when boat fishing, even in freshwater, and would regard lines of 15 lb b.s. more reasonable than lighter lines. For shore casting one's casting range is distinctly less with 15 lb b.s. than with 11–12 lb b.s. so under those circumstances we prefer the latter. But for short casts into rocky gullies we would again go for the heavier line particularly if it became necessary to hustle fish away from kelp beds. Sea spinning does seem to us a more rumbustious, turbulent business and you *need* sturdy gear most of the time, and this means strong traces and ball-bearing swivels as well as heavy line. And, pound for pound, sea fish do seem to fight better than freshwater species, as a generalisation.

There is another sphere of sea spinning which can teach freshwater spinners a thing or two, and that is in the field of artificial sand-eel fishing. These are nowadays made of various soft plastics, and whereas in the past they were simply elongated bits of rubber, now they have a 'tail' which is arranged at right angles to the length of the lure so that it really digs water on the retrieve and vibrates and wobbles in an amazing fashion. These can be killers in salt water whether cast and retrieved, or whether simply jigged up and down. (In freshwater they work very well indeed for pike, and we predict that freshwater anglers will turn to them in large numbers in the future.)

One of the techniques applicable to sea spinning is, of course, trolling, either using artificial plugs and spoons or natural wobbled baits. This is one of the techniques of big game angling, essentially beyond the scope of this volume, where mackerel are carefully mounted so that they 'swim' behind the boat without twisting up the line or themselves spinning or wobbling too fast. But trolling can also be used exactly as we described elsewhere for most species of predatory sea fish: as always the place and taking depth must be found by trial and error in the first instance. The making of particular lures can often be judged correct by the response of the rod tip where it sticks over the gunwhale. Each lure has its own particular throb-throb at the rod end, and if that shows then the lure is working properly even if you have it at the wrong depth! If you need to speed up you may have to change to a faster working lure. If you need greater depth you may need to add an up-trace weight such as a Wye lead (which also acts as an anti-kink device). Wye leads are of excellent design and rarely adversely affect the lure action, more especially if attached five feet or so up the line. In some cases much heavier weights than Wye leads are needed, but by then you should perhaps be thinking of jigging instead. It goes almost without saying that an echo sounder at sea is as valuable as it is in freshwater.

Finally, just for those who do a bit of sea spinning whilst on holiday, or who come to sea spinning from a freshwater standpoint, remember that the sea is full of salt! Use either corrosion-proof reels or wash all washable tackle with great care. Not only that but salt water sits over a lot of sand, that other bane of the anglers' life. Both can ruin good equipment in no time. Our advice is to get kitted out for *sea* fishing.